DATE DUE

UPI 261-2505   PRINTED IN U.S.A.

Thucydides, Hobbes,
and the
Interpretation
of
Realism

Thucydides, Hobbes,

and the

Interpretation

of

Realism

LAURIE M. JOHNSON

NORTHERN

ILLINOIS

UNIVERSITY

PRESS

DeKalb

1993

Published by the Northern Illinois University Press, DeKalb, Illinois 60115
Manufactured in the United States using acid-free paper ∞
Design by Julia Fauci

Library of Congress Cataloging-in-Publication Data
Johnson, Laurie M.
Thucydides, Hobbes, and the interpretation of realism / Laurie M. Johnson
        p.   cm.
Includes bibliographical references and index.
ISBN 0-87580-175-7
1. Hobbes, Thomas, 1588-1679.   2. Thucydides.   3. Man.
4. Philosophical anthropology.   5. Justice (Philosophy).   6. Political ethics.
7. Political science.   8. International relations.   I. Title.
B1248.M36J64   1993
320'.092'2—dc20   92-34016
CIP

To my parents,

KEN AND NINA JOHNSON

CONTENTS

List of Abbreviations

References to Hobbes's works in the eleven-volume collection entitled *The English Works of Thomas Hobbes of Malmesbury* are cited by page number. *Hobbes's Thucydides, De Cive,* and *Leviathan* are cited by book or chapter followed by paragraph or section unless otherwise noted in the text.

B	*Behemoth,* in *English Works,* vol. 6
C	*De Corpore,* in *English Works,* vol. 4
THM	*Considerations Upon the Reputation, Loyalty, Manners and Religion of Thomas Hobbes of Malmesbury,* in *English Works,* vol. 4
DC	*De Cive*
E	*Elements of Philosophy,* in *English Works,* vol. 1
H	*De Homine,* in *English Works,* vol. 4
HT	*Hobbes's Thucydides*
L	*Leviathan*
LNC	*The Questions Concerning Liberty, Necessity and Chance,* in *English Works,* vol. 5
PR	*Philosophical Rudiments Concerning Government and Society,* in *English Works,* vol. 2

Introduction

As a student, I had seen the names of Hobbes and Thucydides mentioned repeatedly as examples of realism in the study of international relations.[1] Kenneth Waltz found in Thucydides a reflection of his "third image," a paradigm in which the balance of power that states find themselves in largely determines their actions.[2] Robert Keohane and Joseph Nye, who together have authored some of the best of the pluralist literature, use Thucydides as a representative of their "overall power model," or the "traditional" international relations paradigm.[3] Hedley Bull found in Hobbes a representative of the realist view that a state of war existed in the international realm just as it did in the state of nature among individuals.[4] In the literature of international relations, Thucydides and Hobbes are often used interchangeably, sometimes as symbols, sometimes as straw men, but infrequently with any substantive penetration of the actual philosophic texts. These references intrigued me and actually were one of the primary reasons I became a student of political philosophy.

So as I began writing this book, I still had the questions that the literature of international relations had raised in my mind. But I was very much interested in the kind of thorough analysis that one can only do if one is not intent on covering every angle of both fields, that is, international theory and political philosophy. Those international relations scholars who related their realist theories to Thucydides and Hobbes, or to some other philosopher, could read such a book with profit and form their own conclusions about what

impact it had on their conception of the realism of international relations. They would have the benefit of a work which goes beyond
the less detailed or informed conceptions of these philosophers'
works that have found their way into many an international relations
book or article. I was hoping that the richness in detail and scope of
this book would spawn in them new ideas, new subtleties, perhaps
new understandings of old themes within realist discourse. At the
same time, since my interpretations of Thucydides and Hobbes, especially Thucydides, might be considered innovative (I hope chari-
tably) by some, I also hoped my book might be of use to other
political theorists who are interested in one or both.

I have chosen what at first might seem a counterintuitive procedure in covering Thucydides and Hobbes. In each of three chapters I
have chosen to place the sections on Hobbes before the sections on
Thucydides. Obviously, this is not a chronological arrangement! But
I conceived of their relationship as one in which one raised questions
and challenges that had to be answered by the other. The questioner
and challenger was Hobbes, who himself translated Thucydides'
History of the Peloponnesian War. Hobbes saw in the *History* a confir-
mation of his own philosophy, and he interpreted Thucydides in a
unique fashion in order to do so. I began to wonder what Thucydides would have to say to Hobbes. Would he agree with Hobbes's
reading of his history? What would he have to say about Hobbes's
philosophy in general? I began to suspect that he would take um-
brage at his work being so easily equated with Hobbesian theory by
Hobbes, as well as by today's students of international relations.

And so I posed three questions over which they could debate. The
first, the one from which all else flows, deals with human nature.
Do Hobbes and Thucydides hold the same view of human nature or
do they differ? I believe they differ so widely in their conceptions of
human nature and the perspectives from which they view human activity and conflict are so divergent that they represent two different
schools of thought. The one reduces all human thought and action to
one motivation or cause, leveling in its wake all apparent human diversity of character and culture. The other expands the view, not to
the point of a meaningless and endless clutter of influences on human
behavior but to a much more rich and rounded picture.

The next question to be asked followed from the first. What were
their respective views of justice? I hope that those especially who are

interested in the growing field of international ethics will listen in on this part of the debate, for, again, I believe that Thucydides represents a way of examining justice in international affairs that differs markedly from that of Hobbes. I argue that Thucydides discovered and dealt with Hobbes's argument within the drama and dialogue of his history. Thucydides recognized the strength and impact of the Hobbesian subordination of justice to power; it was alive within the Athenian thesis and the Athenians' actions. But Thucydides has much to say about this thesis, and in what he has to add to and subtract from it and in what ways he wants to criticize it he points the way to a realistic but non-Hobbesian understanding of justice in international relations.

Finally, I asked the age-old question of the best regime. It was on this question more than on any other that Hobbes thought Thucydides would agree with him. The *best* regime for Hobbes, of course, was monarchy. But Thucydides answers differently, having different criteria and different objectives in mind. Thucydides' answers on the question of the best regime follow from his perspective on human nature and justice, as do Hobbes's. Their divergence here serves to point up their divergence elsewhere.

This book contains, then, an argument for the differences between the two. It also carries, clearly, an argument that the Thucydidean approach to viewing and analyzing political conduct, especially international affairs, should be considered as a preferred alternative to the Hobbesian approach. In the conclusion, I apply my findings to some of the best literature of the realist and neorealist theories of international relations. Perhaps it would be useful to outline briefly my concluding argument now, although some readers especially interested in this aspect may wish to turn to the conclusion now and read the rest of the book afterward.

First, I believe that both realism and neorealism (which purports to be more scientific than its forerunner) share philosophic roots in Hobbesian theory. While realists are generally open about the fact that they assume a rather Hobbesian human nature in order to analyze international relations, neorealists cover similar assumptions under the guise of "structuralism," which understands international relations in terms of power relationships in an anarchical world, in which states can be assumed to respond in specific ways to power imbalances and potential threats due to the inherent insecurity they face. In this regard, I point out that Hobbes was a structuralist as well. By assuming a human nature motivated primarily by self-preservation and self-interest, and by assuming a particular type of instrumental rationality, he could turn to an examination of the *situation* in which such beings found themselves. In anarchy, these individuals could be expected to behave in rather predictable ways; and a change in the "structure" (civil society) would produce different kinds of behavior, still as motivated by self-preservation and self-interest as before. Similar assumptions about human nature have to be made by the neorealists in order for the structure of the international system to become the determining element.

Hobbes acknowledged that human beings could be deterred by vainglory from pursuing their interests rationally. It would seem that here, too, the realists and neorealists are like Hobbes: their picture of reality is not only descriptive and predictive but also prescriptive. Those who fail to conform to the realist view of rational behavior are bound to perish. Therefore, the assumption is (at least for realists and neorealists) that such behavior will be rare. But is "irrational" behavior so rare in international relations that we can afford to ignore it for the sake of the elegance of our theory? Thucydides' answer is an emphatic no.

Thucydides' *History* has been misused by theorists of international relations, who take a sentence or two out of context[5] or who equate Thucydides' views with his characters the Athenians. Instead, Thucydides presents a way of analyzing international relations that realists and neorealists would do well to consider. Thucydides, if read comprehensively, often takes seriously the independent role of national character, the individual personalities and characters of statesmen, the role of political rhetoric (he treats the realist Athenian thesis as one strain of rhetoric in his many speeches), and the role of justice in formulating judgments about political events. From his point of view, realism and neorealism become specific forms of political rhetoric, subject to practical as well as moral evaluation by the analyst.

Perhaps it is difficult to imagine what a Thucydidean scholar of international relations would be like, what he or she would write about. After all, are Thucydidean histories very marketable these days? I will suggest that something like Thucydidean history might indeed be very profitable, at least from the point of view of learning about practical politics, that it is already being done to a certain extent, and that there are some indications that we will turn more and more to it in the future.

Of course, to do justice to the issue of the realist/neorealist paradigm in international relations would require another book, not just a concluding chapter. By offering some comparisons and contrasts with today's scholarship, perhaps I can encourage others to use the observations in this book—or their reasoned disagreement with those observations—to begin their own discussions of the philosophic grounding, verity, and usefulness of various approaches in international relations theory.

It might comfort those interested in impartial scholarship that I started my analyses of the respective texts with the goal of proving Hobbes's contention that they were similar, describing in what ways they were similar, and demonstrating how their thought applied to the theory of international relations. I slowly discovered that they were very different, which, as it turns out, presented me with a more difficult but more interesting and fruitful project of exegesis. Although this manuscript has been considerably pared down, the reader must excuse some necessary close textual analysis, for it is the only way my argument can be made and adequately understood, especially in the case of Thucydides. It is hoped that the descriptive analysis of episodes in the *History* will be of some use in and of themselves for those interested in exploring the philosophic possibilities of those particular episodes and that they will retain enough of Thucydides' stark drama to take all readers willingly along to the central points.

I hope that the reader will think of this work as an experiment. It is the first book-length comparison of Thucydides and Hobbes. Such an undertaking has many difficulties and risks. One common objection to this type of analysis—that Thucydides is a historian and Hobbes is a philosopher and that they cannot really be compared—I will allow Hobbes to answer:

> But Thucydides is one, who, though he never digress to read a lecture, moral or political, upon his own text, nor enter into men's hearts further than the acts themselves evidently guide him: is yet accounted the most politic historiographer that ever writ. (HT, "To the Readers," par. 2)

Of course, there are a few places in which Thucydides *does* digress, and these instances are infinitely useful. But the *History* is a work in which generalizations and patterns can be discerned, and in which the author wishes to universalize a particular experience: the Peloponnesian War was so great that it represents war in general; the experience of Corcyra represents civil war *writ large*. Hence it becomes possible, albeit with difficulty, to compare Thucydides with the philosopher Hobbes. Perhaps the simplest defense of this project is that Hobbes compared himself with Thucydides and thought that the lessons Thucydides taught were relevant not only for himself but also for his contemporaries. Hobbes's assertion that Thucydides *History* supported his own philosophy forms the underlying and unifying question of this book.

There are several people who have influenced my thought during various stages in this project. Larry Arnhart, my dissertation director at Northern Illinois University, gave me the freedom to pursue my own directions in what was the first draft of this work. At the same time, he gave me good advice, constructive criticism, and suggestions for improvements. I am also in debt to Morton Frisch and Gary Glenn, the latter of whom tried to convince me I was wrong on certain points concerning Thucydides' treatment of justice. Although I didn't give him the satisfaction of conceding openly, I spent half a year rethinking my thesis in this area and eventually found myself coming closer to his position. For that I owe him a particular debt, and I have not, until now, acknowledged it. I am grateful to the Earhart Foundation for giving me a year to work on research and writing free of other duties and to the Department of Political Science at Northern Illinois University for giving me office space one summer when, after I had graduated, it was no longer obligated to do so. I used that space to effect a major project of editing and rewriting that resulted in a much more streamlined, and hopefully more readable, book. I want to thank my fiancé, Tim Bagby, for his innate ability to give me perspective, as well as for his support, friendship, tolerance, and strategic laughter. And I wish to express my gratitude to my parents, Ken and Nina Johnson, for being genuinely interested and interesting people who omitted to tell me there were things I couldn't or shouldn't do.

*Thucydides, Hobbes,
and the
Interpretation
of
Realism*

Human Nature

I t is often said that Thucydides' and Hobbes's ideas of human nature are very similar.[1] International relations theorists are just as much prone to this mistake as others, referring to Thucydides, as they do to Hobbes, as a "realist."[2] In this chapter I will argue that Hobbes's view is close to the view of the famous "Athenian thesis" repeated throughout Thucydides' *History of the Peloponnesian War*. That thesis is similar in many ways to the realist thesis, claiming that human beings are universally selfish and always motivated by fear, honor, and interest. Since they are compelled by their passions, they are not to be blamed for their actions, and, as Thucydides' character Diodotus points out, they can be controlled only through superior power and brute force. But I will argue that, in contradiction to the Athenian thesis, Thucydides' overall treatment of human nature proves that it is not so uniform and that passions do not force people to act. Individuals are responsible for their actions, capable of reason, and therefore guilty when they allow their passions to overcome their good sense. The latter type of analysis certainly does not coincide with the theories of realists.

In Thucydides' view, political problems cannot be permanently solved, because there are elements in human nature that cannot be manipulated. Temporary solutions can be obtained only through human intangibles: character, intelligence combined with eloquence, prudence, and ethics. In contrast, Hobbes sees the problem of pride, for instance, as a mere delusion of self-importance that can be banished through science. Hobbes makes human nature so uniform that he engages in grand reductionism when he considers such attributes as altruism, patriotism, virtue, and intelligence. Because of their disagreement about the uniformity of human nature, Hobbes views as normal those human qualities that Thucydides sees as products of decline. While Thucydides depicts the bloodthirsty violence of civil war as well as genocidal international warfare as products of the extreme pressures of war, Hobbes sees them as events that take place whenever there is no power strong enough to prevent them. Whereas Thucydides attributes the overturning of established values to the specific case of the inflamed passions of civil war, Hobbes takes value relativism as a fact at all times—a situation that makes enforced values a prerequisite for peace. For Thucydides, a decline in good political rhetoric is a sign of immoderation and immorality. For Hobbes, there is no such thing as good deliberative rhetoric (political rhetoric that genuinely contributes to the final, not predetermined decision), since all values are relative to the speakers and all speakers are always self-interested. These differences will be worked out below. Does Thucydides supply us with a model of international realism as we understand it today, or does Hobbes more closely approximate the modern realists' view?

HOBBES

Hobbes's assumptions about human nature condition his entire theory. I will start where Hobbes started, by looking at the basic unit upon which his system is built: the individual. Hobbes's mechanism made it possible for him to depict men as uniformly egocentric individuals naturally at odds with one another. This depiction, along with the assumption of rough equality among people, made a war of all against all the necessary result of the absence of government, necessitated a social contract as the basis of government, and made fear the prime motivator for individuals to enter into any such contract. It would seem from this depiction that Hobbesian men are naturally asocial. But as we shall see, Hobbes's depiction of men in the state of nature includes an element of human nature that is social: pride. Indeed, Hobbes emphasizes pride as the main impediment to rational fear and therefore the main impediment to lasting peace. In order to explain this incongruity I will suggest that the state of nature is, for Hobbes, the state of socialized men who find themselves suddenly without any power to keep them in awe, and that it corresponds closely to the dynamics of civil war.

Next, I will turn to what Hobbes held out as man's hope for a permanent escape from the possibility of endless sedition and civil war. For Hobbes, man's hope rests in the possibility of raising his faculty of reason, through precise speech, to the level of science. If this can be done, that is, if men can be convinced of the necessities of absolute sovereignty and obedience, then governments will no longer be plagued continually by civil strife. Man's downfall, however, can also come via reason and speech if these two faculties are exploited by ambitious and prideful orators or preachers. Hobbes tries to prove that rational fear of the state of nature should make men act as if they had accepted the social contract, which involves the suppression of the harmful aspects of human pride and ambition through (it is hoped) recognition of the laws of nature and (necessarily) the exercise of absolute sovereignty.

The Causes of War

Hobbes attributes conflict to three causes inherent in human nature: 1) desire for gain, which causes competition; 2) fear of one's competitors, which leads to diffidence; and 3) concern for one's reputation, that is, concern with glory (L, 13, par. 6–7). The first two can be explained by Hobbes's mechanistic theory of human nature, which depicts man as radically asocial. But the last cause, glory, is derived from further assumptions that bring into question man's lack of sociability. In effect, Hobbes has two proofs for his political prescriptions, one derived from his mechanism and one from his analysis of society itself. Discerning one proof from the other is made more difficult because Hobbes mingles them together in his description of the "state of nature" or "the natural condition of mankind." The state of nature is at once the consequence of mechanistic human nature left ungoverned and a depiction of civil war taken to its extreme. Both proofs are needed to support Hobbes's prescriptions, even though they are somewhat contradictory. With the first, Hobbes proves that all government is founded on the consent of the governed. But only his consideration of man's pride in society makes absolute sovereignty (preferably monarchy) necessary to ensure order.

Mechanism and Individualism   The extreme uniformity in Hobbes's depiction of human nature is made possible by his mechanistic psychology. While Hobbes thinks all men share common passions, he says that the objects of those passions vary from person to person. Why do they vary so widely, and why is it so difficult to know them in any given man? The answer lies in the physical origins of all passions and of human nature generally.

According to Hobbes, there is nothing in the world but matter and motion. Man's senses are activated when they are moved by outward objects, producing different appearances according to the man (L, 1, par. 1, 4). These appearances are called "fancies," and they are produced in the human body, having no direct relation to external objects. What we see is an apparition that the object produces in the brain and not the actual object (H, 4). Proof of this is that people sometimes "see" things that are not really there, such as light, from pressing on the eyeball (H, 4–5). Color is not actually in the object. Instead, it is an effect in us, caused by the motion of the object. In the same way, sound does not exist outside the human ear (H, 7–8). The consequence of these physiological facts is that man knows not reality but only his impression of it; and because human bodies and experiences differ, each man's impression is bound to be at least slightly different from every other's. This effect Hobbes called the great deception of sense: that what we think is in the world is really an illusion. Each person is bound by his particular perspective. He cannot know the outside world, and he cannot know the perspectives of others with any degree of confidence.

Because people have different bodies and experiences, their passions are produced by and vary with these two factors. They are produced when the action of an object, after activating the senses, continues to the heart and there either stimulates or impedes the "vital motion." The basic passions are therefore appetite (stimulant) and aversion (impediment). Some appetites and aversions are innate, such as hunger. But the rest come from experience of the effects of various objects on individuals. Internal deliberation is nothing but the succession of appetites and aversions, and the will is merely the end of this succession (H, 25–26, 31–32, 68; L, 6–7). Hobbes insists that even though the will is determined by necessary causes, every action is voluntary because it is produced by the will.

Because a man's body is in constant flux, it is impossible that the same things will always cause the same appetites and aversions in one, much less in all, men. Thus people will not be able to agree on what is desirable and what is not (L, 6, par. 2, 4, 6–7; H, 26). This is the cause of the diversity of passions and ends. Whatever a man does desire, he will call good; whatever he is averse to, he will call evil:

> For seeing all names are imposed to signifie our conceptions; and all our affections are but conceptions; when we conceive the same things differently, we can hardly avoyd different naming of them. For though the nature of that we conceive, be the same; yet the diversity of our reception of it, in respect of different constitutions of body, and prejudices of opinion, gives everything a tincture of our different passions. (L, 4, par. 24)

Valuation, then, is radically individual and relative.[3] Because of this, a person must be skeptical when hearing others' words. These words are not only affected by the distortions placed on them by the speaker's perspective but are also distorted by those who listen, because of their different natures, dispositions, and interests. What one man calls wisdom, another calls fear. What one thinks cruelty, another might praise as justice. Because of this, "such names can never be true grounds of any ratiocination" (L, 4, par. 24). The only passion one can generally attribute to all human beings is the desire for power, since power is the means with which to obtain any end and therefore to satisfy any passion.

All of the above point to human beings who are radically individualistic, who cannot have any meaningful discourse, and who look at each other solely as threats. For Hobbes, government must be established in accordance with this human nature. Hobbes's theory consequently concentrates on the individual and his particular needs and desires and shows how these can indeed be compatible with society.

Man's Natural Equality   Having proved man's radical individualism, Hobbes had only to add one last ingredient to show that without government protracted war would result. That ingredient is the basic equality of men. Hobbes recognized that intelligence and character are unevenly distributed among people. But equality has to do with what men can *do* to one another, not with other inherent qualities of individuals. All men are to be considered equal because even the weakest can kill the strongest, due to his ability to think and therefore to plot. If it were not for this rough equality, the few who were more effective killers would eventually subdue or eliminate everyone else. The fact that everyone is vulnerable to being killed outweighs all other sources of inequality in the state of nature.

Because all human beings are equal in their threat and vulnerability toward others and consider themselves equal in every way, if any one obtains too much power others can be expected to try to topple him. Rough equality of ability produces equal hope of attaining one's ends, and when any two men desire the same thing, power, they become enemies and try to conquer one another (L, 13, par. 3). People do vary in the strength of their desires, and some could be satisfied if there were not others who were always hungry for more. Thus, natural man's situation is the classic example of John Herz's "security dilemma": all people must continually seek power simply in order to protect themselves (L, 11, par. 2). In other words, competition occurs not because men are all mad with greed or completely power-hungry but because they are placed in a situation in which they must conform to the most base behavior to survive. They do this because, without government, they have no assurance that anyone else will reciprocate the kind of manners and respect they would like. Hence, the quest for dominion "ought" to be allowed them, as necessary to their preservation (L, 13, par. 4).

Because of men's rough equality in anarchy, a protracted war of all against all develops. No hierarchy will be able to emerge just because some men are better killers than others. With these observations, Hobbes introduces the situation as an important element. Equality of ability makes the situation (anarchy) the paramount problem, one that cannot be solved naturally.

Hobbes defines war not only as actual battle but also as the inclination to fight, that is, living in constant suspicion and hostility and in continual preparation for battle:

> In such condition, there is no place for Industry; because the fruit thereof is uncertain: and consequently no Culture of the Earth; no Navigation, nor use of the commodities that may be imported by Sea; no commodious Building; no Instruments of moving, and removing such things as require force; no Knowledge of the face of the Earth; no account of Time; no arts; no Letters; no Society; and which is worst of all, continuall feare, and danger of violent death; And the life of man solitary, poore, nasty, brutish, and short. (L, 13, par. 9)

In man's natural condition, because of the situation in which he finds himself, there is no propriety. Notions of right and wrong have no place. Nothing can be unjust, justice and injustice being qualities that apply to men in society, not in solitude. Force and fraud are cardinal virtues, because the only modus operandi is survival (L, 13, par. 13). This is not because Hobbes does not believe in a standard of right and wrong but because the penalty for trying to be just in the state of nature would be death.

For Hobbes, the natural condition of mankind manifests itself in varying degrees depending on the situation in which human beings are placed. As we have seen, the pure form of mankind's natural condition appears in the state of nature described in the above quote. Did the state of nature ever actually exist? Hobbes says that it is an abstraction, an inference made from the passions (L, 13, par. 11; DC, "To the Reader," pp. 11–12). But he also says that an analogous situation occurs in relations among states, and in places like America there were savages who, even though they had the simple government of families, lived as he describes. Civil war, which is an example of the degeneration of governmental power into something close to the state of nature, provides an even better glimpse of what men are like without an absolute coercive power to keep them in line (L, 13, par. 11–12).

The natural condition of mankind still prevails in situations in which people are not so isolated as in the state of nature. While civil society is still absent, families can come together and contracts can be made within these families. In nature, men and women are basically equal, for the same reason that all human beings are equal. Mothers, by dint of physical evidence, have first rights to rule over their children. But by pact they can transfer that right to the fathers. This type of cooperation Hobbes still places within the state of nature, even though it contains an element of sociability. Also, the natural condition of mankind, whose brutish character forces men to seek peace, can be deduced from events that occur within society.

Hobbes attempted to prove that uncontrolled human nature and its consequences would produce chaos not only through "inference made from the passions" but also by calling on his readers to test their own experiences. Here was ample proof for those who doubted that the state of nature ever existed, that man's nature was still as Hobbes described. For even though there were laws and policemen to enforce them, who went out on a journey unarmed or unaccompanied? Who did not lock his doors at night, and lock his chests against his children and servants (L, 13, par. 12)?

The Causes of Civil War

So far I have discussed Hobbes's mechanism and its consequences for human nature and human interaction. Man's egoism and inability to escape his own unique perspective give rise to competition. We can see that this competition would produce "diffidence," or fear. But Hobbes's third cause of quarrel, glory, cannot be explained on the basis of mechanism, because it cannot be attributed to radically asocial beings. "Glorying" involves valuing other people's opinions. Therefore, if we are to take Hobbes's three principal causes of quarrel as natural to men, we must reevaluate our initial assumption that Hobbes thinks man is naturally asocial. This will allow us to consider the natural condition of mankind not as a presocial state but as a condition of socialized man either ungoverned or ungovernable. Pride is the one passion that Hobbes considers lethal to civil society, the one that can make man ungovernable. This doctrine of equality and his promotion of absolute sovereignty are attempts to eradicate the sin of pride, from which all sedition in society flows. Therefore I will focus on this passion Hobbes so wanted to counter with its "rational" counterpart: fear.

The Societal Origins of Man's Natural Condition   Pride and envy are emotions that have no meaning apart from interpersonal relationships. A man cannot be proud or envious in isolation or if he cares only about himself and not at all about others. The existence of pride in the state of nature is therefore a puzzling phenomenon if we consider the state of nature to be an actual antecedent to society. Hobbes's social proofs of man's natural condition have suggested to some that Hobbes did not intend for the state of nature and the social contract to be considered actual historical occurrences.[4] MacPherson suggests that the state of nature for Hobbes is the state of socialized men who find themselves suddenly without any overarching power to keep them in awe. This theory is bolstered by Hobbes's assertion that civil war is the closest thing to the state of nature that he has observed. Civil war occurs after men are socialized and thus have become attached to social things, like property and honor. In civil war, people compete for power that is already socially defined. As in the "state of nature," the trouble may be caused by a few overly ambitious men who cause sedition and then involve others in the conflict, stirring their vanity to action. The bad consequences that result from the natural condition of mankind are the same as the results of civil war—individual self-interest and fear rule, people are killed, justice has no place, the meanings of words are relative to the speaker, and the desirability of power is the only point on which all can agree. The situation of both is the same: ineffective or absent government. Hobbes's historical analysis bears this comparison out; all the evils of the natural condition of mankind are to be found in his account of the English civil wars in *Behemoth*.

Many of the sources of human conflict that Hobbes mentions make more sense from the point of view of the breakdown of society than from the point of view of a presocial state. Competition revolves around not simply the means for survival but also riches, honor, command, and praise (L, 11, par. 3). Contempt is produced by being beholden to an equal but is not produced if the benefit derives from someone who is clearly a superior. In a presocial state, in which all that is important is an individual's safety and well-being, does it matter how a benefit is obtained? Hobbes writes that in man's natural condition a promptness to hurt comes from distrust of one's own intelligence, so that men who distrust their intelligence are more likely to be victorious in a sedition than those who think themselves wise. The latter dally in thought while the former take action and strike first. Ignorance gives unscrupulous people endless opportunities for mischief. Ambitious men who think highly of their own political wisdom attempt political office to show it off, using eloquence, which "seemeth wisedome, both to themselves and others" (L, 11, par. 13, 16). But ambition combined with eloquence often leads to faction, conflict, and civil war. All these sources of conflict are socially conditioned. They may be natural to men, but if they are, so is a level of sociability.

If we think of the natural condition of mankind as inferred from civil war, Hobbes's causes of quarrel make more sense:

> So that in the nature of man, we find three principall causes of quarrel. First, Competition; Secondly, Diffidence; Thirdly, Glory. The first, maketh men invade for Gain; the second, for Safety; and the

third, for Reputation.

The first use Violence, to make themselves Masters of other mens persons, wives, children, and cattell; the second, to defend them; the third, for trifles, as a word, a smile, a different opinion, and any other signe of undervalue. (L, 13, par. 6–7)

This statement assumes the existence of family and property. It also assumes enough social structure so that all know what constitutes an insult in "a word, a smile, a different opinion, [or] any other signe of undervalue." It has to do with the nature of social man, not simply man in the state of nature.[5] People *naturally* care what others think. This is the primary cause of conflict within society.

Keeping in mind the limited but still real social content of the state of nature, Hobbes's definition of the value or worth of a man is easier to understand. One would think that the only value that could be placed on Hobbes's radically individualistic man would be his estimation of himself, whatever that might mean for a person so intellectually and emotionally isolated from others. But a man's worth is "his price," or what would be given for the use of his power, and is therefore not absolute but dependent on the judgment of others (L, 10, par. 16). The worth of a soldier, for example, depends on whether there is war or peace. Honor and dishonor have to do with how much a man is esteemed by others compared to how much esteem he expects. Hobbes says all ways of honoring are natural and occur both in and outside of civil society (L, 10, par. 34). He could not have in mind here a completely solitary existence in which the only contact with others means the threat of life-or-death struggle, since honoring includes trusting another, hearkening to his counsel, and doing what law or custom deems an honor (L, 10, par. 20–35).

The Content and Consequences of Pride   To be passionless, says Hobbes, is to be dead. But to have too much passion is madness (L, 8, par. 16). Madness can be caused from some malfunction in the body that produces an overwhelming passion, or it can come directly from the passion itself. The passion that causes madness is "either great vaine-Glory; which is commonly called Pride, and selfe-conceipt; or great Dejection of mind" (L, 8, par. 18). Pride produces anger and excessive desire for revenge, which leads to the madness called rage. Overestimation of oneself becomes "Distraction, and Giddinesse," which impedes reason and blinds men to their true self-interest (L, 8, par. 18–19; H, 40–41). All these defects, produced by an immoderation of the passions, derive from vainglory, which is a false estimation of importance in both individuals and multitudes. The singular passions of men may combine to form into the sedition of a nation; in such an instance, men may adopt the mistaken notion that they have the whole truth, which makes them think themselves special when they are not (L, 8, par. 22). Vainglory, one might say, is a drunkenness produced by one's own conceit. The pride that brings about folly can never be deserved. One cannot possibly have good judgment when under the influence of pride. Thus the natural and common delusion of pride keeps human beings from seeing their true interest, from feeling fearful in situations in which rational fear is justified. Pride stands in the way of the order Hobbes wishes to impose on society, because men will destroy for vanity what is in their own best interests.

As indicated above, the concept of pride, or vainglory, assumes a minimum social setting, because it is only in relation to one another that men can feel superior. But if this is true, and the state of nature is an abstraction from society and not a true historical stage of man's development, then the assumptions many have made about Hobbes's view of human nature as radically asocial cannot be true. Indeed, this view suggests that only in the company of others can man "actualize" himself. To say that humans are naturally competitive is not to say that they are asocial. Indeed, it is the very way they relate to each other socially—boasting and vying—that causes war when the government is not strong enough to restrain them. Hobbes's claim that society is purely conventional is contradicted by his own analysis of its formation and disintegration.

The laws of nature also suggest that once men are in society, the greatest threat to order and therefore to human well-being is not competition caused by self-interest or diffidence caused by mutual fear but the struggle for glory brought about by pride. The laws of nature demand that pride be deflated and replaced by rational fear. A quick survey of the laws Hobbes thought most important to long-lasting peace will show why and how he thought pride endangered society.

The first law is to seek peace but to defend ourselves by any means if peace cannot be obtained. The second law calls for each man to lay down his right to all things and give all others as much liberty as he would give to himself, thus admitting the equality of every man (L, 14, par. 4–5). Significantly, this is a contract among the people, not between the people and the sovereign. Hobbes stresses that all men must accept all others as equals, not so much because they really are equal in every respect but because if they do not treat each other as such, no one will agree to give up his natural rights and subordinate himself to the sovereign. This artificial recognition of equality in all aspects, not just the ability to kill, is the first and most fundamental step in ridding civil society of the ill effects of pride. All the laws following the third, *pacta sunt servanda,* are designed to soften the pride and competitiveness of individuals in society. The fourth law is against ingratitude. A person who receives a gift from another should show thanks, so that the giver will not repent of his decision (L, 15, par. 16; DC, 3, par. 8). No benevolence or trust can develop if the benefactor is deprived of his reward—gratitude. The fifth law calls for every man to accommodate his fellows by not taking what to him is superfluous but is necessary for others. If he cannot do this, he cannot remain in society and will be thrown out (L, 15, par. 17; DC, 3, par. 9). The sixth law is to pardon anyone who repents of his offenses, keeping in mind the future good (L, 15, par. 18; DC, 3, par. 10). The seventh law, similar to the sixth, directs all punishment to be executed for the correction of the offender or the deterrence of future offenses, not simply out of anger:

> Besides, Revenge without respect to the Example, and profit to come, is a triumph, or glorying in the hurt of another, tending to no end; (for the End is alwayes somewhat to Come;) and glorying to no end, is vain-glory, and contrary to reason; and to hurt without reason, tendeth to the introduction of Warre; which is against the Law of Nature; and is commonly stiled by the name of Cruelty. (L, 15, par. 19)[6]

The eighth law is against "contumely"—signs of hatred and contempt given by word, gesture, countenance, or deed. Most men, Hobbes writes, would rather risk their lives than not be revenged for such things, and thus such signs are a cause of dangerous conflict (L, 15, par. 20; DC, 3, par. 12). The ninth law, against pride itself, is the first of three laws concerned with equality in society. Inequality, it seems, is introduced by society; it is not natural. Even if inequality were natural, since people think of themselves as equal and will not enter into agreement unless they are so treated, all men should recognize their fellows as equals by nature. If they do not, wounded pride and threatened egos will lead to war (L, 15, par. 21; DC, 3, par. 13). Derivative of this concept is the tenth law prohibiting arrogance, defined as reserving a right to one's self that one is not willing to give to others (L, 15, par. 22; DC, 3, par. 14). The rest of the laws are procedural, dealing with equality before the law, but even here we see that the main reason they are needed is because of man's pride and ambition.

If we examine Hobbes's account of the English civil wars in *Behemoth* we find that it agrees in large part with the above analysis. That is, the causes and consequences of the English civil wars correspond to the causes and consequences of the natural condition of mankind. We can well imagine that Hobbes constructed his metaphorical state of nature and social contract to show the people involved in these and other seditions who were blinded by their pride just how frightened they should be by the loss of order. The state of nature represents the dynamics of civil war taken to their extreme.

In *Behemoth,* the main instigators of the sedition are individuals— ambitious ministers and gentlemen (B, 192). These individuals are moved by nothing more than their own particular interests and pride (B, 275). The common people are "cozened" into believing ministers and papists, individuals who favor private interpretation of the scripture, those swayed by ancient Greek and Roman philosophy concerning liberty and tyranny, and greedy opportunists wanting war. Their ignorance of the necessity for sovereignty makes them easily seduced (B, 167–68). The motives for sedition are ambition, pride, and mutual envy. The ministers envy the bishops. The gentlemen envy the privy council because they think themselves more wise (B, 192, 275). The Petition of Right is a set of demands, reflecting pride (B, 198). Why were the gentry and nobility of Scotland so averse to the episcopacy (which the king wanted to force on them) (B, 200)? Interlocutor "A" replies:

> Truly I do not know; I cannot enter into other men's thoughts, farther than I am led by the consideration of human nature in general. But

upon this consideration I see first, that men of ancient wealth and nobility are not apt to brook that poor scholars should (as they must, when they are made bishops) be their fellows. Secondly, that from the emulation of glory between the nations, they might be willing to see this nation afflicted by civil war, and might hope, by aiding the rebels here, to acquire some power over the English, at least so far as to establish here the Presbyterian discipline. . . . Lastly, they might hope for, in the war, some great sum of money. (B, 200–201)

During the course of the civil wars, words were used to mean what the speakers intended, and oratory became a dangerous weapon. The papists used scripture to prove the pope should rule (B, 169–70). The Church used Aristotle's philosophy to establish universities, which they then used to maintain the pope's doctrine and authority (B, 184). Those who advocated a popular government harangued the parliament, extolling liberty and crying out against tyranny, using, again, the ancient philosophers to lend themselves credibility. Preachers were like actors, using the art of dramatic oratory to win the people over (B, 192–94). Impudence was the "goddess of rhetoric" in parliament. Perhaps the most stunning misuse of speech was the parliament's frequent pronouncements that it supported the king, or the office of the king, while at the same time it tried to reduce or eliminate his power.

The remedy for the relativism and conflict of civil war was education of the common people in the origins of and the reasons for government. The commoners were ignorant of their duty to the public and thought only of their particular and immediate interests (B, 212). While the House of Commons insisted that the origin of all just power was the people, Hobbes said that they were indeed the origin of government, but they had long ago consented to give sovereignty to the king and his heirs. This was the doctrine that needed to be taught to all citizens. The rules of justice and injustice had been put forth so that a lowly peasant could understand them. But many could not read, and others had no leisure to learn. It seemed impossible that the multitude could ever learn their duty, unless it was from the pulpit or on holidays, which were used instead to subvert the people. The remaining hope was the universities, but at the time they were like a Trojan horse to the commonwealth (B, 212–13). None of the world's great commonwealths had been free for very long from sedition, but Hobbes's suggestions were designed to eliminate that problem. He commented, "The Greeks had for awhile their petty kings, and then by sedition came to be petty commonwealths; and then growing to be greater commonwealths, by sedition again became monarchies; and all for want of rules of justice for the common people to take notice of" (B, 252).

In the end, the king was restored by the new parliament of April 1660, which had little hope of being reelected if it did not recall him. This was because the people now wanted the monarchy restored. The reason of the people is not given, but it is stated that the country "felt the smart of their [parliament's] former service" (B, 417). One can surmise that the people were war-weary and longed for the peace that the king had guaranteed, even if it had come without full democratic rights. Thus, indirectly, it was fear—of continued bloodshed—that restored peace, although by Hobbes's own analysis the peace would not be lasting unless his doctrine was accepted and taught. Only if the people feared renewed civil war enough to accept gratefully the authority of an absolute sovereign would the cycle of sedition come to an end.

The Origins of Society and the Way to a Lasting Social Order

In using the state of nature concept, Hobbes did not intend to say that all societies were knowingly formed to escape that fearful condition by way of an explicit social contract. Hobbes wrote in *Behemoth* that a long time ago the people consented to give supreme power to the kings and their heirs (B, 353), but in order for Hobbes's philosophy to make sense, either they could not have understood their consent to be such or they had long ago forgotten the origins of their commonwealth. As John W. Danford explains:

> In the actual historical circumstances everything was confused, every meaning, rendered ambiguous, by certain "phantasms of the mind" which men invented to cover their anxiety, to explain what they did not understand. Thus justice was understood by primitive men to be dispensed by the gods. It was religion above all which prevented the development of language rationally, but it does not prevent Hobbes from figuring out how political terms would have been invented, that is, what they should have meant, if men had had no delusions or had understood themselves scientifically.[7]

In other words, the social contract is the result of Hobbes's resolutive-compositive method, which reconstructed the origins of government according to pure reason. It is not a depiction of reality, but it is more than a heuristic device. It is an assertion of the true reason for government, or how it should be understood. Indeed, the problem Hobbes sees is that government is not so understood. Hobbes is saying not that there could be no society, no government, without social contracts leading to absolute sovereignty but that there can be no orderly society, no lasting government, free of sedition and chance until people realize the need to behave as if they had made such a contract.

Man's Unique Qualities   With Aristotle in mind, Hobbes addresses the question of why men cannot be social without government (like ants and bees), and in the process he tells us what qualities he thinks are peculiarly human. These qualities simultaneously necessitate and make possible the formation of well-governed civil society. First, humans compete continually with one another for honor and dignity, intangible concepts with which animals are not concerned. Second, in the animals that display sociability, the common good does not differ from the private good—by pursuing their particular ends, the common end is automatically attained. Hobbes observes, "But man, whose Joy consisteth in comparing himselfe with other men, can relish nothing but what is eminent" (L, 17, par. 8). Third, animals do not have reason and therefore do not find fault with their arrangements. But among men, there are many who think they are wiser and better able to govern than the rest, and each strives to make changes until they bring on civil war. Fourth, only human beings have language, which can be used to argue about what is good and evil, causing hatred. Fifth, animals cannot distinguish between injury and damage; as long as they are comfortable they leave each other in peace. Only man can be insulted. For all these reasons, what the animals do naturally, in ignorant bliss (cooperate), men will do only if they are coerced (L, 17, par. 9–12).

All but the fourth distinction have to do directly with human pride. Even reason, which is listed third, is treated as being harmful because of pride. Due to pride, the common good and the private good do not naturally coincide in human society as they do in the societies of ants and bees. Animals and men are alike in caring only about themselves, but the good of the society of animals—survival and sustenance—is the same as the good of each. Men's interests include power and a feeling of superiority, which automatically puts them at odds. Therefore the social and individual good do not naturally coincide, even though society is necessary to achieve the private good.

Deliberation and will are shared with the animals (L, 6, par. 51–52), but human deliberation is special in its degree. Common to man and beast is the process of thought whereby the mind seeks causes. But thought that imagines all the possible effects of some action—that is, imagination—belongs only to man. This forward-looking thought is the extent of man's natural capability to deliberate and does not rely on words. Similarly, Hobbes distinguishes the type of understanding animals enjoy from the more profound type that man possesses. Animals understand words insofar as they will act upon command. But peculiar to man is understanding not only the speaker's will but also his reasons. It is this kind of understanding that interests Hobbes: the type made possible only by speech (L, 4, par. 22). The ability to reason is acquired through man's manipulation of language. But it is usually used for each man's struggle for superiority. For this reason, language becomes another source for contention. What causes conflict, however, is not speech or reason. Instead, it is pride that starts the trouble, and speech and reason facilitate its expression.

To be consistent with his own position, Hobbes must have thought that at least some men (such as himself) were capable of completely surmounting their animal passions, as well as their pride, and holding firmly to reason. Hobbes got around the apparent contradiction between his pessimistic theory that reason is led by human passion and his optimism about science by attributing the quest for scientific truth itself to a passion: curiosity, the "lust of the mind." Curiosity is a passion found only in man, and it exceeds any mere carnal lust in its longevity, if not its force. Thus, scientific reason is led by a passion like all other thought, but the passion that leads it is unique because it alone conducts an objective search for its object, truth. This unique passion, combined with speech and reason, makes man the highest animal, and something beyond animal. It is the final ingredient that makes science possible.

Despite its possible abuses, language is called the most noble and profitable invention by Hobbes precisely because of its crucial role in the development of science. It is man's invention, not God's.[8] Speech is described by Hobbes as formed arbitrarily by men from the sounds they make. Hence it flows from the will of man and no one but man (E, 16). Over time, abstract and universal words developed, becoming more and more remote from actual objects until their original meanings became unclear, a phenomenon, Hobbes maintains, that causes most of the disagreement among philosophers and therefore impedes progress toward true knowledge. But speech made distinctions of true and false possible. Before its development, there was no true or false—a person could be in error but could not be charged with untruth. After speech, general and universal terms made the search for truth possible, so long as speech was used scientifically to affirm or to deny, or to express truth or falsity (E, 30).

Science vs. Rhetoric   According to Hobbes, the scientific use of language involves, at its base, definitions for words that stand for universal ideas (L, 4, par. 12–13). These abstract ideas have, as Miriam M. Reik points out, "a purely logical or linguistic existence."[9] The outside world, as we have seen, cannot be known directly. But our conceptions of it can be known, and it is these ideas that must be manipulated using the proper method. As in geometry, the definitions for first principles cannot be directly disputed. They must be agreed upon beforehand as evident. Science, then, is reasoning about the consequences of well-defined words, not about actual experience. From the calculation of the consequences of these words are derived universal rules universally true (L, 4, par. 9). Hobbes states:

> And therefore, when the Discourse is put into Speech, and begins with the Definition of Words, and proceeds by Connexion of the same into generall Affirmations, and of these again into Syllogismes; the end or last summe is called the Conclusion; and the thought of the mind by it signified, is that conditionall Knowledge, or Knowledge of the consequence of words, which is commonly called SCIENCE. (L, 7, par. 4)

Claiming that reasoning is a "mathematical" activity of adding and subtracting names, Hobbes says that no trust should or could be afforded to other authorities who did not follow this method

(L, 5, par. 1, 4). Precisely because of man's relativism and inconsistency in the use of words, only science makes true knowledge possible. John W. Danforth observes, "The fact that names are entirely a matter of convention, according to Hobbes, points to the fact that a large number of philosophical disputes are nothing but disputes about words whose significations are not settled."[10] Because science involves the geometrical calculation of words alone, the test for truth is not its empirical verification but the soundness of its internal logic and its utility. But this acknowledgment left Hobbes's definitions open to the same type of criticisms that marred even the science of geometry. As Reik states, "If the beauty of geometry is in its logical coherence, the bane of the science has always been the logical status of those initial definitions."[11] As we will see, many of Hobbes's definitions having to do with his theory of justice are not intuitively evident at all.

If speech with method could lift mankind to untold heights, speech without method could lead a man to error, contradiction, and absurdity. Error is innocent enough. It is a mistake in reasoning, and even the most prudent men can fall into it, which is one reason why an arbiter of disputes is needed (L, 5, par. 5). Absurdity comes from words that carry no concrete meaning but instead are mere sounds; that is, we can have no picture of it in our heads. Examples of such terms include "immaterial substances" or "free will," which Hobbes took to be contradictions in terms. Hobbes frequently chastises the scholastics and religious leaders of his day for committing this crime.

Because of his exclusive capability to reason about the future, and therefore to be anxious, man is the only religious animal. His mind insists on a cause for everything, and when it cannot be found he supposes a cause, which he invents himself or trusts an authority figure to invent for him (L, 12, par. 5). Hobbes thinks most, if not all, religion is based on spurious reasoning and depends on ignorant men being led by crafty preachers into assuaging their anxiety in this way. He attacks them for their philosophical terms and suggests that their obscurity is a cover for their ignorance and ambition. He even suggests that gods themselves, as some of the old poets had written, are created by human fear. Instead, reason will eventually arrive at an initial eternal cause of all things, "which is that which Men mean by the name of God" (L, 12, par. 6; H, 59–60).

As with religious speech, Hobbes contrasts science with political oratory or rhetoric. In his "Life of Thucydides," Hobbes criticized the Athenian demagogues as wicked flatterers, all alike in their quest for self-promotion and their willingness to prey on the ignorance and pride of the people (HT, "Life," par. 4). He explains Pericles' success as due to the fact that he was more a monarch than an elected representative and thus did not have to compete with any other orator or (presumably) to rely on oratory at all in order to get his way. Unlike scientific speech, rhetoric does not use rigorous definitions but instead shifts and changes its terms and their meanings according to the speaker's point.

Hobbes's mechanism backs up his thesis that every speaker has a unique perspective and that there cannot be any common understanding unless it is enforced. Likewise, his assumption of universal selfishness and ambition devalues rhetoric. For Hobbes, there is no such person as a disinterested politician, let alone a statesman who uses political rhetoric genuinely for deliberative purposes. The aim of science is the truth, but the aim of oratory is always victory for self-interested orators (DC, 10, par. 12, 15; L, 19, par. 8). As Hobbes explains in his analysis of the English civil wars, all leaders are driven by their personal pride and ambition, and their speech is never more than a cover for their selfishness and a tool for manipulating the ignorant common people. Coming from Hobbes's perspective, then, one would not waste time analyzing a speech or set of speeches in order to explain politics. One would simply ask what the speaker's private motivations are based on a general understanding of human beings' invariable quest for power.

Led by the passion of curiosity, science is objective. Rhetoric, in contrast, is subjective, led by the passion of pride. Science is the path to man's salvation, while rhetoric is the cause of sedition and civil war. Science is in the service of the commonwealth. Rhetoric serves particular orators indifferent to the commonwealth except insofar as it serves their purposes. In short, science is the good use of man's special capability to reason using speech. Rhetoric is the self-centered and destructive use of this capability. Therefore there is a fundamental opposition between reason and rhetoric. David Johnston states, "The fundamental dilemma confronting Hobbes's political theory can be reduced to the simple question: science or rhetoric."[12] Hobbes admits that there is a use for rhetoric, but he deprives it of its usual political role. The purpose of rhetoric, or more precisely eloquence, is to educate people concerning the truth found out by science (L, "Review and Conclusion," par. 1–3).[13] Rhetoric is to have no role in discovering the truth, only in communicating it. Hobbes writes, "[N]o great Popular Commonwealth was ever kept up . . . by the open Consultations of the Assembly" (L, 25, par. 16). As we will see, Hobbes makes this statement so blithely because he thinks that there is a real alternative to such political chaos in his theory, which finds salvation in absolute sovereignty. But Hobbes's theory will work only if human nature is not simply uniform but uniform in exactly the way he describes.

Hobbes's belief that, as David Johnston puts it, "rhetoric is the greatest and most insidious enemy with which reason has to contend"[14] is reflected in his analysis of regime-types and his preference for monarchy over aristocracy or democracy.[15] The two latter forms of government encourage competitive and seditious oratory since more than one person is vying for power within them.

The Social Contract   Man is a product of his physiology and experience, but language allows him to escape this mechanism and the determinism it implies with abstract thought, or science. Scientific thought also holds out the prospect of freedom from the harmful consequences of man's pride. Science is a triumph over nature—both man's nature and the natural world writ large.[16] Man's escape from nature, that is, from his own nature, consists in his ability to think rationally and to communicate that thought to others through speech. Confronted with a choice between continual war and the possibility of peace, he will be forced by fear of violent death to stand on the side of peace. Peace means cooperating with other human beings instead of killing them, but many societies are formed that will not last because they are not established firmly enough on reason. That is, they allow divided sovereignty, either by forming a mixed regime or by giving religious leaders too much power over the sovereign. They do not understand the purpose of government. These difficulties are produced by a lack of science in politics.

Without science to teach how to avoid sedition, mankind will be doomed to repeat its mistakes endlessly and governments will continue to be in turmoil and experience bloody change. Hobbes believes himself to be the first to deal scientifically with politics, the first to point out the incorrect use of language and reason in the service of ambition as the main cause of conflict, and the first to propose a scientifically constructed alternative: absolute sovereignty.

Reason dictates that man should make a covenant with his fellows to transfer their rights to a sovereign who will enforce the laws of nature essential to lasting peace. When framing the right of nature and the laws of nature, Hobbes takes individualism as a base on which to build civil society (L, 14, par. 1). The individual is the only one for whom rights matter. The rights of groups, not to mention any higher social good, will not be considered by such individuals as valid claims to their allegiance. In his natural condition, in which he and everyone else is governed by his own passions and guided by his own reason, each man has a right to whatever is necessary for his preservation and a right to everything, including other men's bodies. This liberty is defined in terms of the individual (L, 14, par. 2), and the restriction of this liberty in the name of peace is likewise framed for the good of the individual (L, 14, par. 3).

Formally, at least, every person in Hobbes's covenant would decide to enter into the contract separately (L, 14, par. 6). That is, each individual would agree to adhere to the majority decision about who the sovereign would be. People who never had the opportunity to formally agree to the government they were placed under (as almost all people had not) could be assumed to agree by their continuing presence under its protection. In other words, an individual, if he did not agree with the authority of the sovereign, could "vote with his feet."

Having contracted for protection, individuals cannot be expected to obey only if obedience is a direct threat to their continuing survival. A covenant not to defend oneself is always void, for "no man can transferre, or lay down his Right to save himselfe from Death, Wounds, and Imprisonment," even if he has consented to the law by which he is condemned. Likewise, a covenant to accuse oneself or one's benefactors is void, as is testimony taken by torture. Information gained in these ways will be corrupt since a man's safety and well-being depend directly on the answers he gives (L, 14, par. 29–30). With these exceptions, Hobbes gives the sovereign (be it democratic, aristocratic, or monarchical) complete and unquestionable control over the individuals who have given up their rights for his protection. So an institution, formed by particular wills for their benefit, ends up being one in which these wills are molded in whatever way the absolute sovereign sees fit.

How could such an authoritarian conclusion have been derived from such radically individualistic origins? It is precisely because of the extremity of individualism and especially pride in man that such an authority is logically necessary; that is why Hobbes's theory stands or falls by his analysis of human nature. If his assessment of human nature is accurate, what is needed is a power great enough to keep all men under control and to force them to cooperate for their own good. Without such a power, people, deluded by pride and vainglory, would destroy the very government that was in their best interests for "trifles." Decisions can never be made on the basis of deliberative rhetoric, because the speaker's purpose must always be selfish and will never coincide with the overall good of society. Only absolute coercive power will keep people from self-destruction. Hobbes writes:

> This is the Generation of that great LEVIATHAN, or rather (to speake more reverently) of that Mortall God, to which wee owe under the Immortall God, our peace and defence. For by this Authoritie, given him by every particular man in the Common-Wealth, he hath the use of so much Power and Strength conferred on him, that by terror thereof, he is inabled to forme the wills of them all, to Peace at home, and mutuall ayd against their enemies abroad. And in him consisteth the Essence of the Common-wealth; which (to define it,) is *One Person, of whose Acts a great Multitude, by mutuall Covenants one with another, have made themselves everyone the Author, to the end he may use that strength and means of them all, as he shall think expedient, for their Peace and Common Defence.* (L, 17, par. 13)

Appeals to long-term self-interest are all well and good, and Hobbes thinks it is worth the effort to reason with men about such interest, but he also thinks that only the immediate fear of sovereign power, and fear of the consequences of its absence, can produce the agreement necessary for long-lasting order. Hobbes sees himself as a teacher of those reasons why men should fear civil war and obey their sovereign. With the help of reason and education, there is hope that the endless cycle of conquest, sedition, and revolution, brought about by ignorance of the origins of government, will end.

Summary

Hobbes first proposes a radical individualism and perspectivism in human beings. According to his mechanistic analysis, men are naturally disassociated from one another. Thus society, if it is to come into being, has to be in every individual's self-interest. However, if men in the state of nature were endowed only with interest in themselves and natural fear of others, there would be no reason why any government they created based on self-interest would not last indefinitely. Reason would dictate that cooperative behavior was in every individual's interest, so that whatever the type of regime established, it would tend to continue. But governments, Hobbes says, have always been in a cycle of sedition and change. The reason this is so is because of man's pride. Without assuming pride's disruptive influence on future society, there would be no reason why men could not function in a mixed regime or a regime with divided sovereignty. Since pride, ambition, and envy are the causes of sedition, their presence in the natural condition of mankind is essential. This is why Hobbes's state of nature, in the final analysis, is an inference not so much from the passions derived from his mechanism as from the passions of civil unrest. Hobbes's mechanism cannot account for self-consciousness, pride, or vainglory. The consequences of this mechanism would be radical individualism and asociability—the assumptions necessary to make civil society appear to be derived from individual consent. But the very asocial human nature it hypothesizes contradicts the limited but real sociability inherent in pride, envy, and vainglory.

Realizing that Hobbes's theory has as its conclusion the avoidance of civil war, it comes as no surprise that he spends much time on that aspect of human nature that contributes to the dissolution of a developed society. The worst kind of bloodshed can result from differences of opinion brought about by vainglory. Thus the laws of nature emphasize rules that squelch the natural pride in men that leads to war in societies: laws against ingratitude, antisocial behavior, revenge, contumely, and arrogance; laws that urge forgiveness and acknowledgment of equality. Hobbes's analysis of England's own civil wars bears out this reading of his philosophy. Hobbes teaches prideful men why they should be fearful of the consequences of their actions by showing them what life would be like without government. Since pride and ambition can cause the slide into anarchy, Hobbes teaches that absolute sovereignty is the safest policy. Reason may convince people that Hobbes's recommendations are correct, but only legitimate force will cause them to continue to be so reasonable.

Hobbes has hope that human beings can control their nature through reason, specifically scientific reason. If curiosity and language are employed in the pursuit of science, there is a chance of surmounting the effects of pride. But if reason is employed by some self-serving orator or preacher, it is supremely destructive. Hobbes stands firmly on the side of science as the alternative to ignorance, superstition, and arrogance in both politics and religion. He believes he can educate leaders and subjects in the causes of and need for absolute sovereignty. If men truly understand why government is necessary and can see beforehand the consequences of erosion in sovereignty, perhaps they will accept an absolute authority as reasonable and end their seditions. Only absolute sovereignty can adequately control the natural urges of ambitious individuals. Hobbes is asking citizens to behave *as if* they had made a contract with one another to escape their natural condition. He is asking them to covenant with one another now, through a new, enlightened understanding of politics.

THUCYDIDES

On the surface, it appears that Thucydides would be in basic agreement with Hobbes on human nature. Thucydides' characters are often "Hobbesian," or say Hobbesian things. Although Athenians are the most outspoken in their claim to be ruled by their passions, their enemies usually agree. A passion for profit is responsible for the beginning of Greek civilization and the tyrannies that followed, and it was the true reason for Athenian imperialism and the war it caused. But even though passions are very powerful factors in the *History*, I hope to show that for Thucydides they are not universal or compelling. His analysis, rightly understood, insists that none of the passions compel or force people to act, even though they may be very strong.

This is not the only way in which Thucydides appears to be neither a Hobbesian nor a realist. As human nature is not driven by passions, it is not as monotonous and invariable as the Athenians would have their listeners believe. Indeed, the differing national character of

Athens and Sparta greatly influenced their actions throughout the war, causing Sparta to be conservative, calculating, and sometimes vicious, while causing Athens to be bold, innovative, and relatively magnanimous until her moral collapse. Likewise, Thucydides explains differing policies by the individual attributes of decision-makers—attributes such as character, intelligence, cruelty, and piety. In addition, Thucydides could not possibly acknowledge the role played by deliberative reasoning without rejecting the idea many of his "realistic" characters profess, that passion necessarily determines men's actions and that therefore men are not responsible for their actions.

Moreover, Thucydides contrasts human nature in a more normal state of affairs, in which interest and sociability coexist with human nature in times of extremism produced by ambition, envy, and party rivalry. Destabilized by the greater Peloponnesian War, many Greek cities fell into civil wars, in which people rejected their own self-interest and chose revenge over life and peace. For Thucydides such violence and relativism, though bound to recur throughout history, represent an inversion of normality. Thucydides, as we will see, treats civil war as he treats Athenian strategic miscarriages during the war: they are unfortunate products of certain aspects of human nature that cannot always be suppressed. They represent the decline of civilization, just as unity and a sense of civic duty represent its peak.

Do the Passions Compel?

Thucydides states, "The truest explanation [for the war,] although it has been the least often advanced, I believe to have been the growth of the Athenians to greatness, which brought fear to the Lacedaemonians and forced them to war" (1.23.6).[17] This is one passage that realists sometimes emphasize in their attempt to make Thucydides into one of their own, supporting the proposition that the fear and mistrust inherent in international relations, combined with each state trying to secure itself by adding to its power, make conflict inevitable when one power rises above another. The question is, why did Athens, unlike Sparta, continue to grow in power and possessions after the Persian War, eventually becoming a "tyranny" to their subject-states? Was Athens's *rise* depicted as inevitable, an attempt to amass security in an anarchical world?

The Athenians who happened to be at Sparta during the debate over whether or not to go to war answered this question by asserting that human nature is under the influence of certain passions, which are universal, lawlike, and compelling: "It was under the compulsion of circumstances that we were driven at first to advance our empire to its present state, influenced chiefly by fear, then by honour also, and lastly by self-interest as well" (1.75.3–4). Later it would have been dangerous to give up the empire, especially since all the defectors would fall into Spartan hands (1.75.5). Athenian actions, they claim, were not inconsistent with human nature or character (1.76.2). But if the Athenians were correct in their assumptions about human nature and the nature of international relations, why did Sparta and Athens act in such different ways, until Sparta was forced to go to war with Athens out of fear? On the contrary, it appears that throughout the *History* the Athenians and their counterparts display a richness and complexity of character that cannot be captured by such a facile and determinative thesis.

Thucydides shows that war between Athens and Sparta had nothing to do with Athens's insecurity and fear, as the envoys claim. The Athenians' fearless ambition alone led to imperialism, which then led, predictably, to war. It generated Spartan fear but was not itself compelled by insecurity or fear to provoke Spartan hostility. At the same time, Spartan reluctance invited Athenian aggression. Hence their differing national characters led them to the hostile situation that crystallized at the war conference.

For instance, after the Persian war, while Athens and Sparta were still allied, Themistocles continued to strengthen the Athenian navy and to build the long walls to the suburb of Piraeus. Themistocles, we are told, had persuaded the Athenians to continue to improve their strength by finishing the walls of Piraeus, with its three natural harbors, because it would be a great advantage to the Athenians in their pursuit of power. Domination of the sea was the key to that power, he told them (1.93.4–5). The Spartans, prodded by their allies, voiced concern about the possibility of Athenian walls being erected and asked Athens to stop but did nothing more (1.90.2). Familiar with their reticence, Themistocles put them off until the work was essentially completed. Then he presented them with a fait accompli. He told the Spartans that the walls were needed. Some of the other confederates had walls already, and Themistocles claimed that Athens could not feel itself to be their equals if it did not protect itself likewise.

As leader of the post-Persian war alliance, Sparta had sent Pausanias as commander in chief of the Hellenic confederacy. But Pausanias's violent and dictatorial style soon alienated the allies, who turned to the Athenians for leadership. The Athenians accepted their offer. The Spartans voluntarily receded into isolation when they saw that the allies would no longer accept their leadership, thereby conceding openly to the Athenians, with whom they were still friendly and trusting, despite the Athenians' defensive measures (1.94). The Athenians now determined the tribute that would be paid by the allies for the maintenance of the confederacy, either in money or in ships. And soon, Thucydides says, "their supremacy commenced," first against independent allies, then against the barbarians, and finally against their own imperial possessions. They began to confront the Peloponnesian cities they had contact with (1.95.7).

Athens subdued her first allied city, Naxos, after it left the confederacy (1.98–99). The Athenian-Spartan alliance was broken over the town of Ithome. Sparta called on Athens for help in besieging the rebel town. But when the Athenians came, the Spartans feared they would try to foment political change there and asked them to leave. Athens was offended by this dismissal and broke off the alliance, allying instead with Sparta's enemy, Argos (1.102).[18] All this time, the Athenians were heading sallies into Persian territory. They abandoned an expedition to Cyprus for a more promising invitation from a Libyan king who wanted help in his quest to foment revolution in Egypt. This expedition ended in military disaster for the Athenians (1.104, 109). They also battled the Corinthians and Epidaurians near Haliae and the Peloponnesian fleet near Cecruphalia. War broke out between Aegina and Athens.

In time, Themistocles' "defensive build-up" was achieved. Sparta's resistance, even when it did occur, was relatively mild. A five-year truce was established between the Spartans and Athenians, and then a thirty-year truce. But neither side's behavior seems to have changed as a result. This truce was in place as the events leading up to the declaration of what became known as the Archidamian war (the first half of the Peloponnesian War) unfolded (1.112, 115). No passion compelled any of these Athenian actions, nor was Sparta compelled to acquiesce in Athens's actions. Instead the Spartans acted out of a chosen inwardness and reticence that the Corinthians were later to criticize. A look at some of the speeches leading up to the war will provide a clearer picture of the differing motives of the major antagonists.

In his first speech, Pericles affirms the great difference between Spartan and Athenian motivation. He compares the imperial system of Athens, in which the leading city decides strategy and its allies follow, with the inefficiency of the Peloponnesians' more "democratic" alliance system, in which all cities have a say in strategy. He is so confident of the superiority of the Athenian system that he is more afraid of the Athenians' mistakes than of the enemy's plans (1.144.1–2). For Pericles, the danger is that fear will cause the Athenians to compromise with the Peloponnesians, and he warns that they must never be driven by such fear.

In his funeral oration, as Pericles describes the greatness of the Athenians, their culture, and their character, he again compares them to the Spartans. Athens cannot help but look better in this comparison, and this relative greatness or glory is Pericles' justification for the empire and the war. If the Athenians are worthy and courageous warriors, he says, even if they lose, their actions will be redeemed by their fame in history. Each citizen's private interest is in striving for this type of glory (2.46.2). Athenians must become lovers of their city, taking an erotic satisfaction in Athens's beauty, culture, and exploits: "For the love of honour alone is untouched by age, and when one comes to the ineffectual period of life it is not 'gain' as some say, that gives the greater satisfaction, but honour" (2.44.4).

Periclean rhetoric indicates that what moved the Athenians to wage war was a sense of glory, achievement, and daring. The Athenians, as opposed to the Spartans, have these characteristics in abundance. There is something mercurial about the Athenians as Pericles depicts them, something unpredictable but undeniably admirable. It is more noble than mere national self-interest or fear and decisions based on fear, and it is a matter of choice, not compulsion. Pericles, as the chief supporter of the war, gave the Athenians their reasons to commit to the war, and these reasons were chiefly honor-based, even though he on occasion resorted to sterner admonitions. In another speech he claims that Athens's empire is a tyranny and so must now be kept down out of necessity. Yet the ultimate reason for keeping the empire was, for Pericles, the glory or honor history would reflect on Athens for even attempting to do so.

At least Pericles' enemies agreed with him that the Athenians were risk takers, unlike the Spartans. At the Spartan War Conference, rejected by Athens in favor of Corcyra, Corinth sought to win a Spartan declaration of war. The Corinthians ask the members of the Spartan assembly why they cannot see that the Athenians have long been preparing for an imperialistic war. They point to Athens's alliance with their enemy, Corcyra. Corcyra had given the Athenians both ships and a strategic location with which to wage war. The Spartans are to blame, they claim, for allowing Athens to build up its strength after the Persian War and for letting Athens fortify itself with walls: "For the state which has reduced others to slavery does not in a more real fashion enslave them than the state which has the power to prevent it, and yet looks carelessly on, although claiming as its preeminent distinction that it is the liberator of Hellas" (1.69.1–2).

Sparta had waited until the Persians were in the Peloponnesus before resisting them. Now they treat the Athenian menace in the same manner, waiting for their attack instead of boldly preempting it. Yet the Persians failed mostly because of their own mistakes, and the Corinthians argue, "[I]n our struggles with the Athenians themselves we have so far often owed our successes rather to their own errors than to any aid received from you" (1.69.4–6).

By blaming the Spartans' lack of initiative more than the Athenians' grasping for empire, the Corinthians sanction as natural both the endless pursuit of power and the defense against it. But, ironically, the men they are trying to convince, the Spartans, are proof that such grasping pursuit of power is not as natural or blameless as they suggest, nor is the prompt defense against others' aggrandizements.

The Corinthians contrast the national character of Sparta with that of Athens. Such a comparison is geared to embarrass the Spartans, although the Corinthians insist they speak as friends. The Athenians are innovative, imaginative, and decisive. They are "bold beyond their strength, venturesome beyond their better judgment, and sanguine in the face of dangers." They look on foreign entanglements with hope instead of fear. In battle, they push victory to the limits and retreat as little as possible if they lose. Looking always to future accomplishments, they are never satisfied with what they have. They feel they deserve everything and so feel robbed of a possession if they do not manage to take it (1.70): "In this way they toil, with hardships and dangers, all their life long; and least of all men they enjoy what they have because they are always seeking more, because they think their only holiday is to do their duty, and because they regard untroubled peace as a far greater calamity than laborious activity" (1.70.8).

The Corinthians at least agree with Pericles that Athenian striving goes beyond mere calculations of interest. It is a striving for more power and for glory as well as profit. The Athenians are active simply because they enjoy activity. The Spartans will act only if fear compels them. Spartan behavior is old-fashioned; Athens's behavior is modern. But the modern must always prevail over the old. Athens's innovation will win if Sparta does not change its attitude in time (1.71). Sparta, they threaten, should attack without delay before Corinth and other friendly cities are forced to find allies elsewhere.

At this same war conference, some Athenians who are in Sparta on other business take it upon themselves to deny the Corinthians' assertion that they are different from the Spartans in matters of war, peace, and power. After all, they maintain, the Spartans establish oligarchical governments in their allied states for their own advantage. The Athenians insist that what Athens has done is only normal human behavior, adding, "It has ever been an established rule that the weaker is kept down by the stronger" (1.76.1–2). No one has ever put a priority on justice when faced with the opportunity to get what was wanted by force. If the Spartans had not withdrawn from leadership at the end of the Persian war, they would have become just as disliked and resented by their allies. They, too, would have been compelled to treat their allies harshly. But, of course, the Spartans did withdraw, a fact the Athenians do not want to take into account in the theory of human action they propound.

Again contradicting their own theory by revealing mixed motives, the Athenians go on to state that Athens also deserves her empire for moral reasons. She is to be commended, because while she yields to the "instinct of human nature to rule over others," she observes justice more than she has to (1.76.3–4). Athens's law courts try the complaints of her allies on commercial matters and apply the law on an equal basis. Accustomed to equal treatment, the allies become angry when they feel they are slighted in any way, not remembering that those who can use might do not need to appeal to right. Indeed, the allies would be less offended if Athens resorted simply to might. Men "are more resentful of injustice than of violence; for the former, they feel, is overreaching by an equal, whereas the latter is coercion by a superior" (1.77.3–5). As a final indication that the Athenians are not compelled to go to war, or to do anything else, they offer to let their differences be settled by arbitration (1.78), an offer the Spartans were to reject.

The Corinthians at Sparta characterized the Athenians in terms Pericles would approve. In their estimation, Athenian striving went beyond mere calculation of interest, indeed beyond good judgment, into desire for glory at almost any cost. It was the opposite of fear—courage and daring—that they thought motivated the Athenians. It is only when the Athenians come before the Spartan assembly in an effort to dissuade them from war that we hear the claim that they took and held their empire chiefly through fear. They naturally try to put all of Athens's actions in the best possible light. They blame the temptations of human nature for any action that might have seemed wrong. Who are they to ignore the law that the stronger rule the weaker?

It is safe to say, though, that regardless of the famous claims of the Athenian envoys, the empire was taken chiefly for Athenian interests and, starting with Pericles, was held for the sake of their interest and glory. Moreover, Thucydides' assumption is that great statesmen, namely Themistocles and Pericles, made decisions that led to the imperial policy of Athens. They are not depicted as being *compelled* by fear or any other passion to secure their empire. This fact, along with the frequently acknowledged differences in motivations between Athens and Sparta, disproves the Athenians' thesis, promoted by them throughout the war, that such violence is natural, ungoverned by free will, and therefore blameless.

Human Nature in the Breakdown of Civilization

The breakdown of order is a theme in the *History,* from the plague that wreaked havoc on Athens, to the party rivalry that ripped apart various cities, to the factions and personal competition that existed in Athens itself. The next section will examine the accounts of the plague of Athens and the Corcyraean stasis. I hope to show, by the example of behavior during the plague, that Thucydides does not believe that even under duress are people always naturally as antisocial and violent as they appear during civil war. Under certain conditions, individuals have the capacity for such behavior, but it is not an expression of what is natural and normal for human beings, even in a state of anarchy, when, according to Hobbes (and realists), radical mistrust and preemptive violence should prevail.

The Plague   The account of the plague that descended upon Athens in the second spring of the war is inferior only to Thucydides' description of the Corcyraean civil war in its graphic depiction of human behavior in crises. A disease began to appear that was worse than any other in memory. It was made worse by the crowded conditions in the city. The physicians were unable to treat it. It did not discriminate between poor and rich, weak and strong, virtuous and vicious. Indeed, people caught the disease while caring for the sick (2.51.6).

As the victims realized that all efforts to save themselves were futile, they became "careless of all law, sacred as well as profane." Burial rites were discontinued and bodies were disposed of by the easiest means possible (2.52.4). Eventually people stopped appealing to the gods or oracles, since it did them no material good (2.47), and they began to scorn customs and written as well as unwritten laws. It is worthwhile to quote at length Thucydides' description of the mood of these people in such misery:

> In other respects also the plague first introduced into the city a greater lawlessness. For where men hitherto practiced concealment, that they were not acting purely after their pleasure, they now showed a more careless daring. They saw how sudden was the change of fortune in the case both of those who were prosperous and suddenly died, and of those who before had nothing but in a moment were in possession of the property of others. And so they resolved to get out of life the pleasures which could be had speedily and would satisfy their lusts, regarding their bodies and their wealth alike as transitory. And no one was eager to practice self-denial in prospect of what was esteemed honour, because everyone thought that it was doubtful whether he would live to attain it, but the pleasure of the moment and whatever was in any way conducive to it came to be regarded as at once

honourable and expedient. No fear of gods or law of men restrained; for, on the one hand, seeing that all men were perishing alike, they judged that piety and impiety came to the same thing, and on the other, no one expected that he would live to be called to account and pay the penalty of his misdeeds. On the contrary, they believed that the penalty already decreed against them, and now hanging over their heads, was a far heavier one, and that before this fell it was only reasonable to get some enjoyment out of life. (2.53)

Faced with indiscriminate death, the Athenians disregarded social and religious mores. They developed a "live for today" attitude. When they could see no future in cooperating with the government and their faith was shaken by the deaths of the pious, they chose to commit crimes and squander money. Considering their indiscriminate punishment, this seemed only just: "Justice, such as it was—such as it still figured in these lives of utmost desperation—was now itself a force tending to the dissolution of society."[19] If they were probably going to die before they could be sentenced, what was the point in obeying laws? If the gods did not exist or did not care for men's suffering, what good did it do to worship them? The Athenians freed themselves from these social restraints when they could see no benefit to themselves in keeping them.

Thucydides seems to say that human beings obey laws and worship gods because they perceive some benefit in doing so. People are capable of following their enlightened self-interest, but the result is that mores are easily rejected when they no longer serve. Civilization appears, in Thucydides' description of the plague, to be a luxury that is very tenuous indeed. But we cannot conclude from this episode that civilization is an artificial construct invented by man to avoid the hideous perils of a war of all against all. We might as easily conclude that society and social mores naturally develop whenever men are not faced with mortal danger and that the psychic response to this danger is an extreme exception, a perversion of what it means to be human. After all, the plague was not created by humans; it was imposed on them. The behavior associated with it might be very unnatural, or it might be only natural in unnatural circumstances.

It cannot be said, at any rate, that all sociability died along with the more civilized behavior the Athenians abandoned. But even the worst behavior of the plague victims does not resemble relentless hostility, and their behavior never constituted a uniform reaction to the crisis. On the contrary, the Athenians responded to this terrible situation in a variety of ways. In the midst of the crisis, Thucydides shows doctors who continued to care for the sick and who died because of their efforts, family and friends who also died caring for the sick, as well as others who could safely show compassion after surviving the disease. Plague-ridden Athens is depicted not as a battleground in which every man is forced to attack for fear of being attacked; instead, it is a state of hedonism, a mad rush to enjoy life while it can still be enjoyed.

In addition, Thucydides states, political and religious thought did not completely perish. After the second Peloponnesian invasion and the attack of the plague, Athenians temporarily rejected Pericles' policy and were eager for peace. They sent embassies to Sparta, but unsuccessfully (2.59). They imagined that the gods were on the Peloponnesians' side, and they recalled an oracle that predicted Peloponnesian success.

In sum, the episode of the plague shows the utilitarian motives of most peoples' adherence to social mores. It demonstrates that law is only effective when the punishment is feared and thus that law relies on the threat of punishment. It does not show that faced with imminent death, when they no longer see the usefulness in law or religion, human beings revert to radical insecurity and hostility. Law and piety may be partly conventional, but society is not.

The Passions That Cause Civil War   In the fifth year of the larger conflict, a civil war broke out in Corcyra that served as Thucydides' prototype for all the civil wars to follow. The Corinthians had released some prisoners, 250 of the leading men of Corcyra,[20] with the agreement that they would foment revolution in Corcyra. Under the influence of the returned prisoners, the Corcyraeans still remained allies of Athens, but they also befriended the Corinthians and their Peloponnesian allies. As the former prisoners spread propaganda, squabbles erupted between the oligarchs and democrats. The oligarchs brought Peithias, a leader of the popular party, to trial, accusing him of attempting to bring Corcyra under Athens's control. But Peithias was acquitted. In retaliation, suits were brought against the five wealthiest of the former prisoners, and the sentencing produced fines so high that even they could not pay. Following the traditional alternative, they became suppliants at the temples, hoping to be allowed to pay the fines by installments. But Peithias convinced the senate to let their sentences stand. Because of this, and also because they knew that Peithias would continue to ask the people to conclude an offensive and defensive alliance with Athens, the oligarchs "banded together and suddenly rushing into the senate with daggers in their hands killed Peithias and others, both senators and private persons, to the number of sixty" (3.70.6).

The oligarchic conspirators, now in charge, adopted a position of neutrality toward Athens and Sparta. One ship on either side in the war would be received into Corcyra's port, but if more than one came, either side's ships would face hostility (3.71). When a Corinthian ship arrived with Spartan envoys, the now dominant oligarchic party attacked the people and defeated them. The commoners took refuge in the Acropolis and the hills surrounding the town and began to organize (3.72.2). The Corcyraean slaves quickly deserted to the people, while the oligarchs hired eight hundred mercenaries. Thus prepared, both sides attacked each other again. This time the commons won. The oligarchs were forced to burn their own homes and businesses in order to stop the people's advance (3.74.2). The Corinthians abandoned their mission when they saw the people had retaken their city (3.74.3).

Nicostratus, an Athenian general, arrived in Corcyra and tried to restore order. He proposed a settlement whereby both sides would prosecute the leaders of the revolt and Corcyra would enter into an offensive and defensive alliance with Athens. This settlement was concluded but did not last. The popular party convinced him to leave five ships at Corcyra and then began to enroll its enemies as crews. The oligarchs, afraid that this was a trap to send them to Athens, again sought refuge at a temple, and the commons took this as proof that their pledge to fight alongside the people in the war was insincere. They "took this pretext to arm themselves" (3.75.4). Seeing their precarious position, the rest of the oligarchs (about four hundred) became suppliants in the temple of Hera. The people convinced them to move to an island across from the temple and kept them in supplies, thus respecting for awhile their right to asylum (3.75.5).

At about the same time, a sea fight broke out, with the Corcyraeans and the Athenians together on one side and the Peloponnesians, angered by the turn of events against their oligarchic allies in the city, on the other. To prevent the Peloponnesians from attempting a rescue, the Corcyraeans brought the suppliants back from the island and deposited them in the temple. Confusion and fear broke out in the city at the thought that the Peloponnesians might invade. The people were about to negotiate with the oligarchs for peace in order to keep the Peloponnesians from invading, when sixty additional Athenian ships approached (3.80). The Peloponnesians fled when they found themselves outnumbered. No longer threatened by immediate invasion, the people killed any personal enemies they could find. "They also put ashore and despatched all those on board the ships whom they had persuaded to go aboard, then went into the temple of Hera, persuaded about fifty of the suppliants there to submit to trial, and condemned them all to death" (3.81.21–3).

When they realized what had happened to these men, the remaining suppliants in the temple committed suicide. Now, a full and bloody civil war broke out in the disorder and panic. The people "slaughtered" whomever they thought were their personal enemies: "The charge they brought was of conspiring to overthrow the democracy, but some were in fact put to death merely to satisfy private enmity, and others, because money was owing to them, were slain by those who had borrowed it. Death in every form ensued, and whatever horrors are wont to be perpetrated at such times all happened then—aye, and even worse" (3.81.4–5).

As inhabitants of the twentieth century, we can certainly imagine what kind of horrors are implied. According to Clifford Orwin, Thucydides shows us "in short order the collapse of the three fundamental institutions: kinship, human law, and divine law."[21] He gives us an extremely detailed account of the effects of this civil war and generalizes his description to account for the dynamics of the civil wars that spread throughout Greece as the international conflict continued. In fact, the various revolutions fed off each other so that each new one was worse for cruelty and revenge (3.82.4).

Thucydides' account of this episode is not only lengthy but also uncharacteristically emotional. We cannot escape the feeling that Thucydides is as close to giving us "value judgments" here as he will ever get. But the tone is one of lament, not entreaty. The effects of the revolutions are as important as the causes, if not more. For while we may be able to know the causes, there is no indication that

Thucydides believes that similar catastrophes will not take place again, given the same type of circumstances. We are faced in these passages more than anywhere else with Thucydides' fatalism, his lack of acquaintance with the notion of progress in the way we think of progress, as humans' ability to use reason to permanently change a situation for the better:

> And so there fell upon the cities on account of revolutions many grievous calamities, such as happen and always will happen while human nature is the same, but which are severer or milder, and different in their manifestations, according as the variations in circumstances present themselves in each case. For in peace and prosperity both states and individuals have gentler feelings, because men are not then forced to face conditions of dire necessity; but war, which robs men of the easy supply of their daily wants, is a rough schoolmaster and creates in most people a temper that matches their condition. (3.82.2–3)

Thucydides does not say that this brutality is the basic nature of mankind any more than he would claim that the gentleness of peace and prosperity is natural. Instead, both are natural and are strongly influenced by the climate produced by the decision-makers of the time. Both brutality and gentility are possible within the context of society. Indeed, in civil war, men are all too social, that is, too concerned with their fellow men. There is no more social an emotion than the desire for revenge. But there is no indication that Thucydides believes that the emotions that surface in civil war are the only natural emotions of which people are capable, even when orderly society fails.

We must return to Thucydides' thoughts on the causes of civil war in order to understand what, in the human nature he describes, is responsible for so much evil. The true cause of civil war is not the broader war between Athens and Sparta. Thucydides says only that the war gave factions a pretext for their sedition. The Athenians represented democracy and the Spartans oligarchy, and the corresponding parties in each city sought to bring in the side that could establish their power. The war gave them a legitimate reason for asking for Athens's or Sparta's intervention (3.82).

The cause of the civil wars is also not the "ideologies" themselves, that is, a genuine zeal for either democratic or oligarchic government. Thucydides notes the important role that the class-based parties played in the strife. Familial loyalties, "the true north of the Greek moral compass,"[22] according to Orwin, were replaced by loyalties to party. Sons were killed by fathers in the political struggle (3.81.5). But Thucydides looks behind this vehement partisanship. He does not believe that such violent discord is brought about fundamentally by idealistic adherence to parties. The source of the trouble is found not in the ideas but in a particular passion of individuals, and a decision to indulge it. As Thucydides writes:

> The cause of all these evils was the desire to rule which greed and ambition inspire, and also, springing from them, that [party spirit] which belongs to men who once have become engaged in factious rivalry. For those who emerged as party leaders in the several cities, by assuming on either side a fair-sounding name, the one using as its catch-word "political equality for the masses under the law," the other "temperate aristocracy," while they *pretended* to be devoted to the common weal, in reality made it their prize; striving in every way to get the better of each other they dared the most awful deeds, and sought revenges still more awful, not pursuing these within the bounds of justice and the public weal, but limiting them, both parties alike, only by the moment's caprice; and they were ready, either by passing an unjust sentence of condemnation or by winning the upper hand through acts of violence, to glut the animosity of the moment. The result was that though neither had any regard for true piety, yet those who could carry through an odious deed under the cloak of a specious phrase received the higher praise. And citizens who belonged to neither party were continually destroyed by both, either because they would not make common cause with them, or through mere jealousy that they should survive. (3.82.8)

Personal ambition and self-aggrandizement are the roots of civil war, which then need a particular climate and the willingness to unleash them. As W. Robert Connor observes, "Just as the Athenian dominance (*arche*) is deeply rooted in human nature, the stasis at Corcyra is a manifestation of a tendency within human beings that can take especially pernicious forms."[23]

Thucydides' tone of condemnation is strong throughout his description of the stasis, suggesting that the different warring parties in Corcyra are to be *blamed* for their lack of self-control. Party leaders use their ideologies in order to gain power for themselves, not in the pursuit of some transcendent good. Even piety is used for personal gain; the more deftly it is employed to cover deceit, the more it is to be admired. Neither fear for one's safety nor self-interest (it is not in one's true interest to be reckless or to risk one's life to kill a rival) is responsible for the extreme cruelty that prevailed, but instead envy and thirst for revenge (3.82.7).

All these things, according to Thucydides, have happened and will happen again from time to time as a result of humankind's capacity to change its spirit to one of faction, ideology, and bloodthirstiness. The evils of civil war are not caused by circumstances or nature if by "caused" we mean "determined," for Thucydides' condemning tone and his outright disapproval suggest very strongly that human choice or free will was involved in the succumbing to certain pressures and those particular tendencies of human nature. That is, simply because Thucydides believes that these events will recur does not mean that human beings are not in control of events or are mere slaves to their impulses or circumstances. It means, instead, that given human fallibility we cannot expect the right choices to be made or the right attitude to be adopted all the time.

Thucydides' account of this turn toward ambition and away from reason and deliberation is one of the saddest commentaries on human nature of all time. Predictably, moderation was the greatest victim of the conflict. Those who were not inclined to take sides were destroyed as the society became more and more polarized. The two strongest influences on the side of moderation—piety and intelligence—by their very natures could not survive the immediacy of the violence. On the one hand, "that simplicity, which is the chief element of a noble nature, was laughed to scorn and disappeared" (3.83.2). From the comments that follow this observation, we can surmise that men of such simplicity were trusting and still believed in the binding nature of oaths. These individuals were ruined by the far more prevalent type of men who with no hope for law enforcement "were rather disposed to take precautions against being wronged than able to trust others" (3.83.3). In the context of civil war, Thucydides described a radical Hobbesian insecurity that made men think of preemption first and deliberation not at all.

The intelligent were destroyed along with the simple, because of the incompatibility of their natures with the situation they faced.

Those of "meaner intellects" prevailed over the more subtle by simply using force, "for being afraid of their own defects and of their
opponents' sagacity, in order that they might not be worsted in
words, and, by reason of their opponents' intellectual versatility find
themselves unawares victims of their own plots, they resorted boldly
to deeds" (3.83.3–4).

It is not surprising, considering the fate of the intellectuals, that
language was also a victim of civil war. Thucydides writes, "The ordinary acceptation of words in their relation to things was changed as
men thought fit" (3.82.3). The extremity of the situation itself, the
total lack of trust and security, and the vehemence of hatred forced a
revaluation of words or changed their referents.[24] What Conner refers to as "revolutionary newspeak" took over, because people now
spoke of behavior that was formerly considered bad or shameful as
commendable.[25] Thus, recklessness came to be respected as courageous loyalty to party. Prudence and moderation were viewed as
cowardice and unmanliness. To be clever in everything was to be
seen as a do-nothing.[26] "Frantic impulsiveness was accounted a true
man's part, but caution in deliberation a specious pretext for shirk-
ing" (3.82.5–6). Sophisticated deception was accorded the highest
honors.

Language—and thus customary morality—was debased by more
than this "newspeak." Thucydides' account of the revolution
contains many references to persuasion, but persuasion from any
side was powerless to stop the escalating violence.[27] Communication among individuals, parties, and states continued, but it became less and less effective. Just like the inversion of values that
occurred within Corcyra, this inability of communication to work
was a product of the general mistrust and, indeed, hysteria that
mounted with each passing day. It was a symptom of the problem,
not a cause.

As noted above, the normal moderating influence of fear and
reasoned self-interest gave way to the urge for revenge. Revenge
was more highly valued than personal security. Men gave themselves over to plotting the most satisfying double-crosses, regardless of the risks. Oaths were violated not simply for fear of the
other side reneging but out of spite. They were violated when the
revenge would be the sweetest, when the enemy was off-guard
(3.82.7). Leo Strauss notes:

> While not every civil war is a consequence of foreign war and not
> every foreign war culminates in a civil war, there is nevertheless a
> kinship between war and civil war: both cities and individuals have
> better thoughts in peace and when things go well than in war. . . .
> This means that moderation, justice, and piety and the praise of these
> ways of conduct are at home in the city at peace rather than in the city
> at war.[28]

By lamenting the inversion of customary values, Thucydides re-
assert their objective meaning and indicates that what occurred in
the civil wars was an inversion, or perversion, of human nature that
nevertheless will occur from time to time. The distortions of self-
interest, as Connor observes, are the "drive for dominance, self-
aggrandizement, and ambition,"[29] but they are just as natural as,
though thankfully less frequent than, their more gentle peacetime
counterparts. Lowell Edmunds writes, "The ethical inversions experienced in stasis are a particular expression of a general ineluctable
tendency of human nature to invert the established and proper way
of things. Stasis, as the expression of such a tendency, is inevitable
and will recur."[30]

The Role of Hubris

Some scholars have characterized Thucydides' *History* as a monumental tragedy, in which the pride and lust for power of the Athenians inevitably brought about Athens's fall in Sicily and her eventual
defeat at the hands of the Spartans.[31] Certainly, Thucydides has
much to say about pride, and at first reading one might think that
Thucydides' opinion was that pride pushed men on until they surrendered of necessity to failure. But instead of looking at this theme
of pride as if it occurred in a tragedy, I suggest that we consider
that it occurred in a book at least partly intended to teach future
statesmen.[32]

It is, of course, difficult to take such a decisive stance on Thucydides' purpose, just as it is difficult to glean the true meaning from
Thucydides' famous statement:

> And it may well be that the absence of the fabulous from my narrative
> will seem less pleasing to the ear; but whoever shall wish to have a
> clear view both of the events which have happened and of those which
> will some day, in all human probability, happen again in the same or

similar way—for these to adjudge my history profitable will be enough for me. And, indeed, it has been composed, not as a prize-essay to be heard for the moment, but as a possession for all time. (1.22.4)

Does Thucydides mean that human beings will always react the same way to the same type of circumstances and that his book will only help people to understand that fact, or does he mean that similar events (similar wars and even similar inclinations) will happen and that his book will be profitable for dealing with them? Is the *History* a book mainly of contemplation or of instruction? In support of the latter option, there are certain episodes in the *History* in which Thucydides goes out of his way to emphasize the details of an event that lead to the conclusion that some particular decision was wrong and that there were alternatives. Many of those episodes involve the element of pride. They read not as though the hazards of pride are inevitable (for then there would be no need for the chastising way in which the episodes are written) but only as though they are predict-able. This section will explore three instances in which Thucydides treats pride in this manner, with the aim of ascertaining Thucydides' purpose. I hope this will suggest that Thucydides treats pride as a powerful snare that future statesmen might avoid, not as an over-whelming force sentencing men to failure.

I will focus here on two Athenian political-strategic mistakes: the rejection of Spartan peace offers in 425 B.C. after the fortuitous blockade of Sphacteria and the decision to undertake the expedition to Sicily. These examples show that for Thucydides mistakes are of-ten made as a result of hubris. Thucydides thinks that this human tendency cannot be permanently corrected but suggests that it can be overcome by certain individuals at certain times, recognizing that at other times it is allowed to dominate human events. It inevitably re-curs, it is a product of genuine human greatness, and it is in that sense tragic. But in the *History* it still seems to be treated as a product of human choice.

Pericles, illustrating that choice, once said that he was more afraid of Athens's mistakes than he was of the enemy's successes. Pericles was able, during his lifetime, to see Athens take the measured or prudent course, but Thucydides remarks that later Athenian leaders did not do so:

For he had told the Athenians that if they would maintain a defensive policy, attend to their navy, and not seek to extend their sway during the war, or do anything to imperil the existence of the state, they would prove superior. But they not only acted contrary to his advice in all these things [after his death], but also in matters that apparently had no connection with the war they were led by private ambition and private greed to adopt policies which proved injurious both as to themselves and their allies. . . . (2.65.7–8)

As we read of the events leading up to the disaster in Sicily, it is difficult not to think as Thucydides himself thought, that the Athenians defeated themselves because they gave in to their hubris.

Spartan Peace Overtures   Thucydides' battle vignettes sound a theme at the "micro" level that is repeated at the "macro" level: pride goes before a fall.[33] Clearly Thucydides wanted to teach his readers about human folly by demonstrating that overconfidence can lead directly to defeat. In the case of Spartan peace offerings after the taking of Sphacteria, Thucydides' reporting of the events and speeches indicates that he thinks the Athenians' overconfidence led to a diplomatic and strategic mistake that in hindsight was enormous. In the seventh year of the war the Athenians occupied Pylos and blockaded the island of Sphacteria, gaining thereby a bargaining chip so important to the Spartans that they sued Athens for peace on very favorable terms. Yet Thucydides writes about the episode as though the Athenians stumbled into their position on Pylos with no plan and no idea of the strategic value of the place.

The Athenian fleet had orders to sail to Sicily under the command of Eurymedon and Sophocles, and it was to put into Corcyra in order to help the harassed democrats there. Demosthenes, an Athenian general who was acting in this case as a private citizen, was granted permission to use the fleet while on the way to Sicily to attack the Peloponnesian coast (4.2.4). As the fleet started out, news arrived that Peloponnesian ships were off Corcyra, and the two other generals wanted to go there immediately. Demosthenes wanted to stop at Pylos, a small peninsula on the southwestern coast of the Peloponnesus some forty-six miles from Sparta, "as it was for this purpose that he had sailed with them." While they were arguing about this, a sudden storm blew their ships to Pylos's shore (4.3.2). Upon landing, Demosthenes still could not persuade the other generals or the soldiers to fortify the place, but after awhile the soldiers began fortification anyway, out of boredom (4.4.2). They used whatever stones they could find to build walls, not cutting them, but fitting them together as they could.

The Spartans, upon hearing the news that the place had been taken, did not do anything immediately. Instead they made light of it, "thinking that the Athenians would not await their attack when they got ready to take the field, or, if they should, that they could easily take the place by force" (4.5.2), being occupied with a festival. Pylos was thus fortified in six days, and Demosthenes was left there with five ships. The rest of the fleet went on its way to Corcyra and Sicily (4.5). The Peloponnesians, who had been invading Attica, now rushed to the scene (4.6.1). They placed some soldiers on Sphacteria, an island directly south of Pylos that covers up most of the opening to the Bay of Navarino, so that the Athenians would not occupy it. With the Peloponnesians preparing to attack, Demosthenes called on the help of an Athenian fleet, which luckily had gotten no farther than Zancynthus (seventy miles away) on their voyage to Corcyra. But the fleet could not arrive immediately (4.8). Battle began between the Athenians on Pylos and the Spartans attacking by sea. The two armies' usual roles were reversed: neither fought in its natural element (4.11). The next morning the Athenian fleet from Zancynthus arrived. The battle began anew, and by the time it was over there were Spartans in position on Pylos. However, Athenian ships now circled Sphacteria, besieging the Spartans by sea (4.13). An armistice was concluded, and Spartan envoys were allowed to go to Athens to plead their case (4.15–16). The Spartans regarded what had happened as a catastrophe since the besieged men were some of the best of their men.

The Spartan envoys offered peace, friendship, and alliance in return for the men trapped on the island. They argued that Athens should take the opportunity to consolidate her wins, got mainly by good fortune, instead of always being led on by hope to "grasp at more" (4.17.5). The vicissitudes of fortune, they said, were clear from Sparta's present state. It was not through weakness or hubris that the Spartans had been placed in this situation but only through lack of judgment, so the Athenians should not feel that their good fortune would be with them forever (4.18.2–4). Athens's current prosperity should not make them arrogant or give them a feeling of invincibility, because chance plays such a large part in war. Disaster might follow Athens's refusal, but to agree to Sparta's offers would make Athens look powerful and wise:

> We believe, too, that a permanent reconciliation of bitter enmities is more likely to be secured, not when one party seeks revenge and, because he has gained a decided mastery in the war, tries to bind his opponent by compulsory oaths and thus makes peace with him on unequal terms, but when, having it in his power to secure the same result by clemency, he vanquishes his foe by generosity also, offering him terms of reconciliation which are moderate beyond all his expectations. (4.19.2)

Spartans would be obliged to repay this generosity (*arete*)[34] in kind, instead of seeking vengeance out of having terms forced upon them, and would want to honor the agreement to avoid disgrace (4.19.3). Moderate behavior from Athens, in other words, would elicit a moderate response. The peace would be more stable if it were not bitterly imposed. Besides, peace was desirable for both parties at that moment. Athens should conclude it now, before Sparta's hatred became permanent. Besides, Spartan friendship had its advantages—with Athens and Sparta allies combining their forces, all others would be their inferiors. Thus the Spartans held out a future Athenian-Spartan hegemony over all of Hellas (4.20.4) (this suggestion made their claim that they were warring to liberate cities from the Athenian yoke seem less genuine).

This speech had all the elements necessary to convince the type of Athenians described by the Athenian envoys at Sparta before the war—those who were driven by fear, honor, and interest—that the time to make peace had arrived. The Athenians were told that they should fear war's uncertainty and the threat of permanent hatred between Athens and Sparta. They should desire the honor that would come from having concluded an honorable and advantageous peace after a successful battle. They should look forward to the gain to be had by an Athenian-Spartan condominium. The argument seemed foolproof: the decision to make peace seemed completely rational and in Athens's long-term interest.

The Spartans, having made this offer, thought the Athenians would be glad to accept. But the Athenians, still holding the men on

Sphacteria, "believed that, since they held the men on the island, peace could be theirs the moment they cared to make it, and meanwhile they were *greedy for more*" (4.21.2–3; emphasis mine). As Hunter R. Rawlings points out, "The effect of chapters 17–22 is to emphasize the Spartans' farsighted *sophrosyne* and the Athenians', and particularly Cleon's, myopic immoderateness."[35] Cleon (whom Thucydides explicitly criticizes in the Mytilenaean Debate as "violent") persuaded the Athenians to hold out for too many concessions and refused to let the Spartans confer in private, reviling them for wanting to conduct diplomacy in secret. Not wanting to risk open disgrace and being fairly sure that Cleon was purposefully avoiding any reasonable agreement, the Spartans went home with nothing to show for their efforts (4.22). The armistice ended, and both sides returned to the war with vigor (4.23).

To be sure, Thucydides exaggerated the bumbling, lucky nature of the initial Athenian success at Pylos. Francis MacDonald Cornford writes, "There is hardly a sentence in the whole story which is not so turned and so disposed as to make us feel that design counted for nothing and luck for everything."[36] Indeed, this particular episode in the *History* is unique in being truly unbelievable, at least in its details. The Athenian success seems too fortuitous, and it is all the more troubling because of Thucydides' usual concern for accuracy—for "reporting the facts." Yet the very uniqueness of Thucydides' treatment precludes Cornford's thesis that Thucydides saw in this episode the workings of Fortune and that he must have believed in an active "hand of fate," either of the gods or of some other mysterious agency. The rest of the *History,* while occasionally mentioning fortuitous occurrences such as eclipses and earthquakes, does not give us the impression that these things are controlled or planned by any supernatural force.[37] Thucydides never gives any credit to the gods for any occurrence that is natural or man-made. Indeed, the whole bent of the *History* gives one the impression that Thucydides at least questioned, if not rejected altogether, the notion that such forces were at work. The competing explanations Cornford provides, that Thucydides is moralizing about the uncertainties of war or that he is "actuated by some personal feeling of 'malignity' " toward Athens for his exile, are closer to the truth than Cornford's own suggestion.[38] But perhaps the answer lies in the close connection between the way the story of the capture of Pylos and Sphacteria is told and the way the speech of the Spartans who are treating for peace is presented.

The strange treatment of the episode can be explained more easily by surmising that, for Thucydides, Athens's rejecting Spartan peace offerings was a mistake made due to hubris, which was itself encouraged by the leadership of Cleon. The fact that his treatment is out of character with the rest of the *History* underscores how strongly he believed that this was the case. While not engaging in outright fabrication, Thucydides emphasizes the element of luck in the Athenian success and then likewise emphasizes the elements of the Spartans' speech that dwell on chance in war and the benefits of moderation in making peace. The emphasis on *arete* as moderation in victory coincides with Thucydides' preference for moderation in foreign policy generally and with his identification with Spartan values, if not Spartan practice toward other states.[39] He makes the investment of Pylos and the encirclement of Sphacteria look extremely lucky in order to emphasize how correctly the Spartans speak: chance plays a large part in the successes and failures of war, and it is more rational to stop while ahead than to let arrogance lead a state to disaster. The element of chance made the Athenian proclivity for "reaching for more," or their "daring," as Forde puts it, reckless and self-destructive. This "grasping" was not dictated by necessity: the Athenians could very honorably and profitably have concluded peace. But, encouraged by Cleon, the Athenians thought that there was no limit to Athens's possible achievements, a hubris the Spartans claimed they had not succumbed to, which implies their knowledge that the Athenians were in danger of doing so. The Athenians sought an (admittedly) beautiful if reckless glory. Pericles illustrated this aspect of Athenian character when he said that even Athens's failures would reflect her greatness and that the war was therefore worth waging even if it ended in defeat (2.64.3–5). But Pericles still had sought to limit the Athenians' lust for power for practical or prudential reasons, whereas Cleon urged the Athenians to give in to this part of their nature without reservation.

When an honorable and advantageous peace was laid in their laps, the Athenians no longer listened to reason but thought they were capable of obtaining more. For the Athenians, the rejection of peace at this juncture was to compete with the Sicilian Expedition for the biggest mistake of the war. In both cases, the Athenians were motivated by more than fear, honor, or any reasonable conception of interest. Rather, what moved them was a distorted sense of glory or pride and an overwhelming desire for ever more power. In both cases the Athenians were "greedy for more." This is the passion that dominates some of the most crucial Athenian decisions in the war after Pericles dies, the inculcation of which Thucydides blames on Pericles' inferior successors.

Not long after the Spartans leave the negotiations in discouragement, the Athenian besiegers become uncomfortable and discouraged. As the Spartans on Sphacteria use every ruse to get supplies in, the Athenians live on brackish water and dwindling rations. They begin to regret their decision to reject the Spartans' offer. This discouragement leads Cleon to boldly proclaim his ability to take Sphacteria by force and confer the Spartans on it to Athens. After a disgusted Nicias gives up command in favor of the surprised Cleon, the latter actually pulls off the attack and the prisoners are delivered (4.26–41). However, because Thucydides treats this episode in a similar way to the initial success at Pylos and Sphacteria, it is clear that for him the eventual total but lucky success of Athenian military might on this strategic island does not compensate for the failure of political wisdom displayed in the earlier rejection of peace.[40]

The Decision to Invade Sicily   Thucydides records two Athenian incursions into Sicily. The first was relatively minor and was curtailed by a display of Sicilian unity. The second was a huge Athenian effort that eventually led to military (and internal political) disaster. In most analyses of the Sicilian Expedition little is heard of the first incursion, and yet from this example, which Thucydides records in some detail, the Athenian generals and people who championed the great expedition could have learned much and thus might have avoided catastrophe.

Athens's great expedition to Sicily, near the end of the *History*, turned out to be the military move that stretched Athenian resources too thin and precipitated Athens's downfall. Was it an act of hubris that could not have been prevented? If we look back at Athens's previous experience with Sicily, we will see that, confronted with a similar situation, the Athenians once behaved differently. The first expedition to Sicily was a small one, consisting of twenty ships under the Athenian general Laches. The Syracusans and the Leontines were at war, and the Leontines had asked Athens for help based on a previous alliance and Ionian kinship. The Athenians sent the ships ostensibly on the grounds of this relationship but in truth because they thought they could stop the grain shipped from Sicily from reaching Peloponnesian ports "and also to make a preliminary test whether the affairs of Sicily could be brought under their own control" (3.86). The Athenians experienced some military successes after their arrival (3.90, 99). In 426 B.C. they attacked the acropolis of Inessa, which was held by the Syracusans, but could not take it. On their retreat, their allies were attacked by the Syracusans and many of them were killed (3.103). Reinforcements were sent from Athens that same winter, under Pythodorus (3.115). The following spring, the Peloponnesians invaded Attica, but the Athenians, writes Thucydides, sent forty ships to Sicily anyway, as planned (4.2.2–3). These were the same ships that were delayed at Sphacteria. Thucydides records the events in Sicily at this time, between his description of the Spartans' peace offers and his report of the blockade and capture of Sphacteria. In this interlude, the Athenians were again defeated when engaging the Syracusans (who would be their main enemy in the second expedition) (4.25.6–7).

Then, following the account of Cleon's victory on Sphacteria, Thucydides shows that during the summer of 424 B.C. the Camarinaeans and Geloans of Sicily concluded an armistice. After that, all the Sicilian cities sent representatives to Gela to discuss peace. The Syracusan Hermocrates' argument for unity against Athens won the day, and Thucydides gives us his speech in full and unaccompanied by any opposing speech. Hermocrates urges the Sicilians to surmount their particular enmities at least long enough to deflect their common enemy, Athens. Syracuse, he says, is not the weakest or neediest city in Sicily, but as a Syracusan he is still willing to speak in the general interest. On both sides of a war, the motive for fighting is advantage, but if both sides find that it is not to their advantage to fight, some profit may come from a compromise. Each city went to war for its "private interests." Each should now reconcile, for that is again in the interests of each (4.59–60). The Athenians are the supreme argument for bringing Sicily together. In hurting themselves, the Sicilians are paving the way for Athenian supremacy. Someday the Athenians will come with a larger armament to dominate all of Sicily (4.60). Hermocrates argues that prudence dictates that we ought, each of us in behalf of his own state, to call in allies and incur dangers only when we are seeking to win what does not belong to us and not when we imperil what is already ours; and we should remember that faction is the chief cause of ruin to states and indeed to Sicily, seeing that we her inhabitants, although we are all being plotted against, are disunited, each city by itself. (4.61.–2)

Recognizing the common threat, citizen should reconcile with citizen to end dangerous sedition, and city should reconcile with city to save Sicily. Echoing the Athenians at Sparta and Melos, Hermocrates says that he blames not those who wish to rule but only those who will submit to rule without a fight, "for it is an instinct of man's nature always to rule those who yield, but to guard against those who are ready to attack" (4.61.5–6).

After making his argument for unity based purely on what he considers to be the interests of all parties, Hermocrates claims that peace has an intrinsic value as well. All agree that it is highly desirable. Injustice is more likely to be cured in peace than in war; the rule of law can be preserved better when there is order. Peace has its own honors and splendors, and they are less hazardous than those of war. Hermocrates reminds the representatives of the uncertainties of war and revenge—much as the Spartans warned the Athenians earlier when offering peace—thereby pointing out the risks they are taking by continuing to fight. Both the uncertain future and the immediate presence of the Athenians are to be feared, and if particular enmities cannot be put aside forever, they should at least be put off until the greater danger is gone (4.62). Syracuse, being a very powerful city (which until this point had been striving for hegemony in Sicily), is willing to make concessions if others will, "[f]or there is no disgrace in kinsmen giving way to kinsmen" (4.64.3).

Having heard Hermocrates' counsel, the Sicilians conclude peace among themselves. The Sicilian cities that had cooperated with the Athenian forces now tell Laches and Pythodorus that they no longer need help from Athens. Upon hearing this, and realizing that Sicily has indeed achieved unity, the generals take the fleet back home. When they arrive in Athens, however, two generals are exiled and a third fined because it is believed that they left Sicily on bribes. Because most of their military undertakings have lately been successful, the Athenian people expected nothing to thwart them and arrogantly believed that "no matter whether their forces were powerful or deficient, they could equally achieve what was easy and what was difficult" (4.65). This final ironic comment shows that Thucydides thought that Athenian confidence in this matter was misplaced and that therefore fining and exiling the generals who had returned was wrong. By recounting the events of this first expedition, Thucydides demonstrates that taking Sicily will not be so easy.

It was after this experience that the Athenians began to plan their great expedition to Sicily in 416 B.C. during a very shaky peace with Sparta and her allies. Thucydides says most of the Athenians were ignorant of the large size and population of Sicily. Why is this? Were they aware of the Sicilians' ability to unite for the common defense, or had they really believed their own accusations that the leaders of the previous expedition had been bribed to leave? Were they unaware that Syracuse, the largest and most powerful city in Sicily that had been capable of unifying all others, had had the best of Athens in battles already? Apparently so, although when evidence to this effect was brought forward by one of their most prominent generals, Nicias, they refused to acknowledge it.

The Athenians were eager to conquer Sicily. The pretext for their invasion was once again the request of an old ally. This time, instead of Leontine, it was Egesta that was calling for help in its war with the Selinuntines, who were backed by Syracuse. The Egestaeans pointed to two reasons why the Athenians should become involved: 1) to stop the future Syracusan threat to Athens, which might come in the form of aid to the Peloponnesians; and 2) they would foot the bill for the Athenian effort, a promise that later turned out to be a lie (6.6).

Alcibiades, who should have at least heard of the details of Athens's previous experiences in Sicily, seemed totally oblivious to them. Debating him, Nicias argued in the assembly that the expedition was unwise during a time of such unstable peace with the Spartans. The Athenians should not "*reach out* after another empire before we have secured that which we have" (6.10.5; emphasis mine). Nicias warned against being contemptuous of the military might or resolution of the Spartans or Sicilians. The Athenians now unwisely despise the Spartans because they "have got the better of them beyond your expectation—in comparison with what you feared at first—" (6.11.5–7). The Sicilians would mock the Athenians in the same way if Athens were to lose to them. Nicias obviously felt that all human beings had a tendency to congratulate themselves too early, a moral we have earlier seen Thucydides insert into his battle narratives. He warned Athenians that the Egestaeans might be lying about their ability to finance the war, and he questioned Alcibiades' motives for wanting to go to Sicily. Alcibiades, he said, was considering only his own interest, displaying his expensive tastes for popularity and wanting war for fame and profit (6.12). It turned out that Nicias was correct in his estimation both of the Egestaeans and of Alcibiades.

Having claimed that his personal profit and glory was also the city's, Alcibiades responded to Nicias's argument.[41] He disregarded Athens's previous experience in Sicily and ignored Nicias's warnings. He called the Sicilians a "mixed rabble" that had not been able to amass significant arms and had not even achieved agricultural self-sufficiency. Speaking in terms that could roughly be applied to Athens a short while later, he said of the Sicilians:

> whatever each one thinks he can obtain from the common stock by persuasive oratory or by sedition, in the expectation that if he fails he will settle in some other land, this he provides himself with. And it is not likely that a rabble of this kind would either listen to counsel with one mind or turn to action with a common purpose. (6.17.3–5)

Yet this is exactly what had happened not long before in Sicily when the Sicilians had been threatened by Athenian intervention. Alcibiades defended the expedition by defending the idea of empire. To be an imperial power, Athens had to give aid to everyone who asked for it. Echoing Pericles, he said that if Athens did not hold its empire it would be in danger of being likewise dominated (6.18.2–3). Like Pericles' in his earlier incorrect assessment of the Peloponnesians, Alcibiades thought that the Sicilians would not be able to agree among each other and that their factions would be their downfall, contrary to earlier evidence. Many of the Sicilian cities would probably come over to Athens if they were given an attractive reason for doing so (6.17.5). Alcibiades obviously underestimated the unifying effect of invasion. As for the Peloponnesian threat, he claimed it was insignificant by land and sea, even with most of the Athenian fleet in Sicily. "[N]ever were the Peloponnesians more hopeless against us," he said (6.17.8).

With hindsight these expectations look like so much wishful thinking at best and overinflated estimates to gain a policy for personal self-aggrandizement at worst. Alcibiades and the Athenian people did not enjoy hindsight, but they did have previous experience to indicate that the Sicilians were more than a mixed rabble of military weaklings. The people had denied this evidence when they abused the generals who told them of Sicilian unity. Alcibiades helped them to avoid reality further to serve his own purposes, as Thucydides points out. In describing Alcibiades, Thucydides agrees substantially with Nicias's description: he wished to subdue both Sicily and Carthage, "and in case of success to promote at the same time his private interests in wealth as well as in glory" (6.15.3).

Nicias, knowing he had been defeated by Alcibiades' diminution of the Sicilians and Peloponnesians and his glorification of the expedition, tried to frighten the Athenians by telling them that a massive force was needed in order to subdue the Sicilians. He reasoned that either this would deter them from the project altogether or, if it did not, he would at least go on his way in safety. But his requests had the opposite effect on the Athenians—they were more enthusiastic than ever. The elders thought that either Sicily would be subdued or at least that the force would not be destroyed since it was so large; younger citizens favored it "through a longing for far-off sights and scenes"; and the multitude supported it since it would mean more revenue for them now and more tribute from new dominions in the future (6.24). They voted to grant the generals anything they needed to make a safe journey and gave them full freedom of action (6.26.1).

These concrete reasons and actions on the part of the people were overshadowed by the romance and grandeur they attached to the undertaking. Almost everyone in the city went down to the Peiraeus at dawn to see the ships off, "going at once in hope and with lamentations—hope that they would make conquests in Sicily, lamentations that they might never see their friends again, considering how long was the voyage from their own land on which they were being sent" (6.30.2). Only at this moment did they realize the risks of the voyage. But the strength and abundance of the armament before them revived their courage. Everyone came to watch the spectacle, feeling that it was "noteworthy and surpassing belief" (6.30.2): "for this first armament that sailed for Sicily was the costliest and most splendid, belonging to a single city and with a purely Hellenic force, that had ever up to that time set sail" (6.31.1). Private individuals vied with each other for how much they could contribute to the expedition or how extravagant their personal arms were, until the event seemed more like a vast display of wealth and power for the benefit of the Hellenes than an expedition against an enemy:

> And the fame of the armament was noised abroad, not less because of amazement at its boldness and the splendour of the spectacle than on account of its overwhelming force as compared with those whom they were going against; and also because it was the longest voyage from home as yet attempted and undertaken with the highest hopes for the future as compared with their present resources. (6.31.6)

As the ships were departing, however, news of the expedition was already reaching Syracuse, although it was not believed for quite some time. Thucydides again presents us with a speech by the Syracusan Hermocrates, who once more praises unification of his own city and all of Sicily against the Athenians. Speaking to his fellow Syracusans, he warns against despising the Athenians or being incredulous of the stories of their advance (6.33.4). If the Syracusans stop bickering among themselves and accusing those who warn of Athens of being motivated by private interest, they might unify to defend themselves. Seeing their resolve, the rest of the Sicilians might be more likely to join a Syracusan alliance and repel the invaders. If they thus succeed in defeating the Athenians, it would be a truly glorious achievement. There is every reason to hope, Hermocrates maintains, that given a concerted effort they can do just that:

> For few great armaments, whether of Hellenes or of barbarians, when sent far from their own land, have been successful. The reason is that they are not, in the first place, superior in numbers to the people against whom they go and the neighbours of these—for *fear always brings about union*. (6.33.5; emphasis mine)

Hearing this, the Sicilians—and Thucydides' readers—could not help but recognize the allusion to Xerxes' rude awakening as he realized that the squabbling Hellenes were capable of uniting long enough to defeat him. Xerxes' huge expedition from far-off Persia and the Athenians' expedition to Sicily are alike in their splendor and in their arrogance, and in their prejudice against and contempt for their opponents. Fear brought about the unity necessary to defeat the barbarian, just as it would for the Peloponnesians and Sicilians against the Athenians in the present war, while hope for glory was not enough to hold the conquerors together in difficulty. This simple equation, the natural advantage of the defensive position, makes too much sense to be ignored. Thucydides puts Hermocrates' speech one paragraph away from his description of the glorious mood of the Athenians and their allies as they leave home for Sicily. While Thucydides does not necessarily believe that the Sicilian expedition was doomed from the start, he recognizes what the Athenians chose to ignore, that Athens faced great difficulties against a worthy opponent. Indeed, he later characterizes the Syracusans as the most Athenian of all of Athens's opponents (8.96.5).

Hermocrates notes that the Athenian empire grew after the Persians failed through their own inadequacies in their attempt to conquer Hellas. Similarly, he says, greatness would come to the Sicilians even if Athenian defeat was due to lack of supplies rather than to Sicilian efforts. He warns the Syracusans to take the lead in unifying Sicily against Athens and also to ask Carthage, Sparta, and Corinth for help. He also advises the Sicilians to join together to confront the Athenians before they arrive in Sicilian territory, perhaps deterring them from coming any farther. The Athenians are going in the belief that the Sicilians will not defend themselves, "rightly contemning us because we did not join the Lacedaemonians in the effort to destroy them. But if they should see us unexpectedly displaying courage, they would be more dismayed by this unlooked for resistance than by our real power" (6.34.8).

This time, Hermocrates' speech is coupled by the speech of the democrat Athenagoras, who does not believe the Athenians are coming at all and thinks that Hermocrates is instigating a scare in order to gain political power with the faction-ridden people of Syracuse. He deprecates the Athenians' power. The Syracusans should hope the Athenians are so stupid as to fall into their hands. But the Athenians are shrewd and experienced, and it seems unlikely that they will leave for another expedition before they have secured a more solid peace with the Peloponnesians, "for I myself think that they are content that we do not come against them, being so numerous and so powerful" (6.36.4). Athenagoras fears the Athenians less than Hermocrates even if they are on their way because he assumes that the Sicilians will unite against a common threat again, if it materializes: "But of these things, as I maintain, the Athenians are aware and they are, I am quite sure, taking care of their own interests, and men from here are fabricating stories neither true nor possible, men whom not now for the first time but always I have known to be wishing . . . to frighten the mass of you and themselves dominate the city" (6.38.1–3). Athenagoras then extols the benefits of democracy, his speech being more political than military in nature. Hermocrates' reports are a threat to the Syracusan democracy. If the Athenians come, the people will be capable of manning enough ships and providing enough forces for defense, without jeopardizing the liberty of the people by giving too much power to men like Hermocrates and therefore risking slavery (6.40).

Like that of Alcibiades, Athenagoras's speech illustrates the dangers of having contempt for an enemy and of being too caught up in domestic political rivalry to perceive a real external threat. It is also a commentary on the truly daring, if not fantastic, nature of the Athenians' expedition. Athenagoras points out that such an expedition would be irrational because it is not in the interests of Athens at that time. It is very difficult to convince the Syracusan people that Athens might be reckless enough to dare such a feat, especially when it is still practically at war with the Peloponnesians. But Athenagoras's assessment of the Athenians is completely wrong. They *are* extremely powerful and are a hard match for even a united Sicily. They are not so shrewd and experienced that they will wait until they have secured peace with the Peloponnesians before starting a new adventure. Thus Athenagoras's speech only emphasizes the folly of arrogance and contempt for one's enemies, and the dangers of too much pride on both sides.

Summary

The Athenians' rejection of Spartan peace offers after the lucky capture of Pylos and Sphacteria is an example of overconfidence. Thucydides exaggerates the bumbling nature of the Athenian success to show how much of an opportunity they missed. Influenced by Cleon, the Athenians were "greedy for more," disregarding the risks. But their success quickly deteriorated and the chance to negotiate such favorable terms was missed.

In the middle of recounting this Sphacteria episode, Thucydides shows us the Athenians in Sicily finding the Syracusans an equal match for themselves, contrary to Alcibiades' later claims. The effect is a foreshadowing of the difficulties to come in Sicily when the Athenians' "grasping" leads them to launch another large war before the first has been won. Even if the people were ignorant of past battles with the Syracusans or of the Sicilians' ability to unite, Alcibiades should have been more informed. Yet he chose to exploit the idea of a truly daring expedition for his personal benefit and to sell the Athenians on its glory rather than warn them of its dangers. The people, more easily swayed by passion than by reason, listened to Alcibiades rather than to Nicias, who wanted to remind them that their enemy was not as hopeless as Alcibiades described him. One cannot help but wonder what would have happened if Nicias's trepidation had been combined somehow with Alcibiades' eloquence and presence. But it was not, and so history repeated itself. Just as Hellenic unification defeated Xerxes and previous Sicilian unification had dissuaded the Athenian generals from further interference, so the effort of the Sicilians eventually repulsed the Athenians' great expedition. The Athenians had not learned that great threats lead to great cooperation or that it is folly to treat one's enemies with contempt.

Does this mean that Thucydides is telling us the Athenians had no choice but to be dragged down by their own hubris? If this were his message, Thucydides would not have emphasized the element of luck in the Sphacteria episode, which made the Athenians look mistaken in rejecting Spartan peace offers, not hapless or doomed. He would not have shown us that the Athenians had the opportunity to learn in the first Sicilian expedition but did not, largely due to Alcibiades' love of glory and its influence on the people. Indeed, by showing us both episodes he suggests that *some* Athenian generals could choose wisely, even in the face of what must have been the anticipated criticism of the demos.

It is clear from the example of Pericles that reason embedded in effective oratory could at times overcome passion, even a natural tendency to hubris. The importance of rhetoric diminished as the war dragged on, indicating that the various actors in the war took deliberation less and less seriously.[42] By showing us that reason can be effective if it is used by the right kind of orator (like Pericles or Hermocrates), Thucydides presents us with a mixed blessing. Rhetoric, Thucydides' only vehicle for reason, depends on much besides reason. It relies on character and statesmanship. This conclusion puts reason—and the moderation it can inspire—in a precarious position, with its success depending very much on chance, that is, on the emergence of one outstanding man at the right time and place. Thucydides calls Periclean policy "measured," not moderate, because Periclean rhetoric could not be purely reasonable and motivate the Athenian people. Pericles had to work with the material he was given, and it is because of the nature of this material that his achievement of restraint in war is so admirable.[43] Pericles' successors lacked either Pericles' character or his charisma and evoked in the Athenian people as a whole an immoderate response. Thucydides accepts these constraints on reason as natural and rather powerful, which tends to give the *History* its tragic tone. But Thucydides is not as fatalistic as he first appears. His purpose is to show future leaders what statesmanship requires, what it takes to steer men clear of the more irrational and dangerous aspects of their nature, and the consequences if such leadership cannot be developed and maintained. It is possible that Thucydides' *History* was designed to inculcate through vicarious experience and subtle admonitions the very character in future leaders that Thucydides found the successors of Pericles lacked.

Conclusion

The word *character* has been used in this section in the sense of national as well as personal character. It is this dimension of human experience that is clearly emphasized in Thucydides, and yet this is largely forgotten in the modern realist depiction of Thucydides, partly due to a modern prejudice against such supposedly fuzzy notions as "character." Thucydides can be made into a scientist by today's neorealists, who equate the *Athenian thesis* with Thucydides' own. But the above analysis suggests Thucydides' teaching runs counter to this thesis. The Athenian thesis is systematic and easily used to predict behavior. But how accurate is it? Did the Spartans conform to this theory? Their angry allies claimed that they unfortunately did not behave like the Athenians. Even the Athenians themselves did not always behave in the way they described as natural and compelling. As we will see, other actors in the *History* certainly did not conform to Athenian predictions. Thucydides felt that understanding the character of nations and individuals was vitally important for understanding their actions. One could not predict what they would do by way of a uniformly applied theory.

There are philosophic assumptions about human nature that underlie Thucydides' treatment of the war we have just now glimpsed. If character greatly influences actions, and not blind forces or circumstances, it is possible that men are exercising more free will than much of modern science, and modern philosophy, is willing to admit. But if, as Thucydides seems to indicate, this character itself is inherent in the nation or individual, then the appearance of certain types of character becomes itself a matter of chance. What produces great leaders or infamous leaders? Scholars can report on their childhoods, their surroundings, their education. But these do not explain why *this* particular man or woman becomes great and not others with the same type of background. Thucydides, perhaps more of an empiricist than most empiricists, noticed this most mercurial aspect of human experience and granted it a large place in his explanation of the war.

Analysis attributing human success in part to chance is a way of looking at the world that seems especially alien—even immoral—to many people, especially Americans. Political science as we know it today has as its raison d'être the assumption that formulas can be discovered that will rid people of the need to so rely on chance. Hobbes, arguably the father of modern political science, tries to resolve this problem by introducing man's situation as a determining element that can be manipulated in order to change man. He does this, however, only by reducing the variety of human motivations to the single motivation of self-interest. In other words, he takes the Athenian approach. This, I will argue, is the same reduction realists have to make in order to create laws of state behavior that do not take into account national character, internal politics, or the personalities of individual leaders. Thucydides cannot do this without dramatically altering the landscape of the Peloponnesian War. What Thucydides shows us is a fixed human nature, one that is defined by parameters. But it is a nature with many facets, any one of which can become augmented, depending on the individual characters involved. The false sophistication of viewing man in a limiting way, as all-selfish, all-passionate, or ever-fearful, for example, has the defect of being at odds with a more complex reality.

A COMPARISON OF HOBBES AND THUCYDIDES ON HUMAN NATURE

Thucydides' presentation is somewhat tragic because he shows how difficult it is for human beings to rise above base proclivities, especially in war. Hobbes believes he can banish all human tragedy with science. In Hobbes, any contradictions to his theory of human nature are either resolved by further abstraction or ignored. Thucydides can tolerate the paradoxes in human nature because he is not trying to solve mankind's problems permanently. This does not mean that Thucydides does not think his history will be useful to those who read it. Indeed, he says that it will be useful to those who want an exact knowledge of the past in order to interpret the future. But it is useful in understanding a recurring history and educating statesmen to work better within similar situations, not in changing history or human nature permanently. Hobbes's intolerance of contradiction, due to his devotion to science and its solutions, leads him to try to reconcile the paradoxes, even if it means grand reductionism.

The Individual and Society

It is true that both Thucydides and Hobbes make use of psychology to explain individual (and group) motivations. But at the level of his mechanistic psychology, Hobbes asserts a radical individualism and perspectivism that Thucydides does not. It is not that Thucydides' humans are social at the national and international level while Hobbes's are asocial; it is that the type of sociability he assumes differs from Hobbes's. Once we understand Hobbes's natural condition of mankind as socially defined, that is, broaden the concept of the state of nature to include conflict in society and conflict leading to the breakdown of society, the difference becomes more clear. Hobbes's human beings are sociable only insofar as they care what other people think of them. Other than that vanity, they are wholly fearful and mistrustful of their fellows. Each attempts to gain security and power over all others. While the various actors in Thucydides are also concerned about their reputation and glory, some are socially concerned with someone or something apart from themselves as well, whether this is patriotism, concern for family and friends, or genuine religious loyalties.

For Hobbes, while there is such a thing as truth, men will never arrive at it of their own accord because of their radically different perspectives and their narrow self-interest. It is because of his nature that man's *situation* becomes so crucial, why an absolute sovereign is needed to enforce the laws necessary to achieve, artificially, the only common good of peace. There are times, in Thucydides' *History,* in which individualism and perspectivism become pronounced. As I have shown here, the plague of Athens made men disregard law and social mores (but did not make them radically insecure or hostile), while civil war pushed them into violent, antisocial behavior. Thucydides is saying that violence and an overturning of accepted values and definitions can occur under extreme pressures of war, when passions become inflamed. But Hobbes thinks these things happen whenever government is not strong enough to check violence and maintain standards.

For Hobbes there can be no larger social purpose than that of the individual's pursuit of security and power. Society is made for this purpose; and individuals, whether preachers or politicians, always look out for themselves alone. These individuals might fool the people into believing that they represent a higher purpose, such as salvation or democracy, but what they say and their true motives are different things. Thucydides thinks that many people are like this, but he would allow in some people genuine higher motivations. Hobbes would label all professions of sincerity bombast. In civil strife Thucydidean characters behave like Hobbesian men, but at other times gallant actions are not reduced to mere products of selfishness. In other words, for Thucydides, people are capable of being virtuous, and some of the greatest turns in his *History,* good and bad, are accounted for by the presence or lack of virtue.

Thucydides believes that it is possible for individuals to rise above their own particular self-interest to a higher interest, that of the common good. His treatment of Pericles is the proof of this. He takes seriously the motivation of patriotism, love of country, and culture as true motivations for some individuals and nations at least some of the time. Moreover, national character is a real force in the *History.* National character made the Spartans more laconic, the Athenians more daring. This while all city-states operated within a wider Hellenic culture that prescribed certain rules of behavior due to a common religious heritage, such as giving back dead under a truce, maintaining religious sites while occupying enemy territory, obeying oracular directions and interpreting natural events as signs of displeasure from the common gods. When these customs were violated, their violation was an indication of the deepening vehemence of the war or the worsening of civil strife. Violations were acknowledged as such; they were seen as products of an unusually bad situation, not the norm even in war.

Thucydides would disagree that equality has to do with what men can do to one another. Instead, he takes qualities such as character, intelligence, piety, and moderation into account when judging different actors in the *History*. As we will see in the next chapter, Hobbes would agree not with Thucydides on this count but with the Athenians at Melos, who reduce the question of equality to a question of power. To Thucydides, this attitude is a sign of decline, and it is and should be irregular. Proof of this is that Athenian or Hobbesian theories do not provide the set of standards he himself uses when he evaluates individuals. For instance, while Hobbes says that human equality is proved because wise men are often killed by those less wise,[44] Thucydides thinks that this behavior is unjust precisely because it is unnatural—an overturning of normal notions of virtue must take place before this can happen.

The Hierarchy of Human Motivation

For Hobbes, all men are motivated by self-interest. Even altruism can be explained in selfish terms. This self-interest, which is expressed in a general will to power that makes men naturally irreconcilable, causes fear. The most frequent motivation of Thucydidean men, from the evidence of speeches, deeds, and Thucydides' own evaluation, is also self-interest. A comparison of Athenian deeds in the Pentacontaetia with the speeches leading up to the Spartan declaration of war shows that, despite Athenian claims to the contrary, Athens's reason for building her empire was love of gain. In his account of the plague, Thucydides seems to agree with Hobbes that people obey laws and worship gods because they perceive some profit in doing so, as well as because they fear punishment. But without government, Thucydidean men do not turn to radical insecurity, preemption, or violent crime. Instead they turn into hedonists, which suggests that, government or no government, Thucydides' humans are not as naturally fearful of each other and are mainly self-interested without this interest causing life-or-death conflict. In Hobbes's theory, lack of government should precipitate a war of all against all because people's interests are always naturally opposed. Thucydides' men are not as insecure when they are ungoverned and do not automatically seek power over all others.

Hobbes and Thucydides would agree that the worst violence occurs in a social setting, when there is something of social worth to contest. For Thucydides, trouble begins when individuals' ambitions and need for honor become divorced from the common good. At the level of nations, the pursuit of glory escalates conflict and makes it less rational. As Athens achieved enough power to threaten its nearest rival, it adopted the Periclean view that not only gain but also glory was to be had by maintaining the empire. Pericles transformed the idea of war with the Peloponnesians into an opportunity for more Athenian glory, such glorification being worthy in and of itself. For Hobbes, the passion most destabilizing to political order is vainglory, or unwarranted pride. Such pride both cripples common sense and makes conflict much more vehement. But Thucydides is alive to the tragic dimensions of pride. As Athens fails from having overestimated her own potential, it is the cold or insensitive reader who will look on with complete derision or think of Athens as simply foolish. There are reasons for Athens's overestimation, reasons rooted in her true greatness. The failure is all the more poignant because the glory of Periclean Athens has been destroyed through human fallibility. Disappointment is a better word than contempt for how we feel as we watch the Athenians go down to defeat because of their own internal disorders.

Hobbes takes all tragedy out of pride or vainglory. For him it is simply a madness that infects individuals giddy with their own self-conceit. These individuals then spread their madness to the masses, who take up their doctrines and believe themselves to be inspired and especially worthy. There is nothing in men's opinions of themselves besides these illusions. No man is so much better than another that he is qualified to give the latter advice on his well-being. Hobbes has a way of making all human beings look profoundly silly, like children leading fantasy lives and squabbling over possession of insignificant toys. All is truly vanity. There is no room for greatness, and the laws of nature and the laws of God are in concordance in keeping such credulous beliefs from destroying society.

But, regardless of the difference in their forgiveness of human fallibility, Thucydides and Hobbes agree on the effects of hubris. Pericles signaled the initial loss of concern for national interest when he placed more value on posterity than on whether Athens acquired such fame in victory or defeat. For both, pride and envy inspire the worst kind of slaughter, and it is precisely these passions that make civil war so terrible. For both, the need for revenge obscures true interest and is motivated by vanity. Both emphasize that contempt for one's rivals, born of an unrealistic overestimation of one's own value, can lead to defeat. In general, hubris or vainglory causes people to make mistakes, to think less rationally, and therefore to act contrary to their own interests. This makes pride, and not self-interest, the most dangerous passion.

Thucydides and Hobbes agree that the pursuit of interest and glory cause strife among men, which sometimes leads to enough fear to cause unity. But for Thucydides, at the level of internal politics, fear of the effects of civil war was not a strong enough factor to encourage reunification. Love of gain and glory led to civil strife, as democratic and oligarchical factions in the various cities used the war in order to advance themselves. At the international level, however, fear caused city-states to put aside their internal and international differences when faced with a hostile power. Such was the case both for the Peloponnesians and for the Sicilians, and near the end of the *History* for the Athenians as well. Fear caused cooperation within and among nations; narrow self-interest and glory-seeking caused aggression. In this, Hobbes and Thucydides are in basic agreement. While Hobbes thinks that fear is the only means by which society can achieve stability and order, he knows that such fear is not always present. That is the reason civil strife occurs. His task is to teach citizens why they should be afraid, why it is folly to be fooled by those who are more concerned with their own ambitions and glory than with the common good. The true common good lies in realizing that it is reasonable both to be fearful of anarchy and to fearfully obey the sovereign. The sovereign's interest and those of the public coincide because both are (or should be) concerned with the prevention of civil strife. Self-interest, if enlightened, can be good. If self-interest is not enlightened, it and pride work to the detriment of civil society, while fear is society's unexpected ally. The Greek city-states unified when they were presented with an external, tangible threat to their security. Hobbes hopes that he can bring about the same resolve within states by presenting individual citizens with just as tangible a threat: true knowledge of themselves.

Reason and Rhetoric

Although Thucydides differentiates between true and apparent causes in some cases, stating that speeches represent the apparent causes, and although he would agree with Hobbes that men are apt to reject reason when it contradicts their passions (4.108.4–5), he does take rhetoric and rhetorical reasoning more seriously than Hobbes. By giving us speeches rather than simply relating the greater underlying cause, Thucydides reminds us of the essential political content of any collective decision. The reasons the speakers give must be politically acceptable. These reasons allow many individuals to collectively assent to a policy and carry it out. At times in the *History,* rhetoric has a truly decisive effect. In hindsight, Pericles symbolizes reason and restraint lost later in the war. His reason is necessarily embedded in his rhetoric. Indeed, there is no political reasoning in the *History* that is not within more or less successful political oratory. Hence, for Thucydides, reason needs oratory in order to be successful. Rationality carries the day only if the orator can skillfully sway the passions of his audience with his eloquence, stature, and style. This depends not only on the speaker's wisdom but also on his good intentions, and it requires a speaker who can overcome his ambition to achieve a true concern for the common good. For Thucydides there is no scientific or philosophical alternative to political rhetoric and therefore no alternative to statesmanship for us to pin our hopes on.

What Hobbes criticizes as a permanent quality of rhetoric, its "inconstancy," only occurs in Thucydides' view under certain conditions. While Hobbes says that confusion reigns whenever there are no enforced definitions of words, Thucydides notes the decline of quality communication at certain points, especially during civil wars such as that of Corcyra and civil disorder such as that of Athens during and after the Sicilian defeat. As Athenian war plans begin to lose touch with reality, there are fewer and fewer speeches. In the final two books of his history, Thucydides eliminates speeches altogether. In Athens, men such as Alcibiades and the oligarchical conspirators were concerned with their own individual advancement, not with what was best for the state as a whole. Their speeches, if given, would probably have been purely political, emotion-laden harangues, not reasoned contributions to debate. Leading men, fatally infected with their own hubris, could no longer see that their particular struggles for power would lead to their particular ruins in the long run. Compared to the initial direction of Periclean leadership, these men's examples only serve to remind us of the potential of reason if the right person appears. Thucydides laments the passing of good deliberation and identifies this passing with rash, foolish, immoderate, and immoral decisions. By noting the decline of speech and the rise of demagoguery, Thucydides expresses standards of conduct that Hobbes cannot recognize. But still the success of reason depends on chance. It is rare that a great individual will emerge at the right time, capable of eloquence, wisdom, and true patriotism. There can be no permanent triumph over nature. Successful orators may manipulate nature, but they cannot totally subdue it or force it to change.

In contrast, far from making reason dependent on rhetoric, Hobbes believes that rhetorical reasoning is clearly contradictory. Oratory is always a product of the selfish needs and prejudices of the speaker; it is purely political, and as such it is devoid of any true reason. There is no man, not even a king, who is capable of overcoming his own narrow interests. But reason and speech can be used in the spirit of the detached passion—curiosity—to yield science. Hobbes contrasted the scientific use of speech, which employed careful definitions in a geometrical method, with oratory or rhetoric. Science was man's hope, oratory the fomenter of sedition and civil war.

Hobbes hinged his hopes not on chance but on the negation of chance: science. His solution to the problem of sedition that seemed ever-present in ancient Greece was the enumeration of "rules of justice for the common people to take notice of" (B, 252). This might seem to make men far better in Hobbes's eyes than we originally thought they were, until we remember that while reason can be independent of political rhetoric (although eloquence could serve to make it more palatable) it needs a vehicle to be maintained and enforced. Hobbes did not depend on enlightenment to convince people that they must continue to be obedient and peaceable. He relied on enlightenment to show people why they could not maintain any such resolution in the long run without the sword of absolute sovereignty. If Hobbes really believed that reason was enough, he would have set forth only a rational policy, showing how it was in everyone's self-interest to adhere to it. People would read it and conclude that they must change their ways. But Hobbes realized that while human beings can understand what is best for them, they do not always do what they know they should do. Therefore Hobbes replaced Thucydides' statesman, whose appearance depended on chance because excellence is rare, with the sovereign, whose power depended not on excellence but on might. Hobbes rejected the Thucydidean alternative of accumulating wisdom through vicarious experience and of hoping that future leaders could learn from their ancestors' mistakes. This alternative was simply not sure enough. After all, the absolute sovereign might found a regime that, once instituted correctly, could last indefinitely. Philosophy, in the service of the sovereign, could do what previous philosophies (not to mention histories) could not: become the basis for a real and continuing political order.

Thucydides, as a historian, depicted life as he saw it. For him, politics were an unpredictable cycle of highs and lows that depended on many unpredictable factors, including individual personalities and speeches, national characters, previous enmities and friendships, natural events, and religious beliefs. History was cyclical, with human nature manifesting its various facets at various times. Any learning or improvement was temporary. One could not hope for all favorable factors to constantly converge. Hobbes, while not believing in an inevitable Kantian progression toward perfection, did not believe that history had to be cyclical. Science made linear progression possible by stopping the endless cycle of order and disorder, of government formation and sedition. Hobbes himself held the beacon of science that would illuminate the confusion of history and point the way to a better future.

Finally, a few indications of how these differences apply to the realism/neorealism paradigm of international relations might be useful here.[45] The school of realism is essentially Hobbesian in that it (1) counts on the predictability of actors' motivation and behavior; (2) equates anarchy with constant fear, struggle, and danger; (3) claims that the national interest, defined as self-preservation and advancement against others, is a dictate of nature—either a state obeys it or is destroyed; (4) takes all other motivations besides the national interest as irrational and dangerous and therefore to be counseled against, so that such motivations as national pride and ideological or religious fervor cannot be accounted for except as fatal anomalies or covers for power interests; (5) disregards the character of individual leaders as irrelevant, considering the overriding dictates of the international power structure; (6) disregards political rhetoric because it is seen as epiphenominal; (7) counsels prudent adherence to the realist view of the world put forth by the scientists of the realist paradigm, thus claiming that science is a better source for political wisdom than the cultivation of excellence in leaders and their followers. On all these points, Thucydidean "methodology" presents a different, sometimes completely opposite, point of view. Actors' motivations are not so uniform or predictable. Anarchy is not equated with constant fear, struggle, and danger. National interest is important, perhaps even depicted as the preferable route to take for survival, but we have seen (and will see even more clearly in the next chapter) that Thucydides understands that survival may not be a state's top priority. Whether this is attributed to hubris (as in the downfall of Athens) or a sort of moral nobility (as in the forthcoming cases of Melos and Plataea), Thucydides does not think it is possible to so thoroughly denounce these motivations as do Hobbes and the realists. If we can concede that national hubris is sometimes the outgrowth of deserved pride, then we must realize with Thucydides that it is a phenomenon not easily eliminated. The Thucydidean approach, moreover, stresses the important role of the character of nations and leaders, and the role of political rhetoric. In the *History* it was the decline of the quality of both that led to Athens's catastrophe.

Justice

Hobbes's solution to immoderation, immorality, and rash decisions is the abandonment of political deliberation and debate for science. Hobbes's assumption of radical perspectivism makes the scientific solution impossible without absolute power. But on the international scene, even this is not possible,[1] and Hobbes's theory takes away almost all restraints on action, leaving leaders to decide subjectively how far they may go in defense of the national interest. Just as with many realists' theories, Hobbes's theory is descriptive and prescriptive at the same time. It is a description of how international relations are (that is, anarchical, prone to mistrust and violence, which leads states to calculate their interests and augment their power, preemptively attacking those whom they detect doing likewise). It is a prescription for a foreign policy that adheres to what Hobbes thinks of as rational—violence only for self-preservation, never for revenge or glory.

Hobbes realizes the dangers of leaving determination of the national interest solely to subjective judgment, but he hopes that through his persuasion leaders will see how they themselves are injured by needless cruelty and war. Keep in mind, however, that the realist, along with Hobbes, assumes human nature to be compelled by the passions to use whatever means necessary for self-preservation in the uncertain state of nature. As Thucydides' Diodotus points out in the Mytilenaean Debate, when one assumes that individuals and states are compelled to challenge others because of their passions, the only way for the strong state to stop them is to threaten them with overwhelming force. The Athenians at Melos prove that the abandonment of reliance on political deliberation makes reliance on arbitrary force necessary. Thus the Hobbesian/realist view of human nature can lead to extremism in those powers that wish to dominate in order to preserve or to attain hegemony, despite prescriptions for moderation.

I will argue that this is the point Thucydides makes in his treatments of the Mytilenaean Debate, the Plataean Debate, and the Melian Dialogue. Thucydides not only disagrees with Hobbes on the content of human nature but also shows how deplorable the moral and political consequences can be of taking the Athenian/Hobbesian or realist thesis absolutely seriously in action as opposed to speech.[2] I will try to show that Thucydides himself offers a better alternative. He demonstrates that a true exchange of arguments over a particular policy is more likely to have a moderating or just influence. Indeed, one could sum up the difference between Thucydides and Hobbes on the issue of justice by assessing which case is more realistic: counting on the enlightenment of absolute sovereigns to produce good policy or hoping that deliberation and the moral restraint embodied in it will produce prudence and restraint.

HOBBES

In this section I will explore what Hobbes means by *just* and *good*. His definitions are problematic but necessary for the consistency of his philosophy. As we will see, in order to be consistent Hobbes must offer us not only unlikely definitions but also a curious metaphysics as well. In the end, I will examine Hobbes's application of his moral law to international relations.

What Is Justice?

Hobbes uses the word *justice* to mean the dictates of man-made law. Justice is conventional and presupposes civil society (DC, 12, par. 1). The civil laws determine what is just and unjust. But the sovereign is not himself subject to civil law, since he creates it and can change it at his will (L, 26, par. 6). His power should be absolute, and he should always be obeyed. Those who say a king should be obeyed only if he makes good laws are mistaken:

That "just laws are the ordinances of right reason;" . . . is an error that hath cost many thousands of men their lives. Was there ever a King, that made a law which in right reason had been better unmade? . . . I think rather that the reason of him that hath the sovereign authority, and by whose sword we look to be protected both against war from abroad and injuries at home, whether it be right or erroneous in itself, ought to stand for right to us that have submitted ourselves thereunto by receiving the protection. (LNC, 176)

The quote is instructive because in it we see Hobbes's fundamental distinction between *just* and *good*. Justice *is* the law of the sovereign in civil society. Goodness is whatever conforms to right reason. The law of nature is naturally good because it is reasonable. Civil law, in contrast, may be bad if it does not conform to right reason, but it is nevertheless always just and should be obeyed because the consequence of disobedience—civil war—is potentially too dangerous. Likewise, the sovereign can commit wrongs, but he cannot be unjust because, as the origin of all law, he can change laws at his pleasure. By definition, no civil law and no sovereign can be unjust, but both can be good or bad, right or wrong. As Hobbes says, "A good Law is that, which is *Needfull,* for the *Good of the People,* and withall *Perspicuous"* (L, 30, par. 20).

Hobbes tries to show that although the sovereign is bound by no laws, he has an interest in yielding obedience to right reason, which is the natural, moral, and divine law, remembering that the commonwealth was originally formed for the safety of his subjects and for peace (L, 30, par. 1; DC, 13, par. 2). A law that is only for the king's pleasure may appear to be good, but it is not, because what is bad for the people eventually is bad for the king (L, 30, par. 20). The sovereign has a *duty* to yield to right reason even though he cannot be obliged to do so since he cannot be coerced (DC, 7, par. 3).

That sovereigns often do not obey natural and divine laws or do not make good laws for their subjects is a fact of life, and it is one reason Hobbes wrote his works. Hobbes subordinates right to might while at the same time teaching that might will not survive long without right. There is a rational, that is, good, way to govern, and it includes the use of Hobbes's science of politics to enlighten and to guide leaders as well as followers. Hobbes wants the terms *good* and *bad,* as he uses them here, to be objective. They are ascertained by right reason, by science, which is the only way to find the truth.

What is good is reasonable; what is bad is unreasonable, based on long-term self-interest.

Hobbes also distinguishes between bad or good intentions and between unjust or just actions. Every crime is a sin, but not every sin a crime, for sometimes bad intentions (counted as sins) do not lead to bad actions (crime) (L, 27, par. 2). Therefore not every sin is unjust (see L, 27, par. 3).

Law, being rules backed by force, may cease, but the obligation toward the law of nature does not cease even in the state of nature. Because the first law of nature is self-preservation, in the state of nature it follows that it must be permissible to break the other laws of nature. But to do so for evil intentions (other than self-preservation) is a sin, because the laws of nature are written in men's minds, in or outside of society (L, 27, par. 4–6). What is right and good—that is, what would be reasonable in society—does not cease to be known simply because it cannot be heeded.

Similarly, Hobbes makes a distinction between a just man and just actions. A just man obeys because the law commands it and disobeys because of his weakness. An unjust man obeys for fear of punishment and disobeys because of his iniquity. Moreover, a man who tries to fulfill the laws of nature is just, even if he sometimes fails. The justice *of* a man is in his conscience, not in his outward actions. Just actions are those that conform to the law, no matter how unjust the subject's intentions. Hobbes here uses *just* in the sense of good or righteousness. Just and unjust refer to good and bad or righteous and unrighteous (the terms Hobbes says are often used), not conformity to the law (DC, 3, par. 5; L, 15, par. 10; 27, par. 1). But in reality such righteousness is not very useful: Hobbes finds such men to be too scarce to be the basis of his prescriptions (L, 15, par. 10).

The distinction between the just man and just actions holds in the state of nature as well. In the state of nature, a man may do whatever he thinks to be in his best interests to preserve himself. If he does no more than this, abstaining from cruelty or needless fighting, he is just in the sense of good (DC, 3, par. 27n.). Even though there is no real law, there is still the conscience, guided by reason, which provides limits. The natural law is always obligatory *internally;* but it is only obligatory *externally* when it is safe to obey (DC, 3, par. 26). Thus, "to do that which in peace is a handsome action, and becoming an honest man, is dejectedness, and poorness of spirit, and a

betraying of one's self, in the time of war" (DC, 3, par. 27n.). In the
state of war, breaking the law of nature actually fulfills the law of
nature if it is done for peace or self-preservation (PR, 45). Hence,
while the law of nature is eternal, the opportunities for obeying it
outwardly vary—and an individual's responsibility depends on his
circumstances.

Hobbes says that natural law and civil law comprise each other (L,
26, par. 8). This presents a problem in that he seems to be saying that
natural law (which is reason itself) can be subsumed under civil law
(which may be unreasonable). However, Hobbes anticipates this
problem. Natural law is not really law since it has no backing of coercive force; it is simply dictates of right reason that dispose men to
peace in the state of nature. But the necessity for civil law is a dictate
of reason, and so when a commonwealth is established, natural law
become actual law.

It is in this way that civil and natural laws coincide essentially,
though not in the particulars: in obedience to the sovereign's laws,
whether right or wrong, as the best means for self-preservation. All
the laws of nature after the second one, which explains the necessity
of transferring individual rights to a sovereign, are dependent upon
the second. As such, they are not logically necessary to it, although
Hobbes stresses that they are reasonable rules to follow. The people,
upon transferring their natural right to the sovereign, are obliged *by
natural law* to accept any and all other breaches of natural law the sovereign may commit, so long as he observes the most fundamental
law by protecting them from each other and from foreign enemies.
If he does not even do the latter, then are they no longer obliged to
obey him? The subject should endure the sovereign's unrighteous-
ness in all cases unless his personal safety can no longer be assured.
According to Hobbes, the citizen is obliged to refrain from sedition,
even if he thinks the sovereign is an unrighteous tyrant, in order to
maintain peace.

In his search for immutability, Hobbes equates the laws of nature
with the divine laws. Those divine laws encompassing the natural
duties people have to one another *are* the laws of nature. He tries to
tie his analysis of the law of nature to what he perceives as the true
message of Christianity (DC, 6, par. 13). Obedience to the sovereign
in all things, including outward religious signs, is in full agreement
with the teachings of Christ, he writes. But instead, the Church pro-

motes disobedience toward leaders and laws by threatening the people with hell. Hobbes insists that Church doctrine is not correct and is not fundamental in the practice of Christianity (DC, 12, par. 5). For the good citizen to be a good Christian, all he should have to do is obey the sovereign and give God the honor naturally due Him. Such honor consists in holding the opinion, not necessarily vocalized, that God is all-powerful and good (L, 31, par. 8). This allows subjects who are forced by the sovereign to worship in alien ways to avoid sin.

Late in his career, Hobbes tried to assure his critics that he did not mean to sanction the authority of anyone who grabs power or to absolve all subjects who revolt as soon as the sovereign cannot enforce obedience (THM, 413). Hobbes's defense is that *Leviathan* was written to chastise those who sought to usurp the sovereign through sedition or by attacking him openly and that the work absolves loyal citizens from guilt upon submitting to a new sovereign when it becomes obvious that he is truly in charge (THM, 415, 421). In this way Hobbes tries to dodge the question of whether he legitimizes anyone strong enough to get and hold power through unscrupulous means. His work, he claims, merely legitimizes the well-meaning people's surrender. Yet there is no evidence, excepting a few statements in *Behemoth,* to support the notion that Hobbes truly feels that a particular monarch has a special title to rule.[3] It is this implication that got him into trouble later with the king and some of his loyal followers (THM, 424–25).

Indeed, in the name of peace, order, and self-preservation, Hobbes does legitimize the rule of might over right. Though he does not want the sovereign to overstep his bounds, saying it is unprofitable and therefore unwise to do so, he does not sufficiently construct rationally derived safeguards against the abuse of power to make this anything more than a wish. His bet is firmly placed on force and fear as being the surest bases for law and order in a world full of changeable and conflicting individuals. He obviously hopes that reason, guided by his teachings, will be sufficiently strong to replace the moderating force of traditional safeguards such as ethical and religious norms and political deliberation. For a philosopher who so emphasizes the passions, Hobbes places great faith in the sovereign's rationality and ability to be educated correctly. Hobbes, by insisting on the minimal solution, made the attainment of the good life a hostage to the intelligence and humanity of the sovereign. By virtually guaranteeing his fundamental value, self-preservation at any cost, he made the best situation more difficult to obtain.

Morality and Necessity

Hobbes defines *justice* as nothing more than man-made laws. Good and bad, righteous and unrighteous, if used by the average human being not acquainted with the scientific method, are nothing but reflections of personal prejudices. If used as part of the correct method, however, these words have objective meaning. *Good* is reasonable, *bad* is unreasonable. In this section I will consider whether a moral law based totally on reason subverts the normal meaning of *moral* to the point that it is meaningless.[4]

Hobbes's "morality" seems to be missing something. We know that natural law is a set of rules discovered out by reason that promotes the common good. Natural law may also coincidentally be the law of Christ, but there is nothing necessarily supernatural about it. There can be no genuine sacrifices in the Hobbesian world, since everything is done with an eye to one's own good. These two things, that natural law is based on reason and that it operates through individual egoism, are generally unsettling to the moralist. Why does Hobbes find it necessary to base his morality solely on individual selfishness and expediency? The answer lies in his universal mechanism and its consequences for the human will. Hobbes accepts the principle of the Athenian thesis that human passions are compelling and therefore blameless. His mechanism is put forth as proof for this thesis. In addition, Hobbes wants to establish a moral code based on this mechanism and all that falls out from it. Therein lies the difficulty and the incongruity of his moral philosophy.

As already stated, Hobbes's mechanistic analysis of the individual makes it possible for him to depict mankind as a collection of isolated individuals who are entirely egocentric. Man's nature derives from the purely physical; the will is a direct product of outside stimuli acting on bodily organs. Every action is voluntary because it is produced by the will, according to Hobbes. To some of his contemporaries, however, this definition of *voluntary* sounded suspiciously like complete determinism. Such determinism has a crippling effect on ethics, as it is usually understood.[5]

Hobbes wrote on this doctrine of the will in *Human Nature* and in

Leviathan, before he consented to the publication in 1656 of *The Questions Concerning Liberty, Necessity and Chance.* This latter book was a record of the debate between Hobbes and Bishop Bramhall of Derry, mediated by the Earl of Newcastle. In the preface, Hobbes succinctly states his position: "that it is not in man's power now to choose the will he shall have anon; that chance produceth nothing; that all events and actions have their necessary causes; that the will of God makes the necessity of all things." Bramhall maintains quite the opposite: that God has given man free will, and not simply freedom to do what he will; that chance is active in the world; and that therefore man may go against God's will, proving that man has "moral liberty" (LNC, "Preface").[6]

Neither Hobbes nor Bramhall ever gives satisfactory proof for his theory. Hobbes simply reasserts his argument with every new attack by the bishop, claiming that Bramhall has not answered his main point. Bramhall does not directly answer Hobbes's main point (that the will cannot choose to will or what to will) since, clearly, it is impossible to refute. His argument is at its best when it shows the consequences that flow from Hobbes's theory; otherwise he tries to show that there is free will on a commonsense level by showing how chance may intervene in human decision-making, or how a man may choose, for example, to die for duty's sake even though he really wants to live.

Hobbes's answers are tautological. Everything must have a cause, he argues, and if we go far enough back we must logically come to a first cause of all things. This first cause is God, who by definition is eternal, all-knowing, and all-powerful (LNC, 11). The first cause then sets off innumerable chains of causes (LNC, 105). Hence, many causes go into producing the last dictate of the will, and the will then produces a man's action. Man, then, is simply a part and product of the universal mechanism (LNC, 303). If he is not aware of this or thinks himself free, it is because he does not know or understand all the causes that result in his will. A man may encounter a black cat by chance and act quickly based on that encounter, but in truth the cat arrived not by chance but by an ineluctable, predetermined chain of causes and effects, and his will was the product of the last effect as it worked on his senses. Depending on the causes that worked on him, he might run away in terror from the cat or he might stoop down to pet it. "Chance" is an illusion caused by incomplete information.

Likewise, a man may think he is acting contrary to his will in doing his duty, but this is impossible since the action is always a product of the final will. The man is simply unaware of the internal and external causes that would make him choose such a route (LNC, 74, 222, 226; L, 21, par. 4). The internal causes for a bad decision might be natural lack of wit or of previous experience with which to compare. A person always wills what appears good to him, even if his understanding is faulty (LNC, 324).

At this point, Hobbes's theory is irrefutable; it relies on insurmountable human ignorance as the reason why it cannot be proved. Hobbes goes on to say that God, as all-powerful and omniscient, must know beforehand all the effects that will issue from Him. Thus there must be complete predestination. To this the bishop replies that the all-powerful and all-knowing God is also by definition all-good, that He could not be responsible for the evil and sin in the world and that He would not predestine some people to be sinners and then send them to hell because they were. Therefore, he reasons, God must allow sin, even though He disapproves of it, in order to give man moral liberty (LNC, 127). Hobbes responds, quite predictably, that we should not question God's ways, especially since irresistible power naturally justifies all actions (LNC, 115–16). If God permits men to sin, He must also will their sin, Hobbes says, thus denying the bishop's distinction between allowing and determining (LNC, 117). In effect, Hobbes throws his hands up in piety, saying that those who call God "to the bar" through lack of understanding commit injustice:

> I cannot imagine, when living creatures of all sorts are often in torments as well as men, that God can be displeased with it: without his will, they neither are nor could be at all tormented. Nor yet is he delighted with it; but health, sickness, ease, torments, life and death, are without all passion in him dispensed by him; and he putteth an end to them then when they end, and a beginning when they begin, according to his eternal purpose, which cannot be resisted. (LNC, 213)[7]

Hobbes claims that his doctrine of determinism, rather than being impious, is the height of piety. To think of God as all-powerful is to honor him in the highest degree, he says. Worship is nothing more than acknowledging God's power (LNC, 199). God's justice is thus subsumed under His power. For God, there is no eternal and universal right and wrong. God determines good and evil by what He wills; His will is not determined by what is good and evil. We are wrong to censure Him if what He does appears evil to us. The bishops' reply, that power does not measure justice but justice measures and regulates power, hits on the ultimate difference between the two men. For Bramhall, even God is regulated by the rules of justice—He cannot will anything that is not good by certain eternal standards. Truth, what is just and unjust, is eternal. In this one way, man has more freedom than God, because he can will both good and evil. For Hobbes, God is not determined by anything other than Himself. He is not bound by justice; He creates it by virtue of His power. Everything He wills is good and just, because He wills it (LNC, 146, 192). What seems evil to us must be good to God, and it fits somehow into His eternal plan.

In stating this, Hobbes's theory does away with all sin. What Hobbes calls sin or evil does not correspond to ordinary understanding because it does not involve responsibility. It becomes merely an indication of disutility. That the element of moral responsibility is totally missing in Hobbes's theory becomes clear when we arrive at his account of punishment. Bramhall asks if it is not unjust to be punished for a necessary act, one that is by definition beyond our control. Hobbes replies that such punishment is not unjust because it is expedient. It is useful in deterring men from willing to do the same crime in the future (LNC, 153). Praise and blame are not made ineffectual by the doctrine of necessity, either, because what is necessary is still good when "good" means "to my advantage" (LNC, 154).

But this is not moral goodness, Bramhall argues (LNC, 170). Bramhall identifies morality with freedom of the will, the ability to choose between right and wrong (LNC, 45). Only with choice can a person be held responsible for sin. When Hobbes replies that he does not know what "moral liberty" means and that he cannot understand Bramhall's idea of punishment, the two have come to an impasse again. Clearly Hobbes believes that the only use for punishment is deterrence, while Bramhall believes it has a retributive function as well (LNC, 177).

Predictably, Hobbes thinks that natural evil or affliction is God's correction, not His "revenge" (LNC, 183). Since, according to

Hobbes, God controls all things, God would be correcting Himself by inflicting evils of nature such as disease. This has a ring of absurdity to it that Hobbes, if he had been arguing on Bramhall's side, would have targeted for some sly comment. Indeed, concepts not fully explained or contradictory abound in Hobbes's argument. When he cannot prove them adequately he simply declares them true. He also engages in quite a bit of characteristic nastiness: for example, ridiculing "schoolmen" and "divines" for their jargon, finding Bramhall's communications absurd, and refusing to deal with them because of it.

But how reasonable are Hobbes's formal and legalistic definitions: "voluntary" is anything willed, even if the will is determined; "liberty" is the freedom to do what the will is determined to do. Thus liberty is a lack of physical restraints but implies no freedom of choice (LNC, 35, 62, 314, 372; L, 21, par. 2). Choosing and necessity are joined together because "in this following of one's hopes and fears consisteth the nature of election. So that a man may both choose this, and cannot but choose this" (LNC, 72). No one is obliged who can release himself from obligation (because obligation involves force); therefore a man cannot choose to oblige himself (LNC, 144). Sin is a "halting or stumbling in the way of God's commandments" (LNC, 54), but it is not a purposeful stumbling. It is a mistake that needs correcting but that cannot when it happens be avoided (LNC, 229). Good is a measure of utility, evil of disutility, but in a world in which everything is necessarily so, even these judgments are mere fancies in individuals' minds, which themselves are determined.

One must wonder, If Hobbes really believed all this, what motivated him? The bishop wondered too:

> What a presumption is this, for one private man, who will not allow human liberty to others, to assume to himself such a licence to control so magistrally, and to censure of gross ignorance and tyrannising over men's judgments, yea, as causes of the troubles and tumults which are in the world, the doctors of the Church in general, who have flourished in all ages and all places, only for a few necessary and innocent distinctions. (LNC, 257–58)

Hobbes, always formally consistent, declared that he had written his defense of necessity "to show I have no dominion over my will" (LNC, 405). But in the same paragraph he chided Bramhall for calling him a fool, even though the bishop was necessitated to do so (of course, Hobbes was necessitated to chide, and so on). Bramhall thought that Hobbes's doctrine made all human endeavors futile. "Either allow liberty, or destroy all societies," he wrote. Although this is not a refutation of Hobbes's theory, it does make a very important point: Hobbes seemed to think that most people would remain caught up in the illusion of freedom and that this was why the sort of apathy Bramhall described would not occur. For instance, a man may make a free vow to God even if he believes in predestination because he will not know it was predestined until the moment he did it (LNC, 218).[8]

How Hobbes gets around the theological difficulties of his argument is worth relating in brief, although an entire explanation would be impossible here. The bishop points out that if all is predetermined by God, then the frequent biblical references to God's chastisements would be nonsensical. "God's chiding proves man's liberty," Bramhall writes. Significantly, he draws one example from *Genesis,* where God says, "Hast thou eaten of the tree, whereof I commanded that thou shouldst not eat?" Did God openly command Adam and Eve not to eat the fruit while secretly causing them to eat it? What purpose could God have for creating and controlling evil in the world and then punishing his creatures for their sins? Hobbes's solution to this objection is to distinguish between God's hidden will and His revealed will. He cites God's commandment to Abraham to sacrifice Isaac while willing that he not do it (LNC, 103). But in relating this example, he fails to ask why God would want to test Abraham's faith if God Himself was in control of all events. As for the *Genesis* story, Hobbes says that it proves that Adam was so little a master of his own will that he could not avoid eating from the one tree that was forbidden. He states that God did this not to trick man but to instruct him that he could never attain immortality except through the gift of Jesus Christ (LNC, 102).

This line of reasoning is used in several places as a way to escape the difficulties involved in the notions of evil and sin. Redemption rests not in anything human beings can do; it lies not in reform but only in God's gift of his Son. To the question of why God complains about men's sins, Hobbes answers with Paul (Rom. 9:20, 21): "Who art thou, O man, that interrogatest God? Shall the work say to the workman, why hast thou made me thus?" Hobbes quotes Paul again (Rom. 9:18): "Therefore whom God willeth he hath mercy on, and whom he willeth he hardeneth" (LNC, 115). God wills that some people sin in order to show them their fallibility and that their only hope is in Christ's mercy. Likewise, Hobbes says God chooses to open other men's hearts to His forgiveness. Sin, then, becomes a way for God to display his power over men (LNC, 216, 229).

It is hard to believe that Hobbes actually subscribes to everything he says in his debate with Bramhall. While he is generally consistent with the theology in his other works, like *De Cive* and *Leviathan,* when he edges into complete determinism one looks for an escape clause that can explain these works and Hobbes himself. Does Hobbes really believe it when he says his actions are completely determined? As discussed earlier, Hobbes claimed that reason is dominated by the passions, that the last passion of the will gives reason its end. But at the same time Hobbes asserted, both in words and in deeds, that scientific reasoning could overcome passion. Right reasoning leads to the idea of the one first mover and eternal cause, while reliance on authority leads to belief in "things invisible" (L, 12, par. 6; H, 59). Nothing is produced by right reasoning other than "generall, eternall, and immutable Truth" (L, 46, par. 2). From these and similar statements we can conclude that what is genuine in Hobbes's debate with Bramhall is his belief in a first cause and in mechanism. But contrary to his rigid stance in his debate with Bramhall, Hobbes surely did not think himself extrinsically and necessarily determined in all things. Hobbes thought that some men could escape the dominance of their passions through science. He thought himself to be the first philosopher to apply the scientific method to political matters. Therefore he must have seen his philosophy as a unique glimmer of free reason atop a mass of human confusion determined by passion. His teaching, if understood, or at least adopted, even by a few, could make use of what kept most men enslaved in an endless cycle of action and reaction—their passions—in order to make the world a more peaceful place. What was discovered by one could be taught to many, by playing on fears. Prescriptions found out by right reason could be implemented by the prudent sovereign in order for him to maintain his power, which would end up benefiting all citizens. If this is not a usurpation of God's prerogatives as Hobbes himself defined them, what is?

In sum, if we assume that Hobbes believes in a first cause and a mechanism whose chains of cause and effect extend to the will, we can make the following conclusions about his moral philosophy:

1.   All *justice,* whether God's or man's, natural or conventional, is based on power and therefore arbitrary at the deepest level. Truth itself is relative to power. If God or nature were to change, the "truth" of natural law would also change (however unlikely this may be). And if the sovereign changes, the "truth" of the civil law will change.

2.   Terms such as *good, bad, right, wrong, evil, sin, praise,* and *blame* are used to measure relative utility. As such they are devoid of true moral content. Further, since the passions control almost all men, such terms do not denote any kind of moral responsibility. If men are compelled to act, they cannot be blamed. This is why punishment should be used for correction, not retribution, according to Hobbes.

3.   If the law of nature is the complete and only moral law, *moral* means what is advantageous based on right reason. Thus what is rational replaces what is right or just in the common sense of those terms. On the domestic level, this leaves determination of what is good completely up to the sovereign, regardless of his enlightenment or the lack thereof.

The next section will point out the difficulties and drawbacks of putting this theory into practice in international relations.

Hobbes's Natural Law and the Law of Nations

Hobbes's state of nature looks like the realist's image of international politics. The consequences that flow from the state of nature create many of the political and moral prescriptions of realist doctrine. But in order to evaluate this analogy, we must ask what Hobbes really said about international relations. Although he wrote much less about foreign affairs than he did about domestic politics, he produced enough for us not to have to rely on an analogy.

The State of Nature and the State of Nations   The clearest statement Hobbes makes on the state of nature as analogous to the actual practice of states is in *De Cive.* Hobbes classifies law into types. Law for states' relations is called the law or right of nations and falls under natural as opposed to positive law. The same elements of natural law and right previously applied to individuals may be applied to states (DC, 14, par. 4). The state of international relations is a state of nature, that is, a state of war (DC, 10, par. 17).[9]

From these statements, we might gather that Hobbes would approve of the realist's use of the state of nature not only as an analogy but also as an accurate and self-contained description of international relations. Then we would have to study Hobbes's logical progression from this state of nature to the state of civil society via the social contract. The next assumption would be that states, too, may come together and form a government that could stop war by holding a monopoly on violence. However, this would be a false turn according to both Hobbes and realists, and luckily, Hobbes does not leave us with a simple comparison of the state of nature with states in anarchy.

Hobbes tells us that every sovereign has the right and duty to safeguard his "body," the commonwealth. Because of the lack of guaranteed security in international relations, kings must continually assure their safety by striving for more power, which often means going to war (L, 11, par. 2). Any war waged for these purposes is waged justly, because there is no other recourse (L, 17, par. 2). A king also has the duty to obey natural law as much as he can without endangering the safety of the commonwealth. This duty impinges only on his conscience, however, "there being no Court of Naturall Justice, but in the Conscience onely" (L, 30, par. 30). It is a matter solely of conscience because kings keep their citizens safe, and so there is less misery accompanying the state of nature in international relations. The security that comes from numbers makes the "persons" of the international state of nature much more safe and indestructible than the individual persons of the precivil state (L, 13, par. 12). All individuals are vulnerable in nature because they must sleep, but the body politic never sleeps. This is one major reason for government. For the sake of security, the number of men entering into a social contract must be great enough that the desertion of a few to the enemy will not be so important as to guarantee the enemy's victory (DC, 5, par. 3).

Thus external as well as internal threats of violence produce the necessity for the state. The passions that incline *individuals* to peace are "Feare of Death," "Desire of such things as are necessary to commodious living," and "a Hope by their Industry to obtain them" (L,

13, par. 14). But the creation of the state takes away extreme fear of other states that individuals should have for other individuals in the state of nature. In this respect, international relations are different from the state of nature. States also provide the protection necessary for commodious living and the industry to obtain that way of life. The international state of nature therefore does not directly threaten most individuals. For these reasons, peace will not be as urgent a priority as it is in relations among individuals, but the need to violate the laws of nature will also not be as urgent.

Instead of international war, the war of all against all is more closely approximated for Hobbes by civil war, the breakdown of society, and a dissolution to the original precivil state. In this type of war, laws of nature are known, but no man has to observe them because there is no enforcement mechanism, and to obey them without this mechanism would be contrary to the primary goal of self-preservation. It is an old saying, Hobbes writes, that all laws, natural and civil, are silent in time of war. But in a war among nations, all laws—at least natural—need not be silent (DC, 5, par. 2).

How are any laws to be kept among nations without a sovereign to enforce them? Hobbes does not mention the need for or the possibility of a world government among states. He also does not speak of world empire as the corollary to the possibility of government by conquest at the national level. The absolute power of the city is limited from without, Hobbes says, only by the strength of the city (or state) itself (DC, 6, par. 18). While men can truly be free only once they have subjected themselves to the law and order of civil society, states can be free only if they cannot be subdued, because "so soon as a state hath a strong enough to subdue it, it is no more to be thought a free state" (HT, 4.92n.14). For states, not only is world government not a possibility but also states are not thought to be hindered just because they are not fettered by laws and government. But more freedom means more room for choice and thus less extenuation for violation of the laws of nature.

The Laws of Nature Applied to Nations   In the state of nature, there is no justice or injustice because there is no true law (L, 13, par. 13). There is a standard of right or wrong (based on what is reasonable), but this standard cannot be safely heeded until men give up their right to all things and submit to the coercive power of government and its justice. Given the above conclusions, if in international relations there is no possibility of sovereign control, what parts of the law of nature can apply?[10]

First we must have a definition: "A LAW OF NATURE, (Lex Naturalis,) is a Precept, or generall Rule, found out by Reason, by which a man is forbidden to do, that, which is destructive of his life, or taketh away the means of preserving the same: and to omit, that, by which he thinketh it may be best preserved" (L, 14, par. 3). The fundamental law of nature is to seek peace. The reason men must seek peace as much as possible lies in the exercise of their natural right, which is every man's right in nature to defend himself by every means he can, using his own judgment to determine what are the best means (L, 14, par. 1, 4). Johnston points out that "right" in this case means only freedom from obligation, not "an entitlement that other men have a duty to respect."[11] As long as this natural right continues, no one can live in safety, and it is for this reason that men should seek peace through society. These two concepts—natural right and natural law—lead to a general rule of reason: "*That every man, ought to endeavour Peace, as farre as he has hope of obtaining it; and when he cannot obtain it, that he may seek, and use, all helps, and advantages of Warre.*" The second law of nature calls for a man to be willing for the sake of peace and his own security to give up his right to all things and content himself with the same liberty that he would allow to others (L, 14, par. 5). This is to be done by transferring to another such rights as, being retained, would obstruct peace.

Concerning relations among states, the most fundamental law, which comes before the law concerning the social contract, may be acted upon. That is, states may legitimately seek peace whenever possible, but when it is not possible, they should have recourse to war. This is saying no more than that a state should look after its self-interest, narrowly defined as the least costly way to preserve itself. Wars fought not for more power or security but for, say, revenge or religion or over some insult would be against the law of nature.[12] But to seek peace by social contract would be going too far, because, as we have seen, states' reasons for seeking peace are less pressing than those of individuals.

The third law directs men to carry out the covenants they make (L, 15, par. 1). This law of nature is the origin of justice. No action can be counted unjust until men enter into civil society and give up their right to everything. After a covenant has been made, justice refers to keeping the covenant, injustice to breaking it (L, 15, par. 3). We would expect, then, that in the international state of nature, covenants would not oblige because there is no coercive guarantor. However, according to Hobbes, this is not true. Even in the state of nature among men, covenants entered into out of fear are obligatory. As we have already seen, covenants not backed by force and fear are not obligatory because the covenantor can decide to renege. Indeed, coerced covenants are valid in all circumstances, whether in the state of nature among men, or among nations, or even in civil society. For example, if in the natural condition a man agrees to pay ransom to another in order to save his life, he is bound by that agreement. Hobbes sees this as a binding contract in which one person receives life, the other money. Prisoners of war are likewise obliged to pay their ransom. "And if a weaker Prince, make a disadvantageous peace with a stronger, for fear; he is bound to keep it; unless . . . there ariseth some new, and just cause of feare, to renew the war" (L, 14, par. 27).[13]

The strangeness of these propositions is alleviated when we realize that it is *only* the context of force that makes the difference between valid and invalid contracts in or outside of government. In the case of agreements in which force is not an issue, covenants are made void by the first sign of one party's will not to perform. We can conclude that overwhelming force in international relations obliges, quite naturally. But Hobbes does not leave us with that. He reasons that if in international relations coerced obligations are not seen as binding and not regularly or completely performed, there will be no incentive for conquerors not to kill prisoners of war or decimate the populations of the states they conquer. So, a certain common understanding of conduct in war is being upheld by compliance, an understanding from which all may benefit. Moreover, Hobbes shows that contracts not coerced by superior power may still be very much in all parties' interests as a common good. In this category is the contract between sovereigns for ambassadorial immunity. Without such an agreement, he writes, there can be no hope for honest dialogue between sovereigns using representatives to communicate (L, 21, par. 24).

We see, then, that absolutely binding contracts are possible in the international state of nature, but only those extracted and continued in effect by force. All other covenants are more easily broken, since there is no government to ensure that either party abides by its obligations. Justice and injustice, in Hobbes's conventional sense, do not exist, because there is no overarching coercive power (L, 15, par. 4). But Hobbes recognizes that sovereigns may make contracts with each other based on mutual long-term interest and that it is *unreasonable* to break these contracts, whether in order to preserve either the life of the state or the integrity of ambassadorial communications. As he says in *Behemoth*, "It is indeed commonly seen that neighbor nations envy one another's honour, and that the less potent bears the greater malice; but that hinders them not from agreeing in those things which common ambition leads them to" (B, 203).

The fourth law exhorts gratitude, because unless it is shown, there will be no benevolence, trust, mutual help, or reconciliation, all of which are necessary to maintain peace (L, 15, par. 16). The fifth law concerns mutual accommodation. A man who is too greedy, stubborn, or unsociable is to be cast out of society because he provokes conflict. In the case of these two laws, while it might not be damaging for a state to follow them, its incentive for doing so will be less than that of an individual. There is much less need to foster benevolence, trust, and mutual help in international relations, and only an individual must mortally fear being cast out of society. Yet if gratitude or accommodation were the most rational way to safety and prosperity, Hobbes would recommend them, since the king's foremost duty is to preserve the commonwealth from foreign and civil wars. It is not wise for either men or states to "retain those things which . . . are superfluous, and to others necessary," thereby provoking fights for trifles (L, 15, par. 17). The sixth law calls for men to pardon offenders if asked for forgiveness. If forgiveness is not granted to those who sincerely ask for it, this is a sign of aversion to peace, which is against the law of nature, that is, against reason (L, 15, par. 18). The seventh law directs men, in taking revenge, to dwell not on the crime that has been done to them but on the good they may obtain in the future by properly (and not excessively) correcting the offender (L, 15, par. 19). For Hobbes, every action taken in the state of nature must be concerned only with some future good. Punishments should concern only correction or a necessary example to others, or both. Anything else is cruelty or taking pleasure in another's harm without any end. Revenge with no other end than inflicting pain is a "glorying to no end" and is contrary to reason (L, 15, par. 19). When all other laws must be abandoned for the sake of self-preservation, this prohibition still holds good, because obeying it will not prejudice one's safety (C, 119).

Hobbes gives an example of raiding in ancient times, which was, despite the necessity for it, kept within certain limits. Even as raiding was warranted by the law of nature for the sake of security, cruelty was forbidden. Nothing but fear, Hobbes writes, can justify taking another's life. In war, there can be no injury (which requires enforced laws) in the breach of even this law, but there can be dishonor. "In one word, therefore, the only law of actions in war, is *honour;* and the right of war, *providence*" (C, 119). Hobbes repeats this prohibition in *De Cive*. There are certain laws that do not cease even in war, he writes, since cruelty cannot advance the prospects for peace in any possible way (DC, 3, par. 27n.).[14] In *Leviathan* he says that to hurt without reason tends to bring on war, which is against the law of nature. But he says the laws of nature bind men only in conscience: the only thing required is that they desire to obey them. In the state of nature, he tries to perform them when possible and is therefore just. The one conclusion we can make from the above observations is that the prohibition on needless or excessive revenge holds, and its violation is not excusable like that of other laws.

Thus, in the state of nature among men as well as states, whatever is done out of necessity and out of an endeavor for peace is done with right. But what is right can be judged not by the actions but only by the conscience of the actor (DC, 3, par. 27n.). This caveat means that this law, like all others in the state of nature, is unenforceable. However, Hobbes points to the existence of "natural punishments" that somewhat take the place of the sovereign's enforcement in international relations. Injustice is naturally punished with the violence of enemies. Cruelty invites reciprocation (L, 31, par. 40). Clearly, Hobbes would have states obey his minimal injunctions both for the sake of decency and for their own interests.

The eighth law prohibits contumely, or signs of hatred or contempt. Given Hobbes's standard above, that no killing should be done except out of fear, and because all signs of hatred, or contempt, provoke men to fight each other for no good reason, statesmen could safely obey this law as well (L, 15, par. 20). War provoked by a sign of contempt would be caused not by fear but by triviality and vainglory. The ninth law forbids pride. Nature has made men equal because the weakest and dullest can kill the strongest and most wise (L, 15, par. 21). Therefore men should recognize each other as equals in order to enter into society. But the international state of nature is different from that of men because states cannot so easily destroy each other. They therefore have little incentive to acknowledge each other as equals, especially since states may vary quite greatly in power and still survive. Thus, if pride consists in not acknowledging all others as equals, states may retain their pride and manage to continue quite nicely. However, if they act foolishly on their pride instead of on their true self-interests, they would be acting against reason—against their own preservation. That they often do so is an unfortunate fact.[15] The tenth law of nature is against arrogance: *"That at the entrance into conditions of Peace, no man require to reserve to himselfe any Right, which he is not content should be reserved to everyone of the rest"* (L, 15, par. 22). This is the consequent of the law against pride, so although it applies to individuals, it does not as readily apply to states in their dealings with one another. But inasmuch as arrogance provokes *needless* quarrels, Hobbes would say it is against reason and should be avoided. In *De Cive,* Hobbes sums up how he might apply the ninth and tenth laws to international relations: "For such commonwealths, or such monarchs, as affect war for itself, that is to say, out of ambition, or of vain-glory, or that make account to revenge every little injury, or disgrace done by their neighbors, if they not ruine themselves, their fortune must be better than they have reason to expect" (C, 220).

The rest of the laws of nature cannot be said to apply to international relations, since they are actually rules for constructing a workable government (L, 15, par. 20–33). Unless a government is formed, none of these laws can be safely observed, according to Hobbes. But, as we have seen, Hobbes would discount the possibility and desirability of a world government. Unlike men, states are considered free only when they are unconstrained.

The Consequences of the Law of Nations   Logic may lead statesmen to agree that it would be best for everyone in the world if all states would follow these laws of nature. But logic would also lead them to see that at least some cannot be followed at all, because there is no guarantee that any other state will do the same. Hence, statesmen must operate under different constraints than are present at the level of domestic order. While the virtue of the subject is obedience to the laws, the virtue of the sovereign is to maintain peace at home and to resist foreign enemies. Like the statesman informed by the realist theory of international relations, he must think of his actions not in terms of moral good and evil but in terms of what is useful or harmful to the safety and prosperity of the commonwealth (B, 189, 384).

In the name of national interest, all infliction of evil is lawful in war (L, 28, par. 13). Innocents may be afflicted with whatever evil is necessary: all foreigners not having covenant with the sovereign must be considered enemies. No respect is given to mercy in such matters except as it conduces to the good of the sovereign and his people (L, 28, par. 23). This is the downside of Hobbes's rule against unnecessary cruelty and revenge: if it is *necessary,* anything goes. And the judgment of necessity remains the sole province of every sovereign, no matter how ill-witted or enlightened he may be. This subjective judgment is the real danger in Hobbes's teaching. The determination of the national interest must always be an individual (or collective) subjective determination unhindered by any other impediment or inducement.

Given the above theory of international justice, one can only hope that sovereigns know or can learn what is truly in their long-term best interest, that they *will* look to the future consequences of their actions. As mentioned above, Hobbes leaves us with some hope that nature can teach a few lessons on prudence: "And hereby it comes to passe, that Intemperence, is naturally punished with Diseases; Rashness, with Mischances; Injustice, with Violence of Enemies; Pride, with Ruine; Cowardise, with Opression; Negligent government of Princes, with Rebellion; and Rebellion with Slaughter" (L, 31, par. 40). The priority of avoiding these natural punishments is the reason Hobbes prescribes government for warring individuals. But in the international state of nature, in which no governmental order can be brought to bear, these effects will still exist. Perhaps the more secure and independent condition of nations might leave room for decisions to be made in recognition of these natural punishments. If there is to be any "justice" at all in international politics, it follows that statesmen must recognize not only natural laws but also their natural punishments and that they must be capable of prudential reasoning about avoiding them.

It is easy to be sympathetic to Hobbes's rejection of ideals of morality and justice. It is especially easy to identify with it at the level of international politics. Hobbes would have ruled out wars to check one or another ideology or religion, unless they threatened one's own territory. He would also have ruled out military aid or assistance to those countries whose only claim to our help is moral or ideological. We have seen examples of this pragmatic statesmanship throughout American history, as well as its crusading opposite.[16] Is there anything worth dying for simply on the grounds that the cause is right? Are there any values higher than the national interest? Hobbes would say no.

But to give Hobbesian practicality too much praise is to ignore the possibility of its being practiced in excess. Since Hobbes says that justice is situational in relations among states, as it is among people, it never *has* to be violated. He argues that punishment should be used only to redirect another's will. But by removing the enemy's responsibility from the equation, by disregarding his level of guilt or innocence, aggression loses an important measure. Hence, what appears to be a moderating principle, that no punishment should be inflicted except for purposes of correction or example, may become a justification for excess.

Having wrecked all moral norms, Hobbes desperately tried to rebuild from the ground up by reeducation. His hope was that sovereigns would see the usefulness to themselves in being good to their people. He hoped that kings would see how they themselves would be injured by needless foreign wars. But unlike Hobbes's wish for order, his hope for enlightenment was not insured by absolutism. It remained a hope—in reason and in the intelligence of rulers. This hope came from a man who thought that, until his science arrived, mankind was incapable of escaping its passions and finding a solution to the turmoil of political change. The great pessimist of human nature became the greatest optimist when it came to the power of science.

Summary

Hobbes would disagree with those who say there can be no international justice without a world government to enforce it. Because of their relatively secure status, states can reasonably obey some norms without risking their "lives." However, since Hobbes says that justice is situational in relations among states, as it is among people, it never *has* to be violated. Hobbes's "justice" in the state of nature or in international relations is nothing but the rational calculation of self-interest. While many realists still see a conflict between justice and expediency and choose to expound on the latter, they also seem to endorse a dual morality in which the defense of the national interest is the highest moral good of the statesman.[17] Hans J. Morgenthau had his own unique way of dealing with this moral dilemma. Writing of his conception of realism, he stated: "Its last resort, then, is the endeavor to choose, since evil there must be, among several possible answers the one that is least evil"[18] and "To know with despair that the political act is inevitably evil, and to act nevertheless is moral courage. To choose among several expedient actions the least evil one is moral judgment."[19] Nevertheless, for Morgenthau, the national interest must be the guiding light for the statesman, and one cannot miss in his writings the implication that the moral rules are different for the public figure and the private person.

In a much more crude and less agonized fashion, Hobbes says justice *is* expediency, if only rulers would listen to reason. Reason is designed to replace the character and prudence associated with statesmanship, which Hobbes thinks is too rare to rely upon. But when theory turns into practice, Hobbes's reliance solely on what is reasonable and expedient is easily abused.

Hobbes's mechanism has the same effect. It takes the praise and blame from actions, treating them instead as mistakes that need correction. Mistakes become whatever we do not like, whatever we determine is detrimental to our preservation. No nation should punish another for revenge, he says. Punishment should be used only to redirect another's will. But by removing the enemy's responsibility from the equation, by disregarding degree of guilt or innocence, aggression loses an important measure. Justification becomes easier: the correct amount of aggression is determined by what is reasonable. In reality, this means what seems reasonable to whomever is in charge. Who is to be corrected and the reasons for correction are up to the calculations of the sovereign, who no longer has to justify his actions by the normal moral standards of guilt or innocence, but only expediency. What appears to be a moderating principle, that no punishment should be inflicted except for purposes of correction or example, can become an opportunity for excess.

Excessive cruelty is to be measured by the yardstick of national interest. While needless provocation and revenge are still ruled out, there is much room for abuse. Of course, this is not the result Hobbes intended, but by denying any foundation for norms other than expediency he left the door open for massive rationalizations. By establishing reason as the firmest foundation for morality, he actually made the foundation shakier.

Hobbes replaces political rhetoric with the language of science and the scientific method. He denies the meaning and usefulness of moral debate. The norms bantered about in such debate are meaningless because they are subjective, dangerous because their subjectivity causes conflict. To make norms objective, Hobbes makes them totally reasonable—he takes the conscience formed by customary ethical and religious training out of values. He removes their binding character unless they are either manifestly useful to those who obey or forced upon those who would not otherwise obey. The safeguard of open debate is withdrawn in favor of the appeal to pure reason. The consequence of his argument is, ironically, that we must hope for a truly enlightened sovereign who will apply reason the way Hobbes would have him apply it.

All this falls out from Hobbes's foremost concern: the avoidance of civil war. The fundamental opposing question we must ask of Hobbes is whether order is to be bought at any price. Is order always antecedent to justice? Should it always be our first concern? For Hobbes, the only thing worth dying for (or at any rate worth deaths) is the maintenance of order: a few people must sometimes be sacrificed to stop sedition; a foreign war may have to be waged in order to preserve the state. But as far as "ideals" such as freedom or liberty (in the usual sense), speech, religion, way of life—these are not worth the horrors of war. The death of the individual remains the greatest evil and its avoidance the greatest good. The avoidance of death is more apt to be ensured by membership in civil society. This is precisely what resolves the clash between order and justice in Hobbes's mind.

It is easy to be sympathetic to Hobbes's rejection of ideals. It is especially easy to identify with it at the level of international politics, where too many wars have been fought in order to spread or check communism or capitalism, or in the name of one religion or another.

These wars are more vicious and prolonged because of their unlimited ends. They are driven by hate, not simply by greed or lust for power. Their resolution must be complete victory or surrender. These are international wars with the vehemence Hobbes found so appalling in civil wars. Hobbes's warning about the dangers of going to war over trifles pales before the warnings realists issue today, but they are of the same stripe. Hobbes would not only rule out wars to check communism in areas unimportant to Western interests but would be even more likely to rule out military aid or assistance to those countries whose only claim to our help is moral. We have seen examples of this cold, pragmatic statesmanship throughout our history, as well as its crusading opposite. The question remains, is there anything worth dying for simply on the grounds that the cause is right? Are there any values higher than the national interest? Hobbes would say no.

But what would Hobbes's interpreters say? Could they not find a way to identify the national interest with the most extreme measures against anyone who opposes them? Could they not make a war against a nonessential country into a necessary example to others? Where does one stop when it comes to one's safety? Hobbes says that all efforts to advance one's power are done with right. In practice, ideological challenges are just as threatening to our power as are tanks, planes, and missiles. In Hobbes's time, the application of his reasoning to foreign affairs might have led to excess. In the twentieth century it can lead to total war. Ideology, combined with making utility the measure of all means, becomes a deadly force.

Can we blame Hobbes for the unintended consequences of his philosophy? Only if those consequences were not foreseen. But his advice to sovereigns on how their true interests coincide with the interests of their people proves that he knew there was a need to urge moderation. He knew his system left open the possibility for the worst kind of tyranny. Having wrecked all norms not based on expediency and destroyed all belief in statesmanship, Hobbes desperately tried to rebuild by reeducation. His hope was that sovereigns would see the usefulness to themselves in being good to their people. He hoped that kings would see how they themselves would be injured by needless foreign wars. But unlike Hobbes's wish for order, his hope for enlightenment was not insured by absolutism. It remained a hope—in reason and in the intelligence of rulers. This hope came from a man who thought that, until his science arrived, mankind was incapable of escaping its passions and finding a solution to the turmoil of political change. The great pessimist of human nature became the greatest optimist when it came to the power of science. In this attitude, Hobbes and many of his modern followers were naive.

THUCYDIDES

Thucydides' *History* is often commandeered by the realist school as the ultimate example of the workings of power politics and as proof of the uselessness of appealing to notions of justice in relations among states. I believe this view is based on the recurrence of the "Athenian thesis" throughout the *History*, first put forward by the Athenians at the Spartan War Conference before the Spartans decided to wage war (1.75). The thesis is characterized by the assumption that the ambition to become ever more powerful is natural and compelling and therefore blameless. The implications for justice in this theory are grave. But is Thucydides' view of justice in accord with the Athenian thesis? Here we will pursue that question directly.

Lowell Edmunds's study entitled "Thucydides' Ethics as Reflected in the Description of Stasis (3.82–83)" argues that, even though Thucydides nowhere explicitly states his ethical position, his treatment of the Corcyraean stasis provides us with fairly solid proof of Thucydides' ethical preferences: "Since Thucydides' position is explicitly one of censure (n.b. 3.83.1: *kakotropias*), here Thucydides' ethical sympathies, if not a clear-cut ethics, should appear."[20] Edmunds argues that in his description and analysis of the Corcyraean Civil War, Thucydides' sympathies are clearly with reason and moderation. The "depravity" Thucydides notes includes a cruel sophistication that laughs at noble simplicity, the breaking of oaths, the forbearance of true piety while hypocritically masking one's misdeeds behind a false piety, an abandonment of debate in favor of bold deeds so as not to be "worsted in words," and contempt of one's opponents by reason of an overestimation of one's own wit (3.83). The "prestasis" vices that Thucydides says came to be seen as virtues are "unreasoning boldness" and "frantic impulsiveness." The opposites of these vices are both virtues characteristic of the Spartans: "provident delay" and "planning." Prestasis virtues are moderation and intelligence, also considered Spartan characteristics by Thucydides.

Edmunds notes that not only do the Corinthians recognize the Spartan virtue of moderation, but Thucydides later uses this word to describe the Chians and the Spartans (8.24.4). The display of anger is considered a vice before stasis, but after stasis it is viewed as admirable: "This activity was characteristic of Cleon . . . who has already appeared as the representative of stasis vices."[21] All this amounts to Thucydides' praise of forethought, prudence, and moderation as the moral qualities he admired most. But the Corcyraean revolution does not supply the only proof that Thucydides' view may differ from the Athenians'.

The Athenian thesis, articulated by the Athenian envoys at Sparta before the war began (1.75.5; 1.76.2) and most forcefully acted upon at Melos, will be examined here for its moral content and consequences. It is a theory about human nature and justice that Hobbes shared. The outlook that characterizes the thesis—that the ambition to become ever more powerful is natural and compelling—is shared or criticized by most of the main actors in the *History*. The general questions asked here concern what impact this theory of human nature has on the idea of justice and whether Thucydides thinks the urges of human nature, described in the previous chapter, are compelling or simply very strong. Whether or not Thucydides thinks men exercise moral choice in matters of power is important, because if he thinks that they have no choice, then Thucydides must agree with Hobbes that human beings are compelled to act in certain ways. If this is true, then their actions cannot in any intelligible sense be labeled immoral. This chapter will attempt to show that Thucydides has an opinion on justice that differs fundamentally from the Athenian and Hobbesian thesis, one that can be seen when the three great moral dramas of the *History* are carefully read.

The Mytilenaean Debate

In the Mytilenaean Debate, Diodotus explains the full philosophical and practical consequences of the thesis first articulated by the Athenian envoys at Sparta before the war began.[22] As we have seen, the envoys claim that the empire was not acquired by force but was given to Athens after Sparta, unwilling to finish off the remaining Persian forces at the end of the Persian War, retired. The allies asked Athens for her leadership due to this power vacuum. Thus, they say, it was under the *compulsion* of circumstances that we were *driven* at first to advance our empire to its present state, influenced chiefly by fear, then by honour also, and lastly by self-interest as well; and after we had once incurred the hatred of most of our allies, and several of them had already revolted and been reduced to subjection, and when you were no longer friendly as before but suspicious and at variance with us, it no longer seemed safe to risk relaxing our hold. For all seceders would have gone over to you. (1.75.3–5; my emphasis)

The outlook that characterizes this thesis—that the ambition to become ever more powerful is natural and compelling—is shared by some of the main actors in the *History* (cf. 1.69.1–2; 4.61.5). The use of the thesis in the Mytilenaean Debate is particularly interesting because in this case it leads to a policy of moderation. Leniency for the Mytilenaeans emerged largely because they did not defend themselves (from a position of weakness), as did the less fortunate Plataeans and Melians, but were defended by an able Athenian orator, Diodotus. Diodotus, as we will see, used the Athenian thesis rhetorically to save the Mytilenaeans from destruction. Diodotus's speech is an example of how moderation can be won through successful oratory, but it also illuminates for us the philosophical assumptions behind the Athenian thesis. These assumptions, as his argument shows, imply a policy untempered by justice and informed only by the expedient use of force. This section will explore Thucydides' subtle teaching on statesmanship in this opposition between Diodotus's speech and his intentions.

The Debate   Unlike Plataea and Melos, Mytilene, an independent ally of Athens, not only had rebelled but also had attempted to take the rest of the Lesbian cities allied with Athens with her (3.2). She wished to gain hegemony in Lesbos, in hostility to Athens, and enlisted Spartan help in pursuit of this goal (3.4; 3.9–15). Although their fears of Athenian encroachment on their independence may have been well founded, Athens had done nothing to threaten that independence directly, as the Mytilenaeans themselves admitted (3.11). Indeed, there was a good chance Athens never would have attacked Mytilene, since, unlike other allies, she had her own fleet. But Mytilene decided to revolt anyway, due to dissatisfaction with Athenian interference and indirect domination. And even though the

most guilty of the three, Mytilene was treated with the most leniency, while Melos, the most innocent, and Plataea, the most virtuous, were treated much more severely, as we shall see.

The Mytilenaeans had asked Sparta to aid in their revolt. They
received reassurance from a Spartan ambassador who claimed that
"there would be an invasion of Attica and that simultaneously the
forty ships which were to come to their aid would arrive" (3.25).
But the Peloponnesian ships were characteristically slow, and the
Mytilenaeans were compelled to surrender to and negotiate with the
Athenians, who had managed even in their plague-weakened condition to send enough ships to subdue Mytilene (3.27). It was unclear
who in Mytilene was responsible for the surrender. As a last resort,
the oligarchs had allowed the people to carry weapons in order to
attack the Athenians; "but the commons, as soon as they had got
arms, would no longer obey their commanders, but gathered in
groups and ordered the aristocrats to bring out whatever food there
was and distribute it to all; otherwise, they said, they would come to
terms with the Athenians independently and deliver up the city"
(3.27.2–3).

The oligarchs, realizing that they would be placing their lives in
jeopardy if they did not take part in a surrender, joined the common
people in making an agreement with the Athenians (3.28). Athens
then allowed representatives of the Mytilenaean government to
plead their case and await a decision. The Athenian general Paches
sent with the representatives to Athens the Mytilenaeans he thought
were most guilty of the insurrection (3.28).

In this way the fate of the Mytilenaeans ended up in the hands of
the Athenian demos, which was presented by the demagogue Cleon
with evidence of treachery and bad faith. On "the impulse of anger,"
the people decided to put the present prisoners to death, kill the adult
male population of Mytilene, and enslave the women and children.
They sent a ship off to Paches with the appropriate orders. However,
the next day brought "repentance" of the cruelty of the decree, and
the people called for a second vote (3.36.1–5). Accordingly, they
held a second assembly and heard arguments both for rescinding
and for retaining the decree. Cleon, whose arguments had succeeded
in convincing the Athenians to pass the initial sentence, was "not
only the most violent of the citizens, but at that time had by far
the greatest influence with the people." He is the first to speak again

in defense of his policy, and most of his argument revolves around the injustice of the Mytilenaeans' actions (3.36.6). As we will see, Cleon's argument differs from Diodotus's because, even though it may be distasteful, it utilizes the commonsense notions of justice and retribution.

Cleon objects to the softheartedness of the Athenian demos in rethinking its decision. He tries to persuade the people to stand firm on their initial verdict, arguing that by passing a death sentence on the Mytilenaeans the Athenians would be acting justly. He further states that this poses no political difficulties because, at least in this case, justice and expediency coincide. Therefore, he tells them, he will maintain his original position regarding the Mytilenaeans. Any delay in administering justice will only blunt the Athenians' righteous anger and benefit the guilty (3.38) Like Pericles, Cleon says that he has not changed his opinion, but he wonders at those who wish to debate the policy again (3.38). Unlike Pericles, however, his "wondering" turns into a pointed attack on a political opponent. Cleon would like nothing better than to stifle debate altogether, and he tries to do this by besmirching his opponent's intentions. Anyone who would recommend a policy of leniency to Mytilene must have some personal reason for doing so, such as a bribe. Moreover, by claiming that the time to act is now, before the Athenians' anger is blunted, Cleon has questioned the usefulness of any kind of deliberation. He argues that gut feelings can guide men better than reasoned policies, which should be suspect.

Cleon says he will attempt to prove that Mytilene "has done you more injury than any single state." He distinguishes between revolt, which is an attempt by oppressed cities to free themselves, and rebellion or conspiracy, which is what the Mytilenaeans have committed. Rebellion is instigated by men who are not oppressed but are independent—in this case, "men who inhabited a fortified island and had no fear of our enemies except by sea, and even there were not without the protection of a force of their own triremes" (3.39.2). Cleon argues that the Mytilenaeans presumed to put "might before right," even though they were well treated and prosperous. Indeed, he says, it is states that come suddenly into prosperity that prove the most insolent (3.39.5).

Cleon urges his audience not to put all the blame on the oligarchs of Mytilene by exonerating the commons. The common people

joined the oligarchs in their revolt and should be punished in equal
measure. Also, he reasons, the Athenians should consider the effect
of a light punishment on the allies. If the same leniency is offered to
those who voluntarily revolt and those who are forced to revolt by
the Peloponnesians, who will not choose to desert Athens on the
slightest pretext? If such a city succeeds, it wins liberty; if it fails, it
does not have to fear harsh punishment. By setting such a precedent,
furthermore, Athens would have to fight many more rebellious cities, and the devastation resulting from such conflicts would reduce
the value in tribute of those states Athens manages to regain. If Athens were not to recover these cities, it would face even more enemies
(3.39.6–8). Cleon poses the question, Would it not be better to make
revolts so risky that few cities would choose to revolt? Mytilene
would be a prime example and a warning for others who would contemplate rebellion. He says that he has shown that what is just and
what is expedient thus coincide in his advice, but even if the death
sentence were unjust the Athenians must still abide by it, because
their empire is a tyranny and the Mytilenaeans' deaths are useful to it
(3.40.4–5). Cleon is saying that if the Athenians want their empire,
they must do unjust things. But luckily, in the case of Mytilene, they
do not have to commit any injustice: the Mytilenaeans deserve full
Athenian wrath, and their punishment will set a useful example for
the other allies. Cleon seems to subordinate his argument for justice
to the demands of realpolitik; yet when he speaks of justice one can
hear the fervor in his voice: "We must not, therefore, hold out to
them any hope, either to be secured by eloquence or purchased by
money, that they will be excused on the plea that their error was human. For their act was no unintentional injury by a deliberate plot;
and it is that which is unintentional which is excusable" (3.40.1–2).

In this instance, and in only one other (3.39.5–6), Cleon admits
that the Mytilenaeans' action accorded with human nature, or "was
human." Cleon, however, denies what his opponent Diodotus
claims: that what is done because of human nature is done with less
or no blame. Even if it is natural for the Mytilenaeans to want their
liberty and to despise those who cannot directly control them, it is
not without conscious intention. Cleon may be saying, then, that the
impulses of human nature are strong, but he is not saying that they
are in any way compelling. What is unintentional is excusable, but
for Cleon nothing could be unintentional other than an accident or

misunderstanding. Cleon's understanding of what is unintentional is the common understanding. It is the assumption behind most conceptions of morality, for if people are compelled to do "bad" things because of their nature, how can they be blamed in any meaningful sense for doing them?

Cleon ends with another attempt to revive the Athenians' initial rage, clearly showing why Thucydides, who admired those who displayed forethought and prudent consideration, disliked him so: "Do not, then, be traitors to your own cause, but recalling as nearly as possible how you felt when they made you suffer and how you would then have given anything to crush them, now pay them back" (3.40.7–8). As much as we might deplore the harshness, even bloodthirstiness, of Cleon's recommendations, his prediction of what effect this action will have on the other allies also seems like common sense. Would not seeing the Mytilenaeans receive a death sentence for their rebellion discourage others from venturing down the same path? Most of Athens's allies were not nearly so well equipped as Mytilene to defend themselves, and they had little in the way of military might to offer Sparta as incentive for her help. Would not news of Mytilene's fall, the fall of a relatively strong and independent city, effectively deter those in a much less advantageous position? This is precisely what Diodotus, who argues for leniency toward Mytilene, has to deny in order to compete with Cleon's proposals.

Diodotus promises to speak not of right or wrong but of what is in Athenian interest. In doing so, he insists on what Cleon denies: that the impulses of human nature are compelling and therefore those who follow them should not be blamed. This argument is at the root of Diodotus's theory that even capital punishment is no deterrent. Expediency should be the only factor in considering when and how much to punish, he says.

Athens, Diodotus asserts, is "not engaged in a law-suit with them [the Mytilenaeans], so as to be concerned about the question of right and wrong; but we are deliberating about them, to determine what policy will make them useful to us" (3.44.4). The Mytilenaeans should not be put to death, even if Diodotus proves they are guilty, unless it is to the advantage of Athens, and they should not be forgiven, even if Diodotus proves they should be, unless it is for the good of Athens. Contrary to what Cleon says, it is not to Athenian advantage to inflict harsh punishment on the Mytilenaeans. Diodotus warns the Athenians not to heed Cleon's argument, which relies on "legal aspects of the case" and takes advantage of the Athenians' bitterness toward the Mytilenaeans (3.44.3–4). Thus Diodotus does not propose to ignore the Mytilenaeans' "claim for forgiveness" but rather maintains that this consideration should not be the point on which the Athenians decide.

Diodotus claims that the death penalty does not stop people from committing crimes, an argument familiar today. If a city rebels, he reasons, it means that it thinks it can succeed. All men are prone to error in both private and public life, "and there is no law which will prevent them." States will take even greater risks than individuals because the stakes are higher—freedom or empire. The individual leader, when supported by the people, "unreasonably overestimates his own strength" and is thus more likely to recommend the dangerous course of rebellion (3.45.7). He further states, "In a word, it is impossible, and a mark of extreme simplicity, for anyone to imagine that when human nature is wholeheartedly bent on any undertaking it can be diverted from it by rigorous laws or by any other terror" (3.45.7). In making this argument, Diodotus is elaborating on the Athenian thesis, the theory of human nature put forth earlier by the Athenian envoys at Sparta:

> Nay, men are lured into hazardous enterprises by the constraint of poverty, which makes them bold, by the insolence and pride of affluence, which makes them greedy, and by the various passions engendered in the other conditions of human life as these are severally mastered by some mighty and irresistible impulse. Then, too, Hope and Desire are everywhere; Desire leads, Hope attends; Desire contrives the plan, Hope suggests the facility of fortune; the two passions are the most baneful, and being unseen phantoms prevail over seen dangers. (3.45.5–6)

From one perspective, this seems like an argument concerning the justice of the Mytilenaeans' actions. If they were lured or compelled by some irresistible impulse, if they transgressed laws regardless of the prospect of punishment by some natural and uncontrollable urge, how can they be guilty of wrongdoing? The Mytilenaeans committed no injustice, in the usual sense, if they could not help themselves. But Diodotus's argument, while absolving the Mytilenaeans of injustice, actually subverts the common understanding of justice. Justice presupposes the ability to control ones' actions. But Diodotus's human beings cannot control themselves even when faced with the death penalty. They rationalize their situation until they are sure of success, no matter who else has failed. Punishment, if men cannot learn from others' mistakes and others' punishment, cannot be used effectively as a deterrent—a benefit Cleon claims for his policy. It is this question—whether or not Cleon's punishment would serve as a proper deterrent or example for other cities—that Diodotus now takes up.

Cities will surrender more quickly if they think they will receive better terms for doing so, he says. If they have no hope of being treated with leniency, they will be more likely to hold out to the very end, thus making the Athenians spend more time and money on the siege. Current Athenian policy, he points out, enables rebellious cities to surrender early by paying an indemnity and agreeing to keep up their tribute in the future. But Cleon's policy would lead only to the destruction of such cities and thus the forfeiting of any future tribute from them. If they are punished too severely, Athens will inadvertently punish itself. It is better, he says, to punish moderately and to "deem it proper to protect ourselves against revolts, not by the terror of our laws, but rather *by the vigilance of our administration*" (3.46.4; my emphasis). Instead of severely punishing free peoples when they revolt, as they "naturally will," Athens should "watch them rigorously before they revolt, and thus forestall their even thinking of such a thing" (3.46.6). Diodotus is recommending not deterrence but prevention. Laws and the threat of punishment are meant to deter. Rigorous and vigilant administration prevents not only revolt itself but also the idea of revolt, which emerges whenever people are allowed any reason for entertaining false dreams of success.

Diodotus's recommendation, then, is that Athens try to prevent revolt beforehand; if it cannot be prevented, as few individuals as possible should be punished. This is because, while men cannot be persuaded but only prevented from attempting revolt in the first place, following revolt it is possible to persuade those rebelling to surrender when their cause appears hopeless. At present, he points out, the common people of the various cities are friends of Athens. But if Athens kills the Mytilenaean people, she will be killing her allies and encouraging the many to support the few to the bitter end in the future. According to Diodotus, the common people did not take part in the revolt, and they gave the city up to Athens as soon as they could. But even if the people of Mytilene are guilty, they should still be absolved for the sake of Athenian interest (3.47.4–5).

"And whereas Cleon claims that this [Cleon's] punishment combines justice and expediency, it appears that in such a policy the two cannot be combined," Diodotus states (3.47.5). Diodotus seems to insist on paying attention only to expediency because the compelling nature of human drives makes punishment or retribution meaningless. However, Diodotus's recommendations about what to do specifically with the Mytilenaeans might easily have emerged from an argument from justice.

If we accept his claim that the Mytilenaean commons are not guilty of wrongdoing but instead acted correctly, then Diodotus's recommendations for punishment (not punishing them but punishing those leaders who instigated the revolt) are just in the common sense. Furthermore, contrary to Diodotus's claims, justice and expediency do coincide. Diodotus says that if the Athenians decide to kill all the Mytilenaeans, including the commons, they will be *guilty* of killing their benefactors, and this will show all the other allies that the same punishment "is ordained for the innocent and for the guilty" (3.47.4–5). Diodotus has argued that the commons do not deserve to be punished. He argues this even though he acknowledges in the same breath that it appears that in such a policy justice and expediency cannot be combined (3.47.5). But why bother to mention Athens's potential guilt or the innocence of the Mytilenaeans if the justice of their cause does not matter?

This argument, which rests on justice, is opposed not only to Diodotus's claims to be concerned solely with expediency but also to the bulk of Diodotus's reasoning about human nature and the value of punishment. The fact that Diodotus hides his moderate agenda within such an extreme version of the Athenian thesis compels us to question Thucydides' purpose in juxtaposing the two in Diodotus's speech. When Diodotus says men "naturally will" revolt, that they are moved by mighty and irresistible impulses, then it follows that men cannot be held fully responsible for their actions. But how will they be deterred by any sort of punishment or example if they are naturally convinced that, regardless of the precedents, they will succeed? According to this argument, they will not, which is why Diodotus encourages leniency for those who have revolted and strict control over those who have not yet decided to revolt. Leniency will encourage those who have already felt compelled to rebel to surrender early when faced with winning force, thus saving Athens the expense of a long siege. Strict control over the other allies will prevent them from entertaining thoughts of revolution, while neither appeals to justice nor examples of punishment will suffice. This is the natural consequence of saying that men naturally transgress laws: laws themselves become secondary to force.

The only sure way to maintain order, according to this line of Diodotus's reasoning, is through intimidation. Diodotus says that this maintenance of order through constant application of power is more effective than Cleon's idea of making an example of the Mytilenaeans. It is debatable whether Cleon's or Diodotus's analysis of the situation is the harshest, for if Diodotus's logic were to be carried out in full, the remaining allies would have less freedom and would be treated with less respect than before. While Cleon would leave the choice up to them—albeit a fearful choice—about whether or not to revolt, Diodotus would make sure they had no real choice: "We ought, on the contrary, instead of rigorously chastising free peoples when they revolt, to *watch them rigorously* before they revolt, and thus *forestall their even thinking* of such a thing; and when we have subdued a revolt, we ought to put the blame on as few as possible" (3.46.6; my emphasis).

Thus Diodotus's two arguments—that crime is involuntary and that the Mytilenaean people should be forgiven but those Mytilenaeans suspected to be guilty and sent to Athens by Paches should be tried and punished—seem difficult to reconcile. The first argument tells the Athenians to ignore considerations of justice as irrelevant. The second tells them to take the justice of the people's actions into account. As Orwin has pointed out, if Diodotus had stretched his argument to its logical conclusions—that even the Mytilenaean oligarchs could not be blamed and therefore should not be punished—the Athenians would never have accepted it.[23] But effecting his argument's logical conclusions is not Diodotus's purpose or his intention.

What Diodotus claims, that justice and expediency do not coincide in this case, then, is false on one level and true on another. Justice, as Diodotus has defined it, fits perfectly with his prescriptions for

Mytilene. These prescriptions could have been derived from an argument exclusively from justice. But they are not. Diodotus realizes the need to argue on the basis of expediency, and therefore, even if his true aim is justice for the Mytilenaeans and moderation for Athenian policy, his theory contradicts both. Diodotus has built his argument about expediency on a foundation of human nature that admits no reasonable notion of responsibility, guilt, or punishment. Justice not only cannot coincide with this notion of expediency but also cannot coexist with it. Diodotus deceives his audience by using a theory antithetical to justice in order to make the people feel good about changing their minds in a way that, after all, they had wanted to do ever since their misgivings about the morality of their first decree. Diodotus beats Cleon at the "expediency" game and proves that the Athenian thesis is used better in theory than in practice. At the level of theory, the thesis, with its ring of worldly sophistication, appeals to the Athenian people. It moves them to do what they had wanted to do in the first place out of guilt.

Summary   Diodotus claims that a speaker whose proposals are good has to "lie in order to be believed" (3.43). Diodotus's lie is the very theory he puts forward. He manages, by skillful oratory, to capitalize on the Athenians' initial change of heart. They begin to think that their decree is cruel and excessive and that they have been given an opportunity to live up to Cleon's challenge: their decision should be tough-minded and realistic while still rectifying what they see as an immoral decision. Diodotus does not so much change their minds as give them their reasons. Without his reasons it is likely they would have followed Cleon's advice. However, much of Diodotus's argument, while purposefully winning moderation, logically leads to a policy dependent on the raw use of power untempered by notions of justice. Therefore the Diodotean example serves two purposes for Thucydides. First, it is an excellent display of statesmanship. Diodotus wins moderation through an argument whose elements are basically immoderate. Second, more than any other speech in the *History,* it shows us the outcome of assuming that humans are compelled to act by passions such as fear, honor, and interest. The outcome is that a great power must counter humans' natural compulsions with power, not with argument or judicial procedure. The content of Diodotus's argument and his purpose, indeed his very action in making the argument itself, are fundamentally opposed.

Cleon's plea for retribution hides behind a policy of expediency. But his impatience with deliberation, his anxiety to have the thing done before the Athenians lose their rage, shows that he is not truly interested in what is best for Athens in the long run as much as he is interested in revenge.[24] Revenge or retribution has little to do with expediency and more to do with "legality," as Diodotus later points out. Diodotus claims that justice, or legality, should not be a consideration in war among states as it is in peace among individuals (3.44.3–4). He says that Cleon's argument hinges on justice, but that it will be heeded not by a calm consideration of what is just but out of bitterness and anger. The outcome is that the Mytilenaeans receive more justice because the Athenians are persuaded to think of expediency. This implies that speaking loudly of justice in a forum such as this will lead only to extremism, that it will be distorted by the people's anger and perhaps by a speaker's own ambitions.[25]

In the case of Mytilene, in which arguments from expediency are seriously entertained, moderation and enlightened self-interest win. But as we will see at Plataea and Melos, where expediency is either not mentioned or has been decided beforehand and is not open to serious debate, immoderation carries the day. The evidence suggests that political rhetoric must rely overtly on arguments of "national interest" or expediency in order to be successful. Diodotus's speech exemplifies this strategy. Thucydides gives us the example of Diodotus as an agent of moderation within a naturally immoderate regime. But if we admire Diodotus's achievement, we must recognize that the moderation he obtains depends upon his brilliant statesmanship. Thucydides leaves us with the hope that wise leaders will use the art of political rhetoric for prudent ends.

The Plataean Debate

Thucydides' depiction of the siege, trial, and execution of the Plataeans can be taken as realistic, a classic illustration of power politics and proof of the foolishness of appealing to notions of justice in relations among states. According to this view, the Plataeans' fate is an example of the reality of the "Athenian thesis" that appears throughout the *History* and that was first proposed by the Athenians at the Spartan War Conference before the Spartans decided for war (1.75). As we have seen and will see again in the analysis of the Melian Dialogue, according to this thesis, justice itself does not exist but is a product of power relationships, and then only when both sides' power is equal (5.89). The thesis assumes that the ambition to become ever more powerful is natural and compelling and therefore blameless.

Does Thucydides think the urges of human nature make nothing of justice in the face of unequal power? I have argued in the analysis of the Mytilenaean Debate that Thucydides does not think so and that he instead indicates that good deliberation can bring about a desirable moderation, which is as close to justice as can be had in most practical cases. Another question is how Thucydides treats justice in itself. This section will attempt to elucidate Thucydides' views on the place and content of true justice, as opposed to justice filtered through political practice, which at best produces moderation of the type obtained at Mytilene. In analyzing his views I also hope to provide a better understanding of Thucydides' methods, which tend to lead the reader to certain conclusions without any explicit analysis or judgment on Thucydides' part, and perhaps add my voice to those who have doubted that he was the first "scientific historian."

Surprisingly, no articles have elucidated Thucydides' views of justice by fully analyzing the Plataean Debate.[26] Indeed, one cannot find an in-depth treatment of the structure of the two sides' arguments in any of the prominent books that have been written on Thucydides.[27] This may be due to the complexity and apparent ambiguity of the Plataean Debate. Or perhaps it is because scholars have discounted the importance of the arguments, since, in the end, the Spartans make their decision irrespective of either side's argument, according to Thucydides. Even Clifford Orwin, who has in recent memory given us the best analyses of various episodes from the *History*, has yet to publish an article on this episode.[28]

I hope to show by an examination of the conflicting arguments of the Plataean Debate that Thucydides placed contradictions within the Theban argument and between the Thebans' and Plataeans' arguments that strongly validate the Plataeans' claim to justice. By working these contradictions into the debate, Thucydides' writing produces the effect he must have desired: sympathy for the Plataeans as being on the side of right. And yet, unless one carefully sifts through these contradictions, the way in which Thucydides creates such a strong sense of sympathy remains obscure. Thucydides has designed his debate in such a way that he has no need to pass judgment on the Thebans; the Thebans pass judgment on themselves through their own argument.[29] Because of the character of the Plataeans' idea of justice, I will argue that contrary to the Athenian thesis Thucydides here points out that justice and injustice are more than derivatives of power relations. Hence Thucydides' views of justice must differ markedly from those of the Athenians, who argued that human beings are compelled by their passions to strive for dominion and therefore cannot be blamed for what they do. The Plataean Debate, then, can point us in the direction of the content of Thucydides' idea of justice and serve as a supplement to his explicit statements on this subject in his description of the Corcyraean revolution.[30] Proctor writes, "Their [the Plataeans'] speech (which Dionysius of Halicarnassus thought the finest in the *History*) and the Thebans' reply constitute, in fact, the only debate in the *History* which is conducted throughout on a purely moral plane. The fact that it is also the longest of the debates consisting of only two speeches may betoken Thucydides' recognition of its special character."[31]

In order to understand the arguments in the debate, it is important to keep in mind Plataea's relationships with Sparta, Athens, and her Boeotian neighbors in the past. Thucydides is careful to give us the background that gave rise to the final conflict involving Plataea because the two sides' speeches will deal with events both in the distant past (namely in the Persian War) and in the immediate past (what produced the occasion for the destruction of Plataea).

Athens and Sparta, allies during the Persian War, fought the Persians together at Plataea (497 B.C.). There they battled the Persians and the other Boeotian cities that, unlike Plataea, had decided to ally themselves with the enemy. After the victory over the Persians, while Athens and Sparta were still allies, the Athenian leader Themistocles rebuilt Athens's long walls, even though Sparta urged him not to do so, and began to strengthen the Athenian navy as well. As we have seen, the daring that Athens had shown during the Persian War (1.90.2) and Athens's later takeover of the leadership of the postwar alliance caused Sparta and other cities to fear Athens's designs. Eventually the Athenian-Spartan alliance was broken because of Sparta's mistrust of Athens (1.103.4), and then followed a period of hostility between the two. In 431 B.C., a thirty-year truce between

Athens and Sparta was officially broken when the Thebans (allies of Sparta) attacked the town of Plataea (an ally of Athens). This event formally initiated the war between Athens, Sparta, and their respective allies. The fall of Plataea was treated as a major episode out of proportion to its military importance nonetheless.[32]

In an act that cost them dearly, three hundred Thebans entered Plataea by night. They had been invited into the town by the Plataean oligarchs, who were opposed to Plataea's alliance with Athens and who wished to remove the democratic or popular party from power.[33] But once they had invaded the town, instead of immediately seizing the Plataeans' homes, the Thebans decided to negotiate. A proclamation was made that anyone interested could now take up his arms and join the Thebans in the Boeotian alliance. The Thebans were confident that the Plataeans would choose the alliance voluntarily. Frightened by the thought of large numbers of Thebans in their city, the Plataeans did indeed surrender. But during the negotiations, the small number of the invaders became apparent and the Plataean people, not really wanting to leave the Athenian alliance, decided to attack them while it was still night, when they would have the advantage of familiar territory (2.2–3). This attack was seen by the Thebans as an act of treachery.

The Thebans, finding themselves tricked, tried to fight back, but, as Thucydides describes, the Plataean attack was well coordinated and ingenious. The Plataeans blocked all exits to the city and used their knowledge of the environs to take advantage of the dark. Their sense of community allowed them to work together as a team with little or no planning possible, and their efforts overwhelmed the Thebans. Finally, the scattered survivors surrendered, agreeing to be dealt with as the Plataeans wished (2.4).

The rest of the Theban army came too late to stop this disaster, but they still could threaten those Plataeans who lived outside the city gates and use them as collateral for the return of their prisoners inside the city. But the Plataeans, anticipating this, sent a messenger to the army rebuking the Thebans for their impiety in a time of peace. The Plataeans made a counterthreat: if the Thebans harmed any of the country-dwellers, the prisoners inside the city would be immediately executed.[34] Hearing this, the Thebans withdrew; as soon as they did, the Plataeans slew the 180 Theban prisoners despite the former agreement, and Plataean property was taken in from the countryside (2.5). Again, the Thebans viewed this as another act of treachery. After learning of the executions too late to judge whether to stop them, Athens left a garrison at Plataea, and removed the women and children to a safer place (2.6). In all this the Plataeans showed themselves to be shrewd negotiators, fully willing and able to do what it took to beat their opponents. They were certainly capable of great anger and even, apparently, the desire for revenge. Their qualities were certainly not kindness, gentleness, or piety but rather courage, intelligence, and pride in themselves and in their abilities. And yet, even lacking the "kinder and gentler" virtues, the Plataeans already appear the moral superiors of the Thebans, an affect wrought by Thucydides' scrupulous attention to every detail of the Plataeans' defense.

The Siege of Plataea and Plataean Resistance   Later, the Spartans and the Thebans made another expedition against Plataea. Before they could begin to ravage the countryside, however, the Plataeans sent envoys to the Spartan leader Archidamus to persuade him to stop the attack (2.71.2). They accused him of acting unjustly, reminding him that the Spartan commander Pausanias, after the battle of Plataea during the Persian War, had rewarded the Plataeans with the promise of independence forever:

> These privileges your fathers granted to us on account of the valour and zeal we displayed amid those dangers, but you do the very contrary; for with the Thebans, our bitterest enemies, you are come to enslave us. But calling to witness the gods in whose names we then swore and the gods of your fathers and of our country, we say to you, wrong not the land of Plataea nor violate your oaths, but suffer us to live independent, according as Pausanias granted that to us as our right. (2.71.3–4)

Archidamus replies by reminding the Plataeans of their alliance with Athens; Pausanias's gift of independence should have been used to help other states escape Athenian domination. He implies that the Plataeans have broken the agreement with Pausanias because they have forfeited their independence to the Athenians. Although this is to equate independence with neutrality instead of with the freedom to choose sides, Archidamus understandably thinks that the Plataeans' choosing sides has altered the Spartan obligation toward Plataea. The Plataeans define independence as being able to choose neutrality or alliance and are reluctant to acknowledge their current political situation.

Archidamus then asks the Plataeans to allow Sparta either to liberate them or, failing that, to switch to neutrality (2.72). To alleviate the Plataeans' worries about the constantly menacing Thebans, he tells them that the Spartans will allow the Plataeans to leave and will look after their city for the duration of the war, if only they announce themselves as neutral. He reassures them that the Spartans will till the land for them and pay an appropriate rent (2.72.3).

The Plataeans must have recognized the reasonable nature of this offer. Under a truce, they sent envoys to Athens to gain its approval, but Athens refused and assured Plataea that she would not be deserted. Athens requested that the Plataean-Athenian alliance not be broken (2.73.3). The Plataeans agreed to this request and rejected the Spartans' offer. They seemed to want to abide by the letter and spirit of their alliance with Athens even at great risk. Archidamus, upon hearing this, declared that any measures the Spartans took now would be guiltless because the Plataeans had rejected their "many reasonable proposals" (2.74.3).[35]

The reader, at this point, has a sense that while Thebes is in the wrong, its complaint of treachery is at least somewhat valid and that the Spartans, although acting in self-interest, do try to be somewhat reasonable. The Plataeans recognized the latter, and it was only when Athens forbade them to agree that they refused. The moral character of the Plataeans is one not of perfect purity but rather of steadfast loyalty, which is the virtue they valiantly displayed toward all of Hellas in the Persian War.

The Spartans now begin an attack on the walls of Plataea, and the Plataeans circumvent it in many resourceful ways that Thucydides describes in detail, emphasizing the Plataeans' courage. Since Thucydides rarely elaborates in such great detail, it is unlikely that he is simply indulging a great love for military tactics. The Spartans build a mound up Plataea's walls, but the Plataeans counter by building their walls higher and undercutting the mound by removing dirt from beneath it. They build a second inner wall and devise ways to destroy the Spartans' battering rams. Just when the Plataeans' luck seems to be turning, nature comes to the rescue: when the Spartans attempt to burn them out, a heavy rain puts an end to this plan.

Here, too, Thucydides seems to want us to see the courage and intelligence of the Plataeans.[36] They display a great deal of spirit, martial and patriotic, in all their efforts at self-defense. Indeed, the Plataeans' creativity and initiative finally convince the Spartans to dismiss most of their army, put a wall around the city, and leave a guard to carry on a siege. During the winter, some of the Plataeans and the Athenians with them attempt a daring but well-planned escape in the middle of a thunderstorm. This is again described in admiring detail to highlight the Plataeans' intelligence and skill. According to Thucydides, the Plataeans together count and recount the number of bricks in the Spartan wall in order to determine how tall to build their ladders. They wait for a stormy and moonless night that will make them hard to hear or see. They wear a sandal only on the left foot, to keep from slipping in the mud, and carry out the escape in waves. The men with ladders are the first out, then come a few warriors lightly armed to attack the sentinels, then troops with spears, and finally men who carry shields to hand up when others get to the top of the wall. The sentinels begin flashing beacon fires for help from Thebes, but the Plataeans have anticipated this and those who have stayed behind in town also light fires, in order to make the signals unintelligible and buy their comrades time. In the process, the men kill as many of their besiegers as possible (3.21–23). Of those who go through with the plan, almost all succeed in escaping (3.20–24). Given this descriptive accounting of the Plataeans' ingenuity, it is almost impossible not to admire the Plataeans as they continue to fight their enemies with every means at their disposal.[37]

The Plataeans left in the town are finally forced to surrender. They are told that they will get a trial in accordance with justice if they voluntarily submit (3.52.3). This turns out to be a lie. In time, five judges arrive from Sparta to try the Plataeans. The Athenians do not come to the rescue, as they have promised, but this does not stop the Plataeans from being loyal to them. The trial begins as if the verdict has already been reached. The judges ask a single question: "Have you rendered any good service to the Lacedaemonians and their allies in the present war?" (3.52.4–5). Thucydides now turns his method of showing instead of telling to the speeches of the Plataeans and Thebans, embedding within the Theban argument the seeds of its own destruction.

The Plataean Argument   The Plataeans, faced with the stark question of the judges and its obvious answer, ask for the opportunity to speak at greater length, and their request is granted. Their spokesmen, Astymachus and Lacon, express surprise at the Spartans' question and state that they expected a just trial (3.53.1–2). They point out that there has been no real accusation and no opportunity for a true defense, given the seeming inevitability of their fate. They complain that they are appearing before a court that has already decided to punish them in order to please the Thebans (3.53.4–5). This statement shows that the Plataeans understand their situation but still feel the need to speak in order to give themselves whatever chance there may be.

As to the question at hand, the Plataeans state that the Spartans have not been wronged by Plataea's lack of support if they thought the Plataeans were their enemies. If the Plataeans were considered friends, it was rather Sparta that harmed Plataea by attacking it (3.54.2–4). By "wronged" the Plataeans mean damaged in a legal way, as in breaking an agreement, not in a political way, in which merely to be on the other side would have been a wrong. But if their killing of the Theban prisoners is any indication, the Plataeans do not make this "legalistic" argument simply out of blind respect for agreements.

The Plataeans turn to an exposition of their heroic service in the Persian War. They were the only Boeotians who came to the aid of Hellas; they fought beside the Spartan commander Pausanias against the rest of the Boeotians as well as the barbarian; and they helped Sparta during a Helot uprising (3.54.4–5). As for their alliance with Athens, it was forced upon them when their overtures were rebuffed by the Spartans, who *told* them to ask the Athenians for help because Athens was nearby. Still, even though allied with Athens during the current war, the Plataeans have done nothing yet to harm the Spartans. If they have refused to revolt from the Athenian alliance, it is because it would not be honorable to do so now. The Plataeans here display what underlies their supposed legalism—honor. Sparta dishonored them when after all their loyalty it abandoned them in their struggle with the Thebans. When Athens undertook the protection of Plataea, honor dictated that Plataea be loyal and enter into the type of alliance Athens requested. They refuse to revolt now because it would be wrong to go back on their word to the Athenians, even though Athens seems unable or unwilling to help them in this crisis.[38] The Plataeans claim that blame for any wrong actions on either side of the current war rests solely on either Sparta or Athens in any case, and not their followers (3.55.2–4).

They next speak of the immediate quarrel with the Thebans:

> They attempted to seize our city in time of peace . . . therefore we were justified in punishing them in accordance with the law which has universal sanction, that it is right to repel him who comes against you as an enemy; and now we cannot reasonably be made to suffer on their account. For if you shall decide the question of justice by such considerations as your immediate advantage and their hostility, you will show yourselves to be, not true judges of what is right, but rather to be mere slaves of expediency. (3.56.1–4)

The Plataeans point out that they are being punished now for the same type of behavior that won them praise in the Persian War, namely, pursuing "the noblest course though fraught with danger" instead of "intriguing in security" for their own advantage (3.56.5–7). The Plataeans briefly appeal to the Spartans' long-term interest by warning them that if they destroy Plataea simply to please the Thebans, other cities will view this as "monstrous," a grave impiety as well as an injustice (3.57.1–4). They speak of upholding common principles that will benefit the Spartans in the future just as much as the principles will benefit the Plataeans now. These arguments are an afterthought to the main thrust of their speech and are not therefore as convincing as similar arguments made at more length elsewhere. Finally, they call on the Spartans, in the name of the gods and heroes, not to give in to Theban demands (3.58.4–5), and they place their warnings again within the context of what is honorable:

> These things are not consistent with your honour, Lacedaemonians, nor can it be so to offend against the common usage of the Hellenes against your ancestors, to put us, your benefactors, to death because of the enmity of others, when you have not been wronged yourselves. Nay, your good name demands that you should spare us and be softened in heart, regarding us with a dispassionate pity and bearing in mind, not only how terrible will be our fate, but who we are that must suffer, and how uncertain is fortune, whose strokes sometimes fall even upon the innocent. (3.59.1–2)

The Theban Counterargument   The Thebans' speech attempts to counter the Plataeans' speech point by point, but in the process it often counters itself. The difficulty and complexity of the argument are what have allowed its flaws, and Thucydides' method and purpose, to go unnoticed.[39]

First the Thebans tackle Plataea's supposed virtue in the Persian War. They admit that they and the other Boeotians besides Plataea "medized" (went over to the Persian side) during the last great war, but they say they were forced by the oligarchs in their towns to do so. They argue that the Plataeans did not "medize" only because their protectors the Athenians did not (they do not mention that the Spartans were also Plataea's protectors during this time). So the Plataeans are more guilty of "atticizing" (even though the alliance complaint actually occurred after the Persian War) than the Thebans are of "medizing" during the Persian War. The Thebans were involved in the campaign to liberate the rest of Hellas from Athenian rule. If the Plataeans allied with Athens only to protect themselves from the Thebans, why did they enter into an offensive as well as a defensive alliance? No, they reason, the Plataeans willingly "embraced the Athenian cause" (3.63.3–4). They question whether it was not a greater dishonor to help the Athenians destroy the Hellenes than to go back on their promises of alliance to the Athenians.

Speaking of the Plataeans' claim to have little choice but to turn to Athens, the Thebans lamely state, "And yet, surely, not to repay favours with like favours is dishonourable; but it is not so when, though the debt was incurred in a just matter, it can only be repaid with wrong-doing" (3.63.4). Thus the Thebans make the ideology of the current conflict into a measure of past as well as current right and wrong, a frequent mode of thinking during stasis that Thucydides elsewhere criticizes.[40] For them, it is not the keeping or breaking of agreements that constitute justice or injustice (when it comes to the Plataeans, in any case) but rather allegiance to the right or wrong side. They also superimpose the present conflict on the past, since there was no real conflict between Athens and Sparta during and immediately following the Persian War. This was why it was easy for Sparta to tell Plataea initially to seek Athens's protection.

The Thebans then twist the Plataean claim that only Sparta and Athens were responsible for decisions affecting their allies by accusing the Plataeans of wrongly accepting credit "for the virtuous conduct that was due to the inspiration of others." In this, they must be referring to Plataea's success in the Persian War, credit for which should have been given Athens, according to this logic. In saying this the Thebans inadvertently admit that both Athens's and Plataea's conduct was virtuous after all. As for the initial Theban attack on Plataea, they claim that they were not in the wrong since they had been invited by the Plataean oligarchs to end the alliance with Athens and return to traditional ethnic ties: "For it is those who lead that break the laws [the Plataean oligarchs] rather than those who follow [the Thebans]" (3.65.2–3). Their argument discounts the fact that the oligarchs were not in power at the time.[41]

The Thebans then remind the Plataeans that upon first entering the town they had allowed negotiations and the Plataeans had voluntarily surrendered, that is, until they became aware of the Thebans' small numbers. They admit that they "might seem to have acted somewhat inconsiderately in entering [the] town without the consent of the popular party" (3.66.2–3). But be that as it may, the Plataeans did not repay the mildness of the Thebans' subsequent actions in kind and instead convinced them to withdraw and then "lawlessly butchered" the prisoners they kept (3.66.3). It seems that when it affected the Thebans, strict adherence to agreements, even in war, was required, whereas elsewhere strict adherence to Plataea's alliance with Athens is criticized.

The Thebans' ask the Spartans to disregard Plataean tales of ancient virtue. They ironically acknowledge Plataea's virtue in the Persian War when they say that if they were at one time virtuous, then they are to be twice condemned now because they are acting out of character. The Thebans urge them to ignore the Plataeans' cries for pity and their appeals to the graves of the Spartan fathers. They argue that the Plataeans were not suppliants on the field of battle, after all, and that they voluntarily agreed to be judged by the Spartans and to accept their decisions. They ask the Spartans to "make it plain to the Hellenes by an example that the trials [they] institute will be of deeds not words, and that, if the deeds are good, a brief recital of them suffices, but if they are wrong, speeches decked out with phrases are but veils to hide the truth" (3.67.6).[42]

Thucydides tells us that neither speech had much effect on the Spartan decision, and yet he gives us the speeches in full, with all their elaborate internal logic. The Theban speech, by trying to answer the Plataean points, ends up illustrating Theban injustice. It is full of revealing contradictions, omissions, and admissions that are so well placed that it seems highly unlikely that Thucydides rendered this effect unconsciously.

The Thebans' contradictions make them appear small, deceitful, and bloodthirsty. They are woven so skillfully throughout their argument that it has been easy not to notice them. For instance, the Thebans "medized" due to the initiative of their oligarchic government, which they portray as not being representative of the Theban people and which was deposed after the Persian War. At the same time, they imply that the request on the part of the Plataean oligarchs, who are not even in control of the city, was rightly honored and justly intended. Later, they admit that it might have seemed "inconsiderate" to enter the town without the consent of the popular party, but this is seemingly outweighed by the Plataeans' lawless killing of the prisoners they have taken.

Similarly, the Plataeans "atticized" when the other Boeotians were hostile to Athenian tyranny. But the Thebans fail to address the Plataeans' claim that they were forced into "atticizing" because of Theban hostility and Spartan neglect. Later, they admit that the debt to Athens the Plataeans incurred was in a "just matter," and this as much as admits that the Plataeans justly sought Athenian help after being persecuted by the Thebans. The charge that the Plataeans, even if their request for Athenian help was reasonable, showed their willing atticism by undertaking an offensive alliance with the Athenians addresses neither the reasons why the Plataeans felt strongly enough alienated from their own kindred to do so nor the feasibility of a simply defensive alliance with Athens.

The Thebans accuse the Plataeans of wrongly accepting credit "for the virtuous conduct that was due to the inspiration of others" (the Athenians). But this is tantamount to admitting that the conduct of the Boeotians' "medizing" was vicious, while the conduct of Athens and Plataea was virtuous during the Persian War. It also admits that, as the Plataeans have claimed, responsibility for virtuous as well as vicious acts lies with the leaders rather than with those who follow. This contradicts their thesis that the Plataeans were wrong in following the Athenians in an offensive alliance.

Hence, by their contradictions, omissions, and admissions the Thebans neutralize some of their own central arguments:

1. That they were right to enter Plataea because they were invited to do so.

2. That the Plataeans' "atticizing" was unjust, while their "medizing" was just.

3. That the Plataeans were wrong in following the Athenian lead in an offensive as well as a defensive alliance.

4. That agreements made between themselves and Plataea during their attack were valid and should have been respected, but agreements between Athens and Plataea also made in necessity should not have been respected.

Conclusion   Thucydides' treatment of the Plataeans' character and their side of the conflict predisposes us to conclude that the Plataeans and their cause are truly just. The Thebans' actions and speech reinforce our conviction that the Plataeans are in the right. Thucydides has employed several methods to achieve this affect, and an examination of these methods can illuminate how his understated and austere prose can influence the reader to perceive the justice or injustice of one side or the other.

First, Thucydides provides us with the history of the dispute between Plataea and Thebes, so that we can judge the content of the speeches against the deeds. The Theban speech does not always match the facts as Thucydides presents them. This is a method he makes full use of throughout the *History*. Second, he emphasizes those details in the Plataeans' battle against the siege that show their courage and intelligence in outwitting a much stronger opponent. Thucydides' minute description of their thoughts and actions confirms that the Plataean character really is what they claim it to be, both in the past (in the Persian War) and now. They remain heroic against great odds. Third, he juxtaposes the content of the Theban speech with the Plataeans' speech and with past and recent events in order to discredit the Thebans' argument. He does this by having the Thebans speak in a contradictory and revealing manner. In all this, Thucydides does not have to say one word in his own voice to lead his readers to his preferred conclusions.

This analysis suggests that Thucydides' *History* is far less "scientific" or objective than it might first appear. Thucydides' hand is clearly visible in the development of the Plataean Debate into a major moral drama.[43] This does not mean we should indict Thucydides as a defective historian. Rather we must realize that his idea of what makes history accurate is not our own; that is, it is not scientific. By drawing attention to the moral conflicts of war probably at the expense of literal accuracy, here and elsewhere, Thucydides no doubt thought of himself as more than accurate. He was going to the heart of the matter: the truth about war and the truth about human nature.

Finally, the Plataean Debate helps us to understand exactly what Thucydides thought of justice. Thucydides here seems to most admire courage, intelligence, patriotism, and loyalty,[44] which is confirmed by his rare explicit judgments in the Coryraean episode[45] and in his admiring eulogy of Pericles. Although the Plataeans do utter a few words about the gods, most of what makes them appear just are their past and present deeds and the loyal conviction of their speech. It is neither traditional piety that Thucydides admires nor the mere keeping of agreements. The Plataeans certainly broke an important agreement when they slew their Theban prisoners. But the Plataeans are depicted as truly patriotic and loyal to the Athenians above and beyond duty. They have convictions that defy the reason of power politics.

Thucydides' treatment of the Thebans indicates his views on injustice, and these too are confirmed by his comments on stasis. The Thebans are now and were in the past more interested in party loyalty, the ideology of the current conflict, than in being true to themselves or to their Boeotian brethren. They insist that the Spartans not listen to the Plataeans' speech and that deliberation is not a good conduit for decision, and they use language in whatever way they can in order to make their case. Their intelligence is called into question by their very speech, which is full of self-contradiction. Unlike the Plataeans, who are loyal to Athens even though she never comes to their aid, the Thebans hide behind the power of Sparta and use Sparta to wreak their long-awaited revenge.

Thucydides' notions of what makes one side right may not be our own. Perhaps for us, piety or total innocence might be more important in placing the mantle of victim on the Plataeans. This is fundamentally a difference between the pre-Christian and Christian worldviews. Thucydides presents us with a sympathetic treatment of the Plataeans primarily because he believed that, with the qualities they possessed, they deserved a better fate. In the final analysis,

Thucydides identifies the preservation of those qualities with justice and their destruction with injustice.

The Melian Dialogue

Whereas the Plataean Debate took place in the fifth year of the war, the dialogue between representatives of Melos and Athens took place in the sixteenth year. Yet the central issue had altered little. The most noticeable difference between the Plataean Debate and the Melian Dialogue is form: the Melian Dialogue is the only *dialogue* in Thucydides' entire work. The dialogue form is chosen by the Athenians in order to avoid the "fair words" of most speech making. Hence, the dialogue itself is a denial of the worth of the explanations, justifications, and ornamentations of rhetoric. Another noticeable difference is not that self-interest informed the final decision but that it did so openly and was argued extensively on both sides. In the fifth year of the war, the Thebans and Plataeans had argued about justice: the justice of their past deeds as well as their present undertakings. In the sixteenth year, the style of argumentation in a similar situation had changed dramatically, reflecting changed beliefs. Past deeds, according to the Athenians, were irrelevant to present demands. Deeds and justice should not be an issue in the dialogue, but only force and safety. The Melians agreed to abide by these Athenian rules but resorted to a variety of arguments. As we will see, like the Plataeans, they had nothing to lose by doing so.

The Melians were an independent island people, and as such they were unique in their refusal to submit to Athenian rule. At first they took a neutral stance in the war; but after the Athenians plundered their territory, they became openly hostile to Athens. Accordingly, Athens sent two generals, Cleomedes and Tisias, to subdue the Melians. Before doing any harm to their land, the generals decided to send envoys to negotiate with the Melians. The Melians did not want to bring these envoys before the people, preferring to restrict the dialogue to the Melian magistrates and the few.

The Athenians begin the dialogue by criticizing the Melians for thinking that Athenian arguments would seduce the common people and thus keep them out of the proceedings. Then they add a condition of their own: that the discussion should be a dialogue in which the Melians reply to any Athenian statement they find unsatisfactory: "Take up each point, and do not you either make a single speech, but conduct the inquiry by replying at once to any statement of ours that seems to be unsatisfactory" (5.85). The choice of the dialogue form might represent Athenian anger over the Melians' refusal to submit to their request to speak before the people. It is also an acknowledgment that a different venue requires a different mode of proceeding. The Athenians suspect that the Melians do not want their people hearing Athenian speeches because they think the commons are more readily moved by oratory, by "arguments that are seductive and untested." But they also suspect that the Melian oligarchs will be persuaded more easily by unadorned talk, and so they insist on the dialogue form just as they accept the Melians' request that the commons not be present.

The Melians accept this proposal, but they note that the fairness of it is really not open to discussion. They say that the Athenians contradict themselves by choosing the form of a dialogue, since the eminence of their force makes a true exchange of opinions impossible. This statement indicates that the Melians, from the very beginning, understand their situation: the presence of Athenian force makes the entire exchange something of a farce. They comment:

> For we see that you are come to be yourselves judges of what is to be said here, and that the outcome of the discussion will in all likelihood be, if we win the debate by the righteousness of our cause and for that very reason refuse to yield, war for us, whereas if we are persuaded, servitude. (5.86)

The Melians say they might "win" the debate based on the facts presented if it were heard by an impartial judge. But even if they win in this way and thus resolve not to submit, war will be the result. Yet servitude will be the result of being "persuaded" by the Athenians' arguments. For the Melians, servitude must mean at least being tribute-paying allies of Athens (when the Athenians finally offer the fairly moderate terms of servitude, the Melians refuse). No terms have yet been offered by the Athenians, so it is possible that the Melians are thinking of something more dreadful. Why did the Athenians wait so late to deliver their terms? Perhaps it was because they had found the Melians more difficult to persuade than they had originally estimated. Or perhaps it was because the terms really did not matter to them in the context of the immediate question, which was whether or not Melos would be destroyed. If the terms had been put up front, it is possible that the Melians, more aware of what their "servitude" would have been like, might have given in. But it seems the Athenians' point really was that only safety should have been important to the Melians, not the particular terms of the settlement.

From the Athenians' point of view, there is nothing farcical about the dialogue. They are there to persuade the Melians to act in a rational manner to save themselves, now that they are faced with overwhelming superior force. But they do not take the dialogue form as seriously as the Melians. For the Melians, a dialogue means an exchange of views with the aim of reconciling differences. For the Athenians it is a one-way act of persuasion. The Melians object; the Athenians tell them why they are wrong. As it turns out, the dialogue evolves exclusively along these lines, even though the Melians constantly try to turn it into a meaningful two-way exchange.

The Athenians make it clear that they wish to persuade the Melians to give up without a fight. If the Melians want to talk about anything besides their present predicament and how to safely escape it, they might as well stop right now (5.87). The Melians respond that it is natural for men in their position to use many kinds of arguments. However, they acknowledge that the question at hand is their safety, and they agree to abide with the Athenians' requirement. At this point, the only thing the Melians can do to keep the conversation going is to say they agree with the Athenians' conditions. The Athenians say they will not speak of their conduct in the Persian War, nor of how the Melians have wronged them, since the Melians would never accept their claims anyway. The Athenians' abandonment of justifications, including their heroism in the Persian War, indicates what little value they now place on the usual demands of rhetoric. That they say they will not speak of how the Melians have harmed them suggests that there may have been more grounds for their action than we are given here.[46] But since Thucydides gives us little background for the Athenian decision to confront Melos, we are encouraged to see it as without just cause.

The Athenians ask the Melians to omit claims that they did not aid the Spartans or that they have done Athens no real harm. Let us dispense with all customary formalities, they seem to be saying, "since you know as well as we know that what is just is arrived at in human arguments only when the necessity on both sides is equal, and that the powerful exact what they can, while the weak yield what they must" (5.89). The Athenians insist that the traditional trappings of Greek oratory be done away with, since they have nothing to do with the "real thoughts" of human beings and since the real thoughts of human beings dwell not on justice or honor but on safety and power. They do not claim here, or anywhere in the dialogue, that there is no such thing as justice or that both sides are incapable of agreeing on what it is. They argue only that justice is not applicable in the situation the Melians now encounter. To say that the strong do what they can and the weak do what they must is not to say that might makes right. But to say that justice is applicable only when both sides are equal subordinates justice to relationships of power and thus destroys its meaning.

If all talk of justice and honor are mere trappings, why are the Athenians so eager to see them eliminated? The Spartans listened to the Thebans and Plataeans speak of justice, all the while knowing that all parties were aware of the underlying issue of power interests. They allowed the debate to happen as if it were a mere embellishment to their predetermined actions. In a way, this apathetic stance shows more disrespect for such debate than the Athenians' refusal to allow it. What harm would come from letting the Melians engage them in moral argument if the Athenians are likewise convinced that such arguments carry no weight? Instead, it seems that the Athenians understand that political rhetoric is fundamentally opposed and presents an alternative to their mode of conduct.

The Melians next try to turn the dialogue into a genuine argument by turning the Athenian requirements for relevancy around. They distinguish between Athens's apparent interest and true interest. If we must speak of interest and not of right, they say, then we must tell you that it is in *both* our interests not to eliminate arguments from justice or arguments that do not measure up to the criteria of strict rationality. In other words, it is expedient for the Athenians not to rule out the principle of morality as a common good:

> As we think, at any rate, it is expedient (for we are constrained to speak of expediency, since you have in this fashion, ignoring the principle of justice, suggested that we speak of what is advantageous) that you should not rule out the principle of the common good, but that for him who is at the time in peril what is equitable should also be

just, and though one has not entirely proved his point he should still derive some benefit therefrom. And this is not less for your interest than for our own, inasmuch as you, if you shall ever meet with a reverse, would not only incur the greatest punishment, but would also become a warning example to others. (5.90)

Like Diodotus, the Melians have redefined "expediency" to mean enlightened self-interest. But they have taken this argument one step further; enlightened self-interest now means upholding common principles. It means not denying the coincidence of justice and expediency but embracing justice as the ultimate public good. If the Athenians' luck should ever run out, they would greatly benefit from such a rule and thus they should now uphold it. Likewise, if they are overly cruel now, they may be treated in a like manner in defeat. Thus the Melians bring up the possibility that the true Athenian interest lies in upholding the general rules of decency that forbid such behavior. A claim the Plataeans made only weakly is more fully put forward by the Melians, though with similarly ill results.

The Athenians deny that such a long-range view would benefit them in their particular situation. Athens is a great power. If she falls it will be to another great power, Sparta. But such a power has less reason to be vengeful than Athens's own subjects, if they ever were allowed to get the upper hand. Anyway, they say, they are prepared to take their chances, and they remind the Melians again that they want to talk about the preservation of Melos and nothing else. Reversing the Melian argument, they say that it is in both their interests for the Athenians to rule over Melos without trouble (5.91). The Melians would gain by not being destroyed, and Athens would profit by not having to destroy them (5.92–93).

The Athenians reject the suggestion that they should allow Melos to be neutral in the war and declare its friendship for Athens. They insist that Melian friendship would be worse than hostility, since it would tell the other islanders that Athens is not powerful enough to make Melos submit. Melian hostility would at least speak of Athenian power: "for in the eyes of our subjects that would be a proof of our weakness, whereas your hatred is a proof of our power" (5.95).

The Athenians seem now to be implementing the policy Diodotus rhetorically outlined earlier, in order to save the Mytilenaeans: only the threat of ever-present force would persuade the allies not to revolt. The purpose of destroying Melos would be to spread terror throughout the allied cities. But Melos is independent; therefore Athens's colonial possessions would not expect it to act the same way as themselves, say the Melians. The Athenians maintain that the colonial states think that those states are independent that can ignore Athens's power. The fact that Melos is insular and rather weak makes it imperative that Athens show she is strong enough to control her (5.97). Melos is one of two neutral island cities. The Athenians' strategy, therefore, is to show her allies that they should not entertain rebellion by attacking a city that has not rebelled because she was independent to begin with—a city that has done nothing to warrant punishment. The Athenians are conforming in deed to the true, final implications of their own thesis. What could be more in accordance with Diodotus's prescription for how to avoid rebellion than the subjugation of Melos? How far is this policy from his suggestion that Athens, by ever-present vigilance, should prevent her allies from even thinking of revolt? The Athenian action at Melos is not an act of punishment—it is an act of repression, designed to expand the empire and add tribute if possible but chiefly to let the allies know that Athens is strong enough to keep subject all the island cities. If they remain impressed by the power of Athens, they will not revolt. But they will not believe that Athenian power is overwhelmingly superior or that it will necessarily be used against them if there are weak cities that are still independent, flouting that power. What could be a better example of ever-present vigilance than this? Isn't the rationale behind the attack on Melos the necessary outcome of Diodotus's logic that neither rule of law nor punishment will deter rebellion but only constant supervision and notice of force?

The Melians defiantly say that they would be great cowards if they did not resist as much as possible before submitting to servitude. In saying this, they sound familiar: the Plataeans made the question of honor the largest part of their argument. But the Athenians disagree, because their definitions of honor and justice are very different from the Melians' or the Plataeans': "No, not if you take a sensible view of the matter; for with you it is not a contest on equal terms to determine a point of manly honour, so as to avoid incurring disgrace; rather the question before you is one of self-preservation—to avoid offering resistance to those who are far stronger than you" (5.101).

For the Athenians, pursuit of honor as well as justice is reasonable only among equals, a position that makes honor and justice depend on relationships of power. This is an unconventional view of both, a view the Athenians insist is inwardly held by all men, even if they do not admit it or hide it in flowery speeches. However, it is not a view they held in Pericles' time, in which they accorded justice to their inferiors by allowing allies equal treatment in their own courts. But toward the end of the dialogue, when we hear the Athenians repeat the old formula, a part of which is that the stronger should treat the weaker with moderation, it has a hollow ring. It is not true that the Athenians are absolved from having to be moderate because the Melians have violated the other part of the equation: that the weaker should step lightly around their superiors. The Athenians at the beginning of the war did not renounce the practice of letting the allies be judged by the same impartial standards of Athenian justice just because this made the allies impudent. They complained, but they treated this as the price that a great power paid for honor.

The Melians, like so many other characters in the *History*, next mention that fortune sometimes upsets the advantage of numbers. Besides, they say, to give up would be a sign of despair, while resistance at least offers some hope (5.102). The Athenians, doggedly, will let the Melians have no solace. Hope is for those who have abundant resources. But "those who stake their all on a single throw" are more likely to meet disaster than success. They warn against "divination, oracles, and the like" that might inspire undue hopes.

The Melians never mention divination or oracles, although next they do mention hope in the gods themselves. Because they are "god-fearing men standing [their] ground against men who are unjust," the Melians expect the gods to help even out their disadvantage. They also look to the Spartans to help them out of a sense of kinship and, if nothing else, "for very shame" (5.104). But the Athenians have an especially cutting answer for this objection. In the case of the Spartans, they say, if their interest or their own laws are in question, they will give their all. But they are most notable in considering "what is agreeable to be honourable, and what is expedient just."

The gods seem to have an even worse reputation than the Spartans. The Athenians do not expect to be favored any less than the Melians by the gods:

For of the gods we hold the belief, and of men we know, that by a necessity of their nature wherever they have power they always rule. And so in our case since we neither enacted this law nor when it was enacted were the first to use it, but found it in existence and expect to leave it in existence for all time, so we make use of it, well aware that both you and others, if clothed with the same power as we are, would do the same. (5.105)

Thus the Athenians attribute to the gods the same drive for power they attribute to men. In making this claim, the Athenians seem to expound a natural law. They insist that this law is universally applicable in all times to all peoples and even to the gods. There is a fine line between admitting that neither gods nor men can help themselves and making out of justice an empty shell. If urges are compelling, how can anyone succumbing to them be called unjust? We come full circle to the question Diodotus raised in the Mytilenaean Debate.

The Melians choose not to object to these comments, perhaps because the Athenians' suggestions are too disconcerting to contemplate, but they do object to their doubts about the Spartans. They seem to have more trust in the Spartans than in the gods. Because Melos is a colony of Sparta, it would be in Sparta's interest not to betray the Melians, an act that would earn them the distrust of other friendly cities and would only strengthen the power of their enemies (5.106). The Athenians reply that to follow justice and honor is a dangerous course, while the Spartans are the least disposed to risk themselves (5.108–9). They are surprised that, after the Melians promised to talk about their country's safety, they said nothing that ordinary mortal men might hope to be saved by. Surely they will not succumb to that emotion "which most often brings men to ruin when they are confronted by dangers that are clearly foreseen and therefore disgraceful—the fear of such disgrace" (5.111.3–4). Besides, it is no disgrace to submit to the greatest city in Hellas.

For the first time in the dialogue the Athenians offer the Melians concrete terms: to become tribute-paying allies while keeping their own territory. They then offer their own code of conduct for the Melians to consider: not to submit to equals, to defer to superiors, and to treat inferiors with moderation. One wonders how the Athenians can claim both that one should not submit to ones' equals and that honor and justice are applicable only among equals. Honor and justice both often require a form of submission: a discontinuation of unabated hostilities and not insisting on total victory. One also wonders at how the Athenians' definition of moderation has changed. It now means warning the enemy before destroying him. With these words, the Athenians end the dialogue, urging the Melians to consider how serious their predicament is and to choose wisely (5.111). Despite the Athenians' efforts the Melians decide to stand their ground. They offer their neutrality, something the Plataeans had refused the Spartans, but they will not quickly be robbed of one hundred years of liberty (5.112). To this the Athenians respond that the Melians are the only men who regard the future as more certain than the present and who "look upon that which is out of sight, merely because [they] wish it, as already realized" (5.113).

The Athenians followed through on their threat to Melos; they besieged it until it surrendered. Then they killed all the adult males and sold the women and children into slavery. Later they colonized the island themselves. The Melians were in a short time robbed of their liberty in a brutal fashion. An act like this would have been considered cruel and excessive by the standards eventually arrived at in the Mytilenaean Debate. That is, the Athenians, when they repented of their initial decision to execute all male Mytilenaeans and sell the women and children into slavery, did so because they felt that this sentence was cruel and excessive as well as unwise. And yet this is the very sentence that was actually passed on the Melians, and for much less reason. The Athenians could make a sound argument that the Mytilenaeans had done them an injustice. They could not and did not make any such argument about Melos.

But in the end, had the Melians not also shown their own kind of immoderation? They had refused to yield even after it was clear that they had no other choice between submission and death. They chose not to live to fight another day. Thucydides does not openly praise the Melians' bravery in accepting their fate, but to do so would be out of character for him. He simply reports their fates in brief and stern tones. The fact that he records the dialogue and the eventual destruction of the Melians, however, does make something valuable of the Melians deaths; they did not die completely in vain. The Melian episode is an enduring black stain on the Athenians' history, a reminder of the ugliness of injustice as well as a warning of where such excess can lead. The Melian Dialogue is followed by the Sicilian Expedition, in which the Athenians in their hubris go too far. How could the Melians' lives have purchased any more meaning? Their attachment to honor, piety, and courage contribute to the Thucydidean lesson that moderation and justice are often profitable as well as right. The Melians, through Thucydides' eyes, appear more like martyrs than victims. Their deaths illustrate the failure of the Athenian thesis when that thesis is taken to its ultimate conclusions.

Thucydides' Three Great Moral Dramas Compared

Regardless of how justice is ignored by the aggressors in these episodes, there seems to be an agreement on what justice is among the speakers, except in the case of Diodotus and the Athenians at Melos. According to Cleon, the Thebans, the Plataeans, and the Melians, justice involves retribution—getting what one deserves. This position on justice implies that human beings are responsible for their actions and should be held accountable. The only question is over the facts of the cases, the determination of who deserves what.

Cleon's plea for retribution hides behind a policy of expediency. But his impatience with deliberation, his anxiety to have the thing done before the Athenians lose their rage, shows that he is not truly interested in what is best for Athens in the long run as much as he is interested in revenge.[47] Revenge or retribution has little to do with expediency and more to do with "legality," as Diodotus later points out. Diodotus claims that justice, or legality, should not be a consideration in war among states as it is in peace among individuals (3.44.3–4). He says that Cleon's argument hinges on justice, but that it will be heeded not by a calm consideration of what is just but out of bitterness and anger. It turns out that the Mytilenaeans receive more justice because the Athenians are persuaded to think of expediency, which implies that speaking of justice in a forum like this will lead only to extremism and that it will be distorted by the people's anger, perhaps by a speaker's own ambitions.[48]

The arguments on both sides of the Plataean Debate turn on justice and legality. Because of this, both sides dispute each others' facts. Of all the arguments examined, the Plataeans' is the most legalistic. They claim as their right Spartan adherence to a past treaty between Pausanias and Plataea. They speak of their alliance to Athens as if they are duty bound by their word. They say they did nothing in the current war to harm the Spartans, not acknowledging the political harm their alliance with Athens represents.

The Thebans take the Plataeans' arguments seriously enough to answer them, albeit in a contradictory manner. Some of these contradictions are due to their identification of justice with the correct ideology. For them, being ideologically correct is more important than keeping agreements. The only time the Thebans narrow their concept of justice to mere keeping of agreements is when it applies to the Plataeans—their rethinking of their initial decision to surrender and their breaking of the alleged agreement not to harm the Theban prisoners. The contradictions in the Thebans' speech alert us to the possibility that the Thebans are not taking justice as seriously as first appears and are more concerned with giving the Spartans an excuse to let them have their way. Nonetheless, they feel that they have to answer the Plataeans' charges and defend themselves on the grounds of justice.

The Melians conceive of justice much the same as the Plataeans. They argue that the Athenians' actions are not fair, that they do not deserve their fate, and that common principles of justice should be upheld. They believe not only that they should not be attacked because they are not guilty of any wrongdoing but also that if the Athenians attack them they will be acting unjustly as well as unwisely. For them, not only is justice a moral obligation as it appears to be for the Plataeans; it also conforms to rationality at the highest level, that is, maintenance of the common good. Justice is a set of rules that will benefit everyone if upheld consistently. In this assertion the Melians are unique. The Melians' suggestions are radical, but not because there is no evidence of such rules or no precedent for obedience to them. Indeed, throughout the *History* we see Hellenes taking the conventions of war seriously. Their suggestion is radical because of who they are dealing with. Athens claims that she is not bound, because of her imperial or superpower status, to the ordinary rules of just conduct—they do not benefit her as they would others. The Athenians at Melos, in hindsight, are correct in saying that they will not be treated by their possible conquerors—the Spartans—the way they would be treated by smaller states. Athens, because of her power, truly is exempt even in defeat from many rules, if they are judged by present or future usefulness to Athens. To uphold them regardless of how they would benefit the Athenian state would be an exercise in honor that, as Athens grew to be a tyrant city, the Athenians chose not to pursue. As Pericles and Cleon both pointed out, if the Athenians wanted to keep their empire, they could not afford to be too nice. Indeed, the Melian argument would have worked better on the Spartans, who still had to concern themselves with their popularity among allies. But for the Athenians the need for popularity became a sign of weakness. For them to practice justice would have seemed a noble act indeed, while to practice moderation guided by enlightened self-interest was about all one could hope for. Pericles symbolized this type of moderation, as did Diodotus.

The Athenians at Sparta used the Athenian thesis, that the strong do what they will by the compelling urges of human nature, in order to justify their empire. For an imperial power informed by this theory, can we expect more than the Athenians at Melos are willing to give—a warning? The real question is whether Athens was better off in the long run acting on this theory, or whether she would have benefited more from continuing to observe some justice regarding her allies. Certainly, the growing hostility of Athens's allies, as they perceived themselves more and more as outposts of an imperialist power, did nothing to help the Athenians' cause as the war dragged on. Athens may not have lost in the manner of the Melians, but it did eventually lose.

The alternative approach to justice is advocated by both Diodotus and the Athenians at Melos, who subordinate justice to power. Both insist that it is natural for the strong to do what they can and the weak to do what they must. Diodotus's argument denies that there are things such as guilt and responsibility. The Athenians at Melos, while not saying this outright, certainly act as if this is the case; they repeatedly insist that justice should not be a topic in the dialogue. They add, as an explanation for their insistence, that justice and honor apply only among equals. While Diodotus does not make this argument (to do so would hurt his less conspicuous argument concerning the justice of the Mytilenaeans), this is the logical outcome of his theory of human nature. If human beings are compelled to take advantage of their lessers, the only time that they are compelled to act justly is when they are confronted with an equal. "Justice" is then little more than the product of fear of conflict with an equal; it is not the kind of justice that the Plataeans, the Melians, or Cleon would recognize. Thus, Diodotus and the Athenians at Melos both frame the natural will to power as compelling: their position, as we will soon see, is the Hobbesian position.

By the end, no solution short of unconditional surrender is acceptable to the Athenians at Melos. Their action at Melos is a show of force with no purpose offered by Thucydides other than what the Athenians claim. It is not punishment. The Athenians say they must show their allies that no small island state can remain independent or declare independence from Athens and avoid their wrath. Given the thrust of the Diodotean argument, which only elaborates the consequences of the Athenian thesis, with its recommendation of repression, what could be more sensible than making Melos submit unconditionally or destroying her? There is nothing different about this in comparison with Diodotus's statements, except that in his speech the theory seems benign and is used for a cause we consider good: moderate punishment of Mytilene. The theory, however, is not benign, and we can recognize its dark side in the Athenians' attitude and speech as well as their deeds at Melos. The Athenian thesis subordinates justice to power and thus largely empties it of meaning. What seems like justice among equals is really mutual fear and respect. Among those who are not equals, justice is seen either as a catchword for extremism or as a concept employed by the weak when they have no other recourse. "Punishment" also loses its meaning; violence toward others must have a legitimate purpose other than revenge or blood lust. As long as it does have a legitimate purpose, as much violence as is needed is permitted.

To argue about the facts, to speak of justice seriously, is to believe that people essentially have control over their actions and that they choose their course freely. It also assumes that there is some common understanding of right and wrong upon which most people can agree. On what side in the *History* do we find those who would reduce the role of speech to a minimum, and on what side do we find champions of deliberation? Those who would suppress speech are Cleon, the Thebans, and the Athenian representatives at Melos.

Cleon would rather have the Athenians act immediately on their anger and would cast suspicion on anyone who would debate the matter further, while Diodotus disparages such a viewpoint. For Diodotus, such hostility to deliberation is the most dangerous stance the city can take. The Thebans, at the end of their speech, say that it would be better if in future trials the Spartans would simply ask the defendants the crucial question and decide what they will do on the facts alone, not on pleas of virtue and the use of fair words. The Plataeans, obviously, think differently. They ask to speak at length, hoping they can change the course of events, even though they are perfectly aware of the Spartans' predetermined preference for giving them up to the Thebans. The Athenians at Melos choose the form of a dialogue to *eliminate* true argumentation, while the Melians not only defend the usefulness of speeches and true deliberation but elevate that usefulness into a common good. In each case, it is the aggressor who wishes to suppress speech. Deliberation produces unwanted moderation (according to the aggressors) or justice (according to the victims).

In the case of Mytilene, Cleon's political style produces his accusations against Diodotus, which might well have been made about anyone who opposed him. In the case of Melos, the reasons for wanting to stop debate are much deeper. The Athenians have surrendered to their own doctrine that human nature creates a compelling will to power that then creates inevitable situations, like the one facing Melos. There is a positive relationship among their definitions of human nature and justice and their disparagement of debate. Given the inevitability of the Athenians' desires and the availability of the force required to satisfy them, what good is debate about justice? The point of communication is simply to make the other side understand their dire situation.

In contrast, the Spartans do not say a word against the Plataean Debate. The debate takes place, and it is full of the traditional forms. Both the Thebans and Plataeans recall their past deeds in the Persian War and justify their activities then and now, something the Athenians at Melos strictly forbid both for themselves and for the Melians. The Thebans warn against fine speeches, but they do not shy away from justifying their actions. In the end, despite the presentations from both sides, Sparta decides to give Plataea up to the Thebans for reasons of her own self-interest. She has ignored the content of both speeches for reasons of justice. But perhaps she would have listened more carefully if good arguments from expediency had been used.

Diodotus defends the usefulness of calm, reasoned deliberation. But that he gives a speech at all and changes the Athenians' minds is in contradiction with his theory of human nature. He is trying to reason with the Athenians about the essentially unreasonable nature of man, and he is using the most reasonable argument of all—long-term interest—in order to stop them from doing what comes naturally. Who would have guessed that a man who believed the allies could be controlled only by constant repression would think the Athenians capable of abstract reason on such a pressing issue? If Diodotus were to have been consistent with his own theory, he would have let Cleon have his way with the Mytilenaeans, since he and the Athenian people had already decided that course by the force of their passions. Then he would have told the Athenians that in the future they had better crack down on their empire.

The argument that Diodotus expounds in more detail and depth than any other Athenian in the *History* is embraced by the Athenians at Melos and acted upon. What was used as a theoretical point of deliberation by Diodotus and with less penetration by other Athenians—believed or not—found itself, in practice, a brutal and single-minded repressor of speech. It is hard to believe that Diodotus, champion of political debate, would have approved of this consequence of his theory of human nature, which makes us suspect that Diodotus's intention was merely to persuade the Athenians on the occasion of their reconsideration of the Mytilenaean decree, not to have his theory taken to its extreme in practice. Another indication of this is that Diodotus never insisted on the full application of his theory to the case at hand. If he had, he would have had to call for no punishment at all for the Mytilenaeans. After all, their suffering would not deter others from the same crime. But Diodotus instead called for a punishment that seemed fair enough under the circumstances. Diodotus, like the Thebans, might knowingly have contradicted himself in order to get the greatest punch from his argument, regardless of its validity. Diodotus claimed, after all, that a speaker in the assembly had to lie in order to be believed. Diodotus's lie is the same theory he puts forth. He turns the Athenian thesis in on itself by taking it to its extremes. He makes the people feel better about their concern for justice by giving them a more attractive, sophisticated reason for being lenient with the Mytilenaeans. The thesis that Diodotus did not take completely seriously but used rhetorically was accepted completely by the Athenians at Melos, just as it was to be by Hobbes.

By showing us that Diodotus can win, while the Plataeans and

Melians cannot, Thucydides is acknowledging the role of power in deliberation. When one side is faced with a determined enemy more powerful by far than itself, reason and masterful oratory will not help. Thucydides accepted that justice is often ignored among those who are not equals and that the most one could ask for is a prudent moderation of superiors. Pericles and Diodotus promoted restraint, if not moderation; Cleon and the Thebans promoted extremism.

Most (but not all) decisions in the *History* are made, according to Thucydides, on calculations of interest. But the speeches and debates themselves vary in content. Cleon argues that what is just is also expedient and that expediency should be the primary concern. As we have seen, this argument for expediency is largely a cover for a much more retributive scheme. Diodotus also subordinates justice to expediency. But Diodotus uses appeals for expediency because he is challenged to do so by Cleon and because he knows that this is the "sophisticated" position the Athenians want to hear. He too considers what policy would be best for the Athenian empire in the future, and he proves that moderation coincides with Athens's long-term interest. The Athenian demos, then, chooses one of two policy recommendations, both of which claim to be expedient in the long run. Much like the Melians, Diodotus defines expediency as enlightened self-interest, but he does so by claiming that human nature is compelled to transgress and thus that punishment is not an efficient means of controlling men. Unlike the Melians, Diodotus does not say that adhering to the tenets of justice is in Athens's interest; instead he says that to be moderate is expedient in this and similar cases; and in this case, moderation coincides with what is just. He wins moderation by denying justice in favor of expediency.

The Thebans, who win the day, although not by their arguments, say very little about why destroying Plataea would be expedient for Sparta. Instead, they concentrate on telling why they are right and the Plataeans are wrong. The Plataeans for the most part do the same. They speak of Sparta deriving some continuing benefit from her gratitude for Plataea's role during the Persian War, but they do not explain what the benefits are, as though they do not themselves take these arguments very seriously.

Cleon and Diodotus argue about the expediency of severe punishment for the Mytilenaeans, but the Spartans hear no arguments concerning the expediency of their impending action, only those of justice. Yet the Athenians are moved to embrace Diodotus's moderate path while the Spartans, unmoved by either side's arguments, show no moderation at all. If the Plataeans had been more forthcoming in their defense, if they had given more solid reasons for why leniency toward them was expedient, would they have won the Spartans over? All we can say is that in the case of Mytilene, when arguments from expediency are seriously entertained, moderation and enlightened self-interest win. At Plataea and Melos, where expediency is either not mentioned or has been decided beforehand and is not open to serious debate, immoderation carries the day. Thus, while political rhetoric promotes more moderation, we must modify that general conclusion. The evidence suggests that political rhetoric must rely overtly on arguments of national interest in order to be successful. Diodotus's speech exemplifies this strategy. If Thucydides' preference for moderation and traditional values is shown in his analysis of the Corcyraean Civil War, the Mytilenaean Debate, the Plataean Debate, and the Melian Dialogue, and if Thucydides shows that deliberative rhetoric produces moderation while its absence is accompanied by immoderation, then we may conclude that Thucydides places a high value on such rhetoric and speakers who are capable of utilizing it.

A COMPARISON OF HOBBES AND THUCYDIDES ON JUSTICE

It should be clear by now that the impression many political scientists have, that Thucydides and Hobbes represent a common view on human nature, ethics, and international relations, is not without reason. But most of the political scientists who invoke the names of Thucydides and Hobbes are aware that they are using them as archetypes and either know or suspect that the true Thucydidean or Hobbesian position is not as simple or as clear-cut as they make it out to be. The positions of Thucydides and Hobbes on justice are actually very different.

Justice and Expediency

The difference between what should be and what is reverberates in Thucydides' moral dramas. All the characters recognize the tension between justice and the demands of power politics. We have seen that, at the least, Thucydides equates justice with the avoidance of needless and excessive bloodshed and with adherence to basic war conventions such as not killing women and children. In his treatment of Plataea, Thucydides recognizes the value of traditional notions of virtue and justice. But he laments that men are always willing to violate these principles because of envy and need for revenge. Through the speeches he chooses to emphasize, he also clearly states that superpower status makes adherence to common principles even less attractive. If Sparta, which relied much more on its popularity to keep its allies than did Athens, was not willing to consider the future good in upholding principles of justice at Plataea, how could Athens be expected to do any better? As Athens relied in the latter stages of the war more on raw force than on anything else, she could see little benefit in upholding these principles. Thus Thucydides holds out little hope that mankind will at any time recognize the Melian claim that its interests lie in adherence to a common code of justice.

Hobbes thinks that a common code of justice is in the common interest of mankind but that the only way it can be consistently upheld is if there is an absolute sovereign to maintain it. This means that at the international level one cannot expect all the laws of nature to be observed consistently. States need only obey these laws if their unilateral obedience will cause them no harm. In this way Hobbes makes justice and expediency coincide. As does Thucydides, Hobbes condemns unnecessary violence and bloodshed, and he disapproves of war fought for "trifles." Hobbes hopes that these evils can be avoided due to his spreading of the new, rationalistic gospel. While Thucydides mourns the inability of man to recognize his true, long-term self-interest, Hobbes thinks that he *can* recognize and embrace it. But we have hit on a basic similarity and difference between Thucydides and Hobbes. Both consider justice to be in the long-term best interests of individuals and states most of the time. But Thucydides, unlike Hobbes, thinks that some things are simply right, regardless of their utility. We can see his acceptance of the validity of certain values in his treatment of Corcyra, Plataea, and Melos.

The Role of Deliberative Rhetoric

Thucydides presents an alternative to his observation that states can rarely see the benefits of upholding justice when it conflicts with their short-term interests. This alternative is statesmanship. Pericles and Diodotus are models of statesmanship because they know how to extract moderation from a political system prone to immoderation: imperial democracy. For Thucydides, moderation depends on the excellence and intelligence of individual leaders, as well as those they lead. Pericles and Diodotus try to show not that upholding the principles of justice is in the common interests of mankind (even though it might have been) but that their proposals are in the particular interest of Athens. Pericles and the Athenian envoys at Sparta do this by claiming that while Athens does not need to be just, it is a sign of its glory and power that it observes justice when it does not have to. Diodotus obtains moderation from the Athenians by denying the importance of justice altogether and claiming that his only concern is expediency.

Thucydides takes moderation, guided by enlightened self-interest, to be the highest achievement possible in international relations, not adherence to rules of justice that are in the common interest of mankind. It is evident that moderation truly was in the best interests of Athens, for as she became more immoderate and repressive, she began to lose her empire. Her enemies multiplied and her burdens increased. As statesmanship lost out to demagoguery, Athens began her decline. The true message of the Melian Dialogue is not that an imperial power does not have any reason to uphold justice or think about the common good but that it is doubly hard for imperialists to recognize this fact. Without the right kind of leadership, such a state will not act in accordance with its own true interests.

Hobbes has no use for statesmanship and absolutely no use for political rhetoric. There is no need to lie to the people, at least not in order to get things done. The only language needed is the language of science and scientific method. Therefore, unlike Thucydides, he denies the meaning and usefulness of debate about anything, but particularly about what is right and wrong or good and bad. It is not successful rhetoric that makes wills coalesce around a particular policy but force, albeit force derived from an original social contract. The sovereign has only to follow certain rules to be a complete success both in domestic and international affairs. The people have only to remember that they have given up their rights to the discretion of the sovereign and that they have done this for their own good.

Hobbes is *less* realistic than Thucydides when it comes to his expectations. He expects that reason, when it is clear to the average individual, will prevail. He is willing to endorse absolute monarchy, aware of the possible dangers of absolutism, because he has such faith in enlightenment. Likewise he hopes that sovereigns will see that their true interests lie in obeying natural law as much as they can. Thucydides' hope lies in the possibility that a gifted individual will step forward at the right time and persuade others to follow his lead, often using the methods most antithetical to the enlightenment rationale: lying, exaggerating, glorifying, appealing to vanity. This hope is perhaps encouraged by his own written work, which may improve some future leaders, educating them in the ways of prudence and justice.

Justice and Necessity

Hobbes embraces the assumption of the Athenian thesis: that the impulses of human nature that cause quarrel, namely, desire for gain, safety, and glory, are natural and compelling and therefore blameless. But he seems to have discounted the potential danger of this thesis. Hobbes uses the Athenian thesis much the way Diodotus does: in order to produce moderate treatment for the underdog. But while Diodotus gains leniency for the Mytilenaeans, he deepens Athenian understanding of their own philosophy; he exposes the true implications of it. The implications are evident in the Athenians' brutality toward Melos. Hobbesian philosophy can be said to have done the same.

Cleon's view, that the impulses of human nature are strong but actions are still intentional, is consistent with the common view of morality. This is, strangely enough, Bishop Bramhall's view. Cleon proves that this view is easily combined with anger and rage to go beyond what is moral. Diodotus and Hobbes react to the potential consequences of assuming the guilt and responsibility of one's opponents. Rather than being a limiting factor, morality combined with outrage can lead to unlimited aggression. An illustrious modern realist described this problem succinctly in describing the greatest deficiency of the American legalistic approach to international politics:

> That is the inevitable association of legalistic ideas with moralistic ones: the carrying-over into the affairs of states of the concepts of right and wrong, the assumption that state behavior is a fit subject for

moral judgment. . . . It is a curious thing, but it is true, that the legalistic approach to world affairs, rooted as it unquestionably is in a desire to do away with war and violence, makes violence more enduring, more terrible, and more destructive to political stability than did the older motives of national interest. A war fought in the name of high moral principle finds no early end short of some form of total domination.[49]

This is precisely why Hobbes wants to remove responsibility from the equation. His desire for more moral action leads to a denial of morality. Punishment, he reasons, will be more limited if it is not tied to vengeance but is guided only by the wish to correct both the offender and others. Unlike Diodotus, Hobbes thinks that punishment is useful, because it can reform the will of the offender. Diodotus thinks that punishment is useless once men become convinced that they can accomplish great deeds. But both Diodotus's and Hobbes's theories, emerging from a common understanding of human nature, produce the same dangerous side effect. While originally put forward in the name of moderation and humanity, these theories can easily be used for immoderation and inhumanity. Whether punishment should be used only to redirect another's will or should not be used at all, the assumption is still that there is no such thing as guilt or innocence, no responsibility for human actions. By removing responsibility from the equation, punishment, or aggression (which is what it should be called, to remove the tinge of values), loses all measurement except that of expediency. And, practically speaking, the determination of what is expedient is up to the decision maker, who justifies his actions no longer by moral standards but only by standards of expediency. Thus Diodotus's suggestion that the only way to control the allies is through the constant threat of force is consistent with his appeal for the least amount of punishment for the Mytilenaeans. And while Diodotus champions the importance of reasonable deliberations in decision making, the upshot of his theory of human nature is the suppression of debate. When one's actions are determined beforehand by the immutable consequences of one's nature, by the natural will to power, what is the point of debate, especially moral debate? But true, reasoned deliberation, according to Pericles as well as Diodotus, produces wise policy. It serves as a brake on rampant justification, because of the multiplicity of arguments. To deny the usefulness of debate and deliberation is to invite extremism, the worst kind of sophisticated justifications, and finally no justifications at all. This is precisely the position of the Athenians at Melos, who have become utterly and cynically convinced of their own philosophy.

Thucydides shows us, through the Melian Dialogue, the bitter consequences of the Athenian thesis taken to its logical conclusion. But Hobbes, even though he foresees the difficulties and dangers that might arise from his solution to the problem of stubborn human nature—oppression in domestic politics, the triumph of self-interested reason in international affairs—nevertheless clings to the solution without reservations. Not moral debate but a sterile application of reason provides the king with a guide. He decides what is necessary, and any amount of aggression is "just" so long as it is necessary. It is this type of thinking that produces those cruelties we find most unacceptable in "total war"—such as bombing civilians, targeting food supplies, and destroying the civilian economy—all in the name of a quicker peace.

Justice vs. Security

Is anything worth dying for, simply on the grounds that the cause is right? Are there any values that supersede the national interest? I have concluded that Hobbes would say no. The only legitimate reason for war is defense, broadly defined. War for "trifles," for avenging insults, is prohibited as being counterproductive. There is no value higher than the national interest, and so intervention on the side of right cannot be condoned by Hobbes unless it is also beneficial to the defense or expansion of the state. And if the state is faced with extinction or surrender, Hobbes will always recommend surrender. Since death is the ultimate evil, for individuals and states, there can be nothing worth dying for. Order and safety are of such importance to him that as long as the conqueror provides these two goods, all else is to be tolerated. Certainly freedom of speech, freedom of religion, or any other kind of autonomy besides that of being free from bonds would not be worth risking one's life for.

What would Thucydides' position be on this question? Knowing what is likely to happen to them, the Plataeans and Melians decide to die for their freedom. That is, they insist on freely choosing their fate, the most important value for them being autonomy and self-respect. Thucydides betrays his admiration for the Plataeans' courage as he describes their many ingenious devices for thwarting the Spartan siege; and he makes them sound noble and virtuous in the speech they give in their own defense. Their cause is clearly the just cause. The Spartans and Thebans appear cruel and unjust; the Thebans' excuses for their advice are very clearly excuses. Here and in the Melian Dialogue, Thucydides' emphasis is on the intrinsic good of justice and on the side that is just. The deaths of innocent people are singled out by Thucydides because their lives are valuable, and in the end these people are remembered through Thucydides' poignant description along with the Athenians in all their largesse. It would seem that in Thucydides' opinion there are some values that *are* worth dying for and that such nobility, courage, and conviction as the Plataeans and Melians possess are praiseworthy and edifying. These values contribute to the instruction that Thucydides offers his readers, by showing the ugliness of their destruction. The Spartans and Athenians in their role of cynical destroyers are not glorious, and, ironically, they do not appear very powerful.

Underlying Hobbes's position is not only the belief that death is the ultimate evil, to be avoided at any cost, but also the corresponding belief that there are no ideals, no permanent principles of good, and no evils outside of what is useful or not useful for the individual. The Corcyraean Civil War and the Plataean Debate, along with the Melian Dialogue, prove that Thucydides recognizes such permanent principles. Certainly he laments that "men are wont, when they desire a thing, to trust to unreflecting hope, but to reject by arbitrary judgment whatever they do not care for" (4.108.4). But this does not mean that he thinks that all desires are equal in their moral value, that the victims of injustice are wrong for having principles or for being proud of their virtuous past.

From his sympathetic treatment of the Plataeans (as well as his earlier sympathetic account of Periclean "measuredness"), we can surmise that Thucydides would not agree with the Athenians at Melos that pursuit of honor and justice is reasonable only among equals. That is, he would not make the validity of honor and justice depend necessarily on the relationship of the actors' power. Therefore, we might say that Hobbes agrees with the position of the Athenians at Melos that justice is a function of power and subordinate to it. He does not agree with Thucydides, for whom a just cause is still just even if it is challenged by a superior power. And while Hobbes believes that man is entirely the slave of his passions, Thucydides shows, in the person of Pericles and through the Athenians at Sparta, that while men may be driven to conform to their desires they can also observe justice. Indeed, the greater the state's power, the more it can afford to be just, even if it derives no other satisfaction than the knowledge that it is observing justice more than it has to. Thucydides shows that this compromise between the imperatives of power and interest and the principles of justice is in the long-term best interest of the state.

Leadership and Regimes

This final chapter will canvass the similarities and differences between Thucydides and Hobbes on the subject of regimes. Hobbes was convinced that Thucydides had proved the absurdity of democracy and the desirability of absolute monarchy. But Hobbes misread Thucydides on this point. For Hobbes, monarchy was the only regime in which the selfish interests of the ruler and ruled rationally coincided. Revealingly, in order to deal with the leadership of Pericles, Hobbes had to characterize him superficially as a monarch, ignoring how Pericles won and maintained his power (and the true significance of Thucydides' similar characterization). But it is just the type of statesmanship exemplified by Pericles (and later by Diodotus) that Hobbes cannot accept because of his rigid assumptions about human nature. Thucydides' focus on the importance of studying the thought, character, and actions of statesmen is an important difference between the Thucydidean and the Hobbesian realist models.[1]

Hobbes's horror at civil violence led him to lose faith in ordinary human reason and thus in political deliberation. It is because he lost faith in the latter that scientific reason emerged as a powerful alternative. But if human beings are so unreasonable that we can no longer take seriously what they say, how can we expect them to be reasonable enough to accept Hobbes's prescriptions? The Hobbesian solution is that an absolute government must enforce the plan. I will argue that this solution to political problems is even more dangerous than the Thucydidean solution, which relies on political rhetoric and judgment.

Thucydides' treatment of regime types is ambiguous. He does not think that human nature is so uniform that a rational political plan can be devised to eradicate the need for political rhetoric and statesmanship. He does not believe linear progress is possible, with the result that individual excellence becomes the most valuable human commodity regardless of regime type. Hobbesian perfection is perfection of society through the state. Such a state may harbor men and women of excellence, but it will not rely on them for its existence, or for its actualization. But for Thucydides, these are the very people who make or break any particular historical moment. Individual character becomes all-important, while in Hobbesian thinking the plan and the force to back the plan replace individual character. Hobbes's entire project revolved around eliminating the need for personal integrity and excellence, although it did not succeed in this regard. Science is the would-be destroyer of chance, but, as it turns out, chance cannot so easily be destroyed.

HOBBES

It is difficult to have an unmitigated admiration for the Athenian democracy. Yet Hobbes came away from his reading of the *History* with no respect for the Athenian people at all. The somber tones Thucydides employs to show us the follies of Athens's democracy, and later her oligarchy, do not much resemble the mocking and derisive character of Hobbes's treatment of democracy and aristocracy. Hobbes is an omniscient scientist looking down upon the quizzical and perverse actions of specimens bumping blindly into each other, puffed up with their own conceit, fools rather than foolish. As Bishop Bramhall observed, Hobbes's opinion "reflects too much upon the honor of mankind" (LNC, 185). When we read in the *History* of the unwise decision of the Athenians to pursue another war before they had won the first, we do not feel like laughing. But it is difficult not to smile sometimes as Hobbes describes his weak, selfish, ignorant individuals, living in their fantasy worlds and wreaking havoc on the rational order of civil society. While Thucydides stands apart from the Athenians and Peloponnesians, Hobbes stands above his fellows. While Thucydides wrestles with the weaknesses and strengths of men, Hobbes allows the lowest common denominator to be the rule.

Hobbes stated in his verse autobiography, written late in his life, that Thucydides had taught him a fundamental lesson about democracy: its "absurdity." He claimed that one of the reasons he translated the work was to propagate its antidemocratic message. Thucydides' theory that the Athenians lost because of internal disorders chiefly caused by interparty and interpersonal quarrels impressed Hobbes. He claimed that Thucydides would agree with him that monarchy was superior to any other regime, be it aristocratic, democratic, or mixed. This section will explore Hobbes's treatment of types of regimes by following his thought on this subject through several works. It will become apparent, I hope, that Hobbes's preference for monarchy over democracy or aristocracy is intimately linked with his theories of human nature and justice, and differs from the Thucydidean view accordingly. I will devote the first part to a study of the epistle, introduction, biography, and notes found in Hobbes's translation of the *History*. This will show not only that Hobbes thought Thucydides confirmed his theory but also that Hobbes's preference for monarchy and his reasons for that preference were formed early on. I will turn to *De Cive* to find the analysis and critique of regime types, nascent in the translation, articulated more fully. Hobbes favors monarchy because he believes that in this form of government the sovereign's and the people's interests coincide most easily, assuming the monarch will always act in his narrow self-interest. I will then examine Hobbes's treatment of this subject in *Leviathan*, written when Hobbes had reached his maturity. Finally, I will analyze how he applies this theory to the actual history of the English Civil War in *Behemoth*.

Hobbes's Thucydides

In 1628, when he was forty years old, Hobbes published his first translated work, the *Eight Bookes of the Peloponnesian Warre*. Over a relatively short span of time (twenty-eight years), he had managed to fully explicate, in an admirably consistent manner, his philosophy of politics. His consistency was no doubt largely due to the fact that he began writing these works in his middle age, after many years of study and consideration. Thus, many of the ideas contained in his introduction to the *History* are repeated and worked out more thoroughly in his later works.

Hobbes chose Thucydides to translate and praise because he was already inclined toward the lessons he saw in the *History* and because, as he states in his introduction, he thought those lessons well worth disseminating in the English language. In Thucydides' writings he saw a profitable instruction for noblemen (HT, "Epistle," par. 2). The *History* was relevant directly to Hobbes's England, as well as to a "possession for all times."

Hobbes's Early Elitism   The young Hobbes admired and identified with Thucydides on several levels. He agreed with Thucydides' criticism of the multitude and his esteem for the few. His introduction to the translation, "To the Readers," is ostensibly made to convince many readers of his sincerity and to give his reasons for doing the translation, but it is equally an appeal to the few readers who will truly appreciate it, men of judgment and education. It was this elite audience to whom he thought Thucydides intended to speak (HT, "To the Readers," par. 5). Most men like to hear of battles and blood rather than strategy and politics, Hobbes wrote. But he believed that this clamor for entertainment should not carry any weight at all for the author who is addressing himself to the few, better readers. Thucydides himself, after all, wrote his history not to win a popularity contest but as a monument of instruction for ages to come (HT, "Life," par. 8). Indeed, Thucydides was purposefully obscure, to keep the common people in the dark (HT, "Life," par. 22).

Hence, at this point in his life, Hobbes claimed to hold the same opinion as Thucydides of "the better" and "the vulgar" sort of men. When Thucydides mentions the few or the many in a discussion of the possible establishment of oligarchies in Athens's allied states, due to Athens herself becoming an oligarchy, Hobbes notes of the few that they are "[t]he best men, or *Aristocracy,* a difference from the *Oligarchy,* which was of the richest sort only. For the *good men* who in a *Democracy* are the *People's* minions and put the *People* upon all they do, will do the same things themselves, when they have Sovereignty in their hands" (HT, 8.48n.3).

Hobbes's note has no immediate connection with that portion of the text and could have been placed at any point where Thucydides mentions "the few." This note is curious for several reasons. First, he makes a clear distinction here between aristocracy and oligarchy, but in his later works he insists that oligarchy is just a bad name for aristocracy. At this point, it appears that Hobbes still embraced the classical distinction between the two, namely, that aristocracy is government by the best while oligarchy is government by the rich. Another possibility is that Hobbes was only expressing the way the ancient Greeks thought of aristocracy and oligarchy, nothing more. However, the second part of the note makes this reading less plausible than the first, because there is no need to further editorialize if the objective is simply to describe current distinctions. Instead, Hobbes says that the good men in a democracy lead the people well (like Pericles). And in an aristocracy, they will still prescribe the same good policies.

As David Johnston points out, Hobbes's elitism was to fade after his first political tract, *The Elements of Law*. His disdain for the people's intelligence lessened, while his criticism of democracy did not. Hobbes increasingly saw the importance of education, not just for the sovereign but for the people.[2] In *Leviathan*, much of the sovereign's duty consists of education and thus the manipulation of public opinion. Johnston sees this shift away from the exclusion of the common people from philosophy as coinciding with Hobbes's shift, evident in *Leviathan*, away from attributing the causes of civil war simply to objective aspects of human nature and toward blaming their real-life manifestations: orators, preachers, and philosophers.[3] The people had to be educated properly so that they would appreciate the role of the sovereign and not be swayed by these seditious types. By the time Hobbes wrote *Leviathan*, then, he no longer displayed his disgust for the vulgar that was so loudly proclaimed in his translation of Thucydides. But his utter rejection of democracy remained the same, and for the same reasons: the people could be used by ambitious men who were bent on sedition. So, even if we subtract the elitist flavor from Hobbes's observations about the *History*, they will still yield strong indications of his later theory.

Hobbes's Critique of Athenian Democracy   Hobbes read the *History* as a critique of Athenian democracy, and he agreed with it. Three of Hobbes's notes appear in Pericles' Funeral Oration. In these notes, Hobbes seems to favor Sparta even as Pericles is criticizing it in comparison with Athens. A large part of the oration is explicit praise of the Athenian democratic institutions and culture and implicit criticism of the corresponding deficits of the Spartans. Hobbes notes that Pericles is "carping secretly" at the Spartan habit of allowing only nobles to govern (HT, 2.37n.8). In another note he says that Pericles abuses the Spartans because "they ever looked sourly on soft and loose behavior" (HT, 2.37n.9). That is, what Pericles depicts as the virtuous freedoms of all Athenian citizens Hobbes thinks of as soft and loose behavior.

Hobbes thought Thucydides described well the antics of demagogues, the inconstancy of democratic policy, and its faulty decisions. At one point in Hobbes's translation, Cleon says that the demos will follow novel advice but dismiss any tried advice (HT, 3.38). In the note for this passage, Hobbes writes, without adding anything else, "The nature of the multitude lively set forth" (HT, 3.38n.1). Apparently, Hobbes approved of Cleon's ironically correct assessment of the Athenian demos, even though he did not approve of Cleon's demagoguery, having called him a "most violent sycophant in those times, and thereby also a most acceptable speaker amongst the people" (HT, "Life," par. 6). Hobbes observed that Thucydides could have become a great demagogue but did not want to. In those days, he wrote, it was impossible for a man to give good advice and not incur the wrath of the people. The men who endangered Athens the most with their advice were thought wise. The reason Hobbes gave for this folly was that much prosperity made men love themselves, and wise counsel (which would oppose their impulses) would make them love themselves less (HT, "Life," par. 4). In a multitude, this kind of self-destructive behavior was more prevalent, because

> in public deliberations before a multitude, fear (which for the most part adviseth well, though it execute not so) seldom or never sheweth itself or is admitted. By this means it came to pass amongst the Athenians, who thought they were able to do anything, that wicked men and flatterers drave them headlong into those actions that were to ruin them; and the good men either durst not oppose, or if they did, undid themselves. (HT, "Life," par. 4)

Thus, Hobbes pointed out not only the fearlessness of the people brought on by their sense of power but also the fear leaders had of angering the people. He noted a battle between Corinth and Athens, at which Nicias was the Athenian general in charge. Nicias won the battle but sent a herald back to collect two dead bodies left behind, which in the Hellenic code of battle at that time signaled an admission of defeat (HT, 4.44). Of this Hobbes wrote that Nicias would rather renounce victory than to omit an act of piety, since the latter was more important in the people's minds. He implied that Nicias was afraid of what befell the Athenian captains after the battle of Arginussae earlier (HT, 4.44n.7). Later, in his description of the Sicilian expedition, Thucydides makes it clear that Nicias's fear of the demos and concern for his reputation led him to make shortsighted political decisions that were strategically disastrous.

Later in the *History,* Thucydides writes that after the Athenian generals returned from Sicily for the first time, Hermocrates having managed to unify the Sicilians against the common threat, they were accused of being bribed to leave. As punishment, they were banished or fined (HT, 4.65). Hobbes noted that in Athenian assemblies at this time, the accusation of bribery was frequent when things went badly for Athenian interests, "for it was a sure way to win favour with the people, who thought that nothing was able to resist their power" (HT, 4.65n.8). That is, unscrupulous speakers, out to take advantage of some current misfortune, besmirched their opponents' character in order to raise their own popularity. Punishing the supposed wrongdoers and elevating those whom they now favored gave the people a sense of power, since they could so easily decide the fate of their leaders. The fearlessness of the demos and the sycophancy of the demagogues reinforced each other.

Hobbes claimed that what was missing from the advice of the Athenian leaders was fear. Fear would have produced moderate and prudent advice. Instead, because of the inconstant nature of the demos, what they were afraid of was the people of Athens. They told the people what they wanted to hear and feared carrying out plans that would not please them. Reckless demagoguery was thus encouraged, and thoughtful counsel and action became a daring act of patriotism indeed. The result was that only those leaders who encouraged the Athenians into some dangerous and desperate enterprise were considered wise and patriotic. Those who gave temperate advice were thought cowards or fools (HT, "Life," par. 4). Thus, Hobbes's rejection of the art of rhetoric that we have noted in previous chapters was already under way in 1628, and the reasoning behind it was basically consistent with his later works.[4]

Hobbes's Critique of the Oligarchs   Hobbes emphasized the ill effect of individual ambition in the *History.* It was ambition that led unscrupulous orators to manipulate the people, just as it was the envy of the people that caused them to attack their advisors (HT, "Life," par. 5). He had not much more praise for the Athenian oligarchs who usurped the democracy than he had for the demagogues. Of the conflict that erupted amongst the oligarchs as some of them prepared to change their government back into a democracy, Hobbes made two notes. The first is factual or explanatory (HT, 8.89n.7). The second is a commentary on the fight among the oligarchs, of whom Thucydides wrote that "the most of them, through private ambition, fell upon that, by which an oligarchy made out of a democracy is chiefly overthrown." Hobbes took pains to clarify what Thucydides had already said: "Ambition of the oligarchicals amongst themselves overthroweth their government" (HT, 8.89n.8). Armed with this evidence, that the government of the few was not any more effective than the government of the many, Hobbes concluded that Thucydides must have preferred monarchy:

> Nor doth it appear that he magnifieth anywhere the authority of the few: amongst whom, he saith, every one desireth to be the chief; and they that are undervalued, bear it with less patience than in a democracy; whereupon sedition followeth, and dissolution of the government. He praiseth the government of Athens, when it was mixed of the few and the many; but more he commendeth it, both when Peisistratus reigned, (saving that it was an usurped power), and when in the beginning of this war it was democratical in name, but in effect monarchical under Pericles. So that it seemeth, that as he was of regal descent, so he best approved of the regal government. (HT, "Life," par. 5)

Along this line, Hobbes went so far as to italicize, in his translation, the part of the text that referred to the government of Pericles as really being the government of one man only, not a democracy. Without mentioning where Pericles' power came from, Hobbes equated his rule with monarchy. Hobbes's idea of monarchy was that the sovereign, any sovereign, by virtue of the institution of monarchy, would necessarily dominate politics because of his monopoly on power. As we will see, the situation of Pericles was very different, yet Hobbes was reacting not to the reality of Pericles' achievement but to his own preconceived framework.

From 1628 on, Hobbes's preference for monarchy over democracy, aristocracy, or any mixed regime (which he thought was impossible) was a recurring theme in his philosophy. He was concerned not only with conflict among demagogues or oligarchs that could lead to the dissolution of the state but also with the unwieldy character of any type of council or assembly charged with making complex and often pressing decisions. Hobbes interpreted the *History* as emphasizing how universal self-interest made democracy and oligarchy inferior to monarchy. His conclusion that monarchy was the best form of government did not necessarily imply that the monarch was somehow morally superior to any other sovereign. Indeed, it is safe to say that it was because he felt that no one was morally superior and that everyone was inclined to ambition that monarchy was better for the state. Absolute monarchy eliminated competition and therefore the possibility of sedition. Hobbes's later works elaborated this nascent theory.

De Cive

It is fruitful to examine *De Cive* (1642) as the prototype for *Leviathan* (1651). It was written only two years after Hobbes completed his translation of Thucydides. In his Epistle Dedicatory to William, Earl of Devonshire, Hobbes wrote, "I have been long since of this opinion, that there was never yet any more-then-vulgar prudence that had the luck of being acceptable to the Giddy People; but either it hath not been understood, or else having been so, hath been level'd and cryed down." He called the tyrant-hating Romans beasts of prey that brought many nations into bondage (DC, "Epistle," par. 1). Hobbes was impressed with the history of ancient Rome as well as of Greece, especially when he criticized the notions of tyrannicide and the right to revolt, and at one time he listed Plato, Aristotle, Cicero, Seneca, and Plutarch as men who influenced sedition in his own time by supporting the Greek and Roman "anarchies" (DC, 12, par. 3). He questioned, "How many Kings (and those good men too) hath this one error, that a tyrant king might lawfully be put to death, been the slaughter of? . . . And what blood-shed hath not this erroneous doctrine caused, that kings are not superiours to, but administrators for the multitude?" (DC, "Preface," par. 2).

It was Hobbes's purpose to educate readers through universities controlled by the sovereign so that they would accept rule and no longer allow ambitious men to take advantage of them for their own profit (DC, "Preface," par. 7). This humane sentiment was to support Hobbes's advocacy for obedience to even the most autocratic rule in the name of peace and stability. Autocracy could occur in any form of government, he often pointed out, but citizens were obliged to obey whichever was in power—democracy, aristocracy, or monarchy—no matter how tyrannical. What was dangerous, indeed impossible, was divided sovereignty; whatever the form of government, sovereignty had to reside in one body or person. Although he had tried in his writing to produce a belief that monarchy was the best government, he claimed that he had not, in *De Cive* at least, demonstrated but only probably stated that this was the case (DC, "Preface," par. 8). Despite Hobbes's modest claim here, as we will see both in our discussion of *De Cive* and in our subsequent examination of this topic in *Leviathan,* Hobbes put forward some very solid arguments in his case for monarchy and against democracy and aristocracy. These arguments rested on the logic that all men being equal in their basic nature, it was not character that made good leaders but circumstances. In other words, contrary to the Thucydidean notion, it was the type of regime that dictated how leaders and led would behave, not individual character.

Hobbes judged the three forms of government that tended most to the preservation of peace and to the subjects' advantages (DC, 10, par. 1). The greatest inconvenience that could befall any city, he observed, was anarchy. But any stable sovereign could supposedly provide against that. The question then became which form was best for the stability that fostered peace and advantage. Hobbes put forth several arguments to prove that monarchy was best. First, there were operational considerations. In some ways democracy and aristocracy proved unwieldy; times and places had to be set to convene for deliberation. The monarch, in contrast, because he represented the "person" of the state but was also one natural person, was always ready to exercise his authority (DC, 7, par. 13).

Other considerations were more political or moral in nature. In chapter 10, after dismissing praise of monarchy based on what he admitted were examples and not solid reasoning, Hobbes went on to discuss why life is more difficult under the people than under a monarch (DC, 10, par. 6). Some people complain that monarchs overly enrich themselves. But compared to those who will be enriched in any government, there will not be as many in a monarchy, since there is only one person to accumulate riches. In a democracy, all the demagogues and their children, relatives, friends, and hangers-on will have to be rewarded, since all want to be as powerful and wealthy as possible. (DC, 10, par. 6)

Because of his power, a monarch *may* appoint unworthy people but is not compelled to do so for fear of them. But in a democracy all the popular men appoint unqualified people whom they need for one reason or another because it is necessary; if only some did it, these few would increase in power disproportionately to the rest (DC, 10, par. 6). Hobbes is saying that this type of behavior is compulsory in a democracy—honor does not pay when one is struggling for power with an indefinite number of others possibly willing to use less scrupulous methods.

Hobbes also made a claim that there was less abuse of power under monarchs than under popular governments. Subjects are less often unfairly condemned under one ruler than under the people. This is because only the ambitious people suffer in a monarchy—those who give bad advice or in some way challenge the king's authority. But in a popular government, leaders will not punish those who have slain citizens if those citizens stand in their way or have privately angered them (DC, 10, par. 7).

Hobbes emphasized the problem of democratic and oligarchical competition. It is no disadvantage to the subjects that they do not all take part in public deliberations, he wrote. It may seem like a problem of monarchy that everyone cannot participate. But if everyone did, there would be constant conflict, much useless advice, hatred, and neglect of one's family. Prohibiting everyone from participation, then, might be as much a grievance as keeping men from attacking one another just because they enjoyed it (DC, 10, par. 9).

As for the quality of deliberation, this went up as the numbers deliberating went down. Deliberations were less successful in great assemblies than in smaller counsels, Hobbes maintained, because very few men in great assemblies had enough knowledge on foreign and domestic matters to deliberate well. Hobbes emphasized that this was because most were unskilled in such things, not that they were incapable of learning (DC, 10, par. 10). But he seemed to take for granted that a society of highly informed and competent deliberators was not possible. Given his opinion on the Athenian democracy, a small and relatively public-minded society, he must have thought even less of English chances of having a well-informed public. Instead, he opted for a public drilled in the values of obedience he taught.

In a great assembly, he wrote, everyone would want to make a long, eloquent speech. But the nature of eloquence, "as all the masters of Rhetorick teach us," is not truth but victory, not information but allure (DC, 10, par. 11). Naturally, orators practicing this form of rhetoric end up hating each other. They fight each other for personal glory, and from this there arises faction, sedition, and civil war (DC, 10, par. 12, 15). What is decided at one assembly is brought up again when the other side has worked out a plan for outvoting the previous winner. This is a faction, and if it does not get its way in this manner it will try to force its way, thereby producing civil war (DC, 10, par. 12). The laws change whenever the majority faction changes (DC, 10, par. 13). This is why, presumably, democracies (and aristocracies) are considered less lasting than monarchies by Hobbes.

Hobbes again emphasizes the difference in policy outcomes in a monarchy from that in a democracy or aristocracy near the end of chapter 10, where he says the subjects are safer in the hands of a ruler who sees the people as his inheritance, since every man eagerly tries to preserve his own inheritance (DC, 10, par. 18). Hence, even though a monarch by definition cannot be bound by any law because he is the source of law, Hobbes still expounded on his duties. Indeed, Hobbes observed that in a democracy or aristocracy, only the individuals who voted for a breach in natural law actually sin, not the government as a whole. But in a monarchy, the monarch himself sins as well as the government, because the civil and natural will are combined in him (DC, 7, par. 14). It would appear that Hobbes thought the monarch would be more apt to observe his duty because he could not hide behind others or in some other way abdicate responsibility for his actions: "Now as the safety of the People dictates a Law by which Princes know their *duty* so doth it also teach them an art how to procure themselves a benefit; for the power of the Citizens, is the power of the City, that is to say, his that bears the chief rule in any state" (DC, 13, par. 2).

Those who have acquired dominion want their subjects to be strong in body and mind so that they may serve better. Therefore rulers should provide subjects not only with the means to live but also with whatever it takes to grow strong. If they did not do this, they would be acting against themselves (DC, 13, par. 4). This argument, that the power of the sovereign is only as great as the power of his citizens, was given less emphasis in the corresponding chapter in *Leviathan*. We are instead given an extensive argument that the duty of the sovereign consists mainly in his keeping and maintaining power and teaching his subjects why it is good for him to do so. However, the argument remains intact, even if overshadowed. In addition, the interest of the people as Hobbes now defines it in *Leviathan* (as the maintenance of safety and the provision for the pursuit of happiness within the confines set by the needs of the sovereign) still coincides with that of the sovereign. The fact that Hobbes assigns to sovereigns a duty to educate their citizens to the reasons for obedience implies that people can be made to see that obedience is in their best interests even if it means putting up with autocratic rule. Indeed, most of *Leviathan* is devoted to pointing out this coincidence of interests to both rulers and ruled.

Leviathan

Chapter 19 of *Leviathan*, "Of the Severall Kinds of Commonwealth by Institution, and of Succession to the Soveraign Power," corresponds to chapter 10 of *De Cive*. Again, Hobbes says that in a monarchy public and private interests are identical for the sovereign. A prosperous country makes a prosperous king, whereas an ambitious man in a democracy or aristocracy may profit more from giving bad advice or committing treachery or sedition than from working for the common good (L, 19, par. 4). From this it can be extrapolated that the king may be as corrupt as any man in a public assembly and still rule well. Even a corrupt king will want his government to be well liked and his country to be prosperous, the more to enrich himself. A demagogue or a jealous aristocrat may compromise that health if in the short run he can convince his peers that he is right, thus gaining the crucial popularity.

Likewise, a monarch can get good advice, while an assembly is subject to demagoguery (L, 19, par. 5). Assemblies are susceptible to envy or to private interest, and this corruption may lead to civil war. An assembly can be seduced by orators and can be filled with individuals who become "one an others Flatterers, serve one anothers Covetousnesse and Ambition by turnes." For "to accuse, requires lesse Eloquence . . . than to excuse; and condemnation, than absolution more resembles Justice" (L, 19, par. 8). Hobbes devotes chapter 25 to counsel, and it is here that we see the intimate link in Hobbes's mind between oratory or rhetoric and the evils of democracy. Exhortations and dehortations rely on tugging at the common passions using the tools of oratory. They are directed toward the private good of the counselor, not the counseled. They are used only in speaking to a multitude, because if they were directed toward an individual the speaker could be interrupted and questioned, whereas the multitude can do nothing but listen, according to Hobbes. To avoid this type of bad counsel, the counselor's ends should be the same as the sovereign's, and this may happen only in a monarchy. The speaker should avoid obscure or inflammatory speech and be well versed in his subject. Advice is best received from one advisor at a time, not from groups, in which people tend to end up agreeing with one another. In an assembly of many, there will be those with private interests whose passionate and eloquent oratory can set the commonwealth on fire under the pretense of counseling it (L, 25, par. 15). Private consultation is better than what is to be had in an assembly, where the discourse will dazzle, not inform.

The damage done by demagogues is not to be confused with what achievements the people are capable of if left on their own or if guided by the appropriate leader. Indeed, Hobbes wrote that the best counsel on domestic issues comes from the people affected, who know best what they need and "ought therefore, when they demand nothing in derogation of the essentiall Rights of Soveraignty, to be diligently taken notice of" (L, 30, par. 27).[5]

One might see in Hobbes's treatment of rhetoric the same linkages between democratic oratory and bad policy as are made by Thucydides in his characterizations and speeches of Pericles, Cleon, and Alcibiades. As we have seen, Cleon and Alcibiades, interested first and foremost in their own *private* advantages, often used their oratory not to lead the people toward prudent policies but to incite their anger against a rival or to endorse a policy that would lead to the personal glory of the speaker. Simply winning the debate was glorifying in and of itself, and very often to the disadvantage of the state. Such was Cleon's policy to exterminate the Mytilenaeans or Alcibiades' exhortation to conquer Sicily. But Hobbes's position on rhetoric cannot deal with a Pericles, or for that matter a Diodotus. For

Hobbes, orators were always dangerous to the regime and to the maintenance of the laws, and demagoguery was the natural out-growth of a democratic government: "Men that have a strong opinion of their own wisdome in matter of government, are disposed to Ambition. Because without publique Employment in counsell or magistracy, the honour of their wisdome is lost. And therefore Eloquent speakers are enclined to Ambition; for Eloquence seemeth wisdome, both to themselves and others" (L, 11, par. 13).

Eloquence and flattery make men trust such leaders. The vain-glory of popular men encourages people to violate laws, through a hope of intimidating the sovereign power (L, 27, par. 15; 11, par. 16). The popularity of a powerful subject is dangerous to the monarch because the people, by the flattery and the reputation of some dem-agogue, can be lured from obedience to the laws. This situation is even more dangerous in a popular government because the army might easily believe its interests are the same as the people's and be-come accomplices in the destruction of the government (L, 29, par. 20). Vainglorious men may seem to be of little consequence because they delight in egotistical fantasies but never act courageously, since this would expose their inadequacies (L, 11, par. 11). But Hobbes thought such men were really the most dangerous. They may be in-clined to rashness and prone to run away in danger, but they will return to incite the people with their seditious oratory whenever the danger is not immediate. It is in their words, in their very coward-liness of relying mainly on oratory, that they are most dangerous.

The minds of the common people are like clean slates, Hobbes wrote (L, 30, par. 6). They should be taught to love their own form of government, not to adhere to popular men who flatter and seduce them (L, 30, par. 8). By educating his subjects, the sovereign can counteract the poisonous effects of ambitious individuals. In this way, Hobbes redeems the people, taking the burden of guilt from them and placing it on their leaders. The problem of the masses is their ignorance, not their stupidity. They can be used by those who know how to manipulate them, but only if they do not know better. The ultimate responsibility rests with the sovereign, who must pro-vide this form of education to his subjects. If used solely by the sov-ereign for his purposes, rhetoric seems to be redeemed. The people cannot or will not respond to dry scientific discourse, Hobbes says. Science must be filtered down to them through educational institutions such as universities and the pulpit, which can make it palatable. But even Hobbes, as we have seen, calls this "eloquence." It is not deliberative rhetoric but pretty language to sell what has already been decided.

Behemoth

A brief look at *Behemoth* reflects the view of regimes contained in Hobbes's philosophic works. Hobbes attributes the events of the English Civil War to hypocrisy and conceit (B, 167–68). Ambition and envy motivated parliament and others to quarrel with the king and with one another, which led to chaos. Hobbes portrayed the contending preachers as actors who used dramatic oratory to win over the people (B, 193). Many leaders of the sedition had read the histories of the ancient popular governments of the Greeks and Romans, in which kings were "hated and branded with the name of tyrants, and popular government (though no tyrant was ever so cruel as a popular assembly) passed by the name of liberty" (B, 193). The same thing had happened in England when, after the reign of Queen Elizabeth, ministers who would have the people believe that they were oppressed by both the Church and the king allied with democratic men who received these ministers into their counsels in order to change the government from monarchical to democratic (B, 196).

Hobbes described the Presbyterians and other anti-Catholic sects of his day as democratic because they promoted individual interpretation of the scripture. He argued that the Presbyterians became powerful, beginning in the reign of Queen Elizabeth, when local ministers led the people to dislike the Church government, the canons, and the common prayer book. They were helped by gentlemen who desired a popular government in the civil state as much as the ministers did in the Church. These gentlemen incited the people to favor democracy by their harangues in the parliament and their communication with the country folk suggesting that the monarchy was a tyranny that by rights could be overthrown (B, 192). After Queen Elizabeth's reign, men with democratic sympathies allied more openly with these ministers, with the design of changing the state from a monarchy to a popular government (B, 196). When the Scots invaded the country to deliver a petition of rights to the king, the English parliament, instead of giving the king money to fight them, spent their time airing grievances and tended to side with the Scots, who shared their ambition of bringing down the monarchy. The king then raised an army from the nobility and the gentry. The nobility had caused trouble for the king in parliament. But now it helped him because it did not want popular government. The nobility wanted instead a mixed monarchy, with power divided among the king, the House of Lords, and the House of Commons (B, 202–5). The Scots proceeded to capture a few towns, and the king made a treaty with them agreeing to call a parliament on 3 November 1640, at which all problems would be discussed. But the English parliament, almost wholly Presbyterian, were sympathetic to the Scots. Supporters of the king and some of his ministers were imprisoned or forced to flee (B, 208). This was the beginning of the conflict between the king and parliament that Hobbes depicts as being a one-way attack on the king.

Reflecting on all these things, Hobbes wrote that such "a multitude of ignorant people" would naturally elect bad representatives. The common people are ignorant of their duty to the public because they never think about anything besides their particular interests. They follow their immediate leaders, either preachers or powerful men, the way soldiers follow their captains. The miseries of the civil war would not make them any wiser, since they would quickly forget them (B, 212). The rules of just and unjust had been put forth so that even a fool could understand them. The real problem, Hobbes explained, is that many could not read, and others had no leisure to learn. Those with leisure spend it on private business or pleasures. Thus, he continued, it is impossible for the multitude to learn its duty except from the pulpit on Sundays and on public holidays, but these occasions have been used instead to subvert their interests. The universities would have to teach the correct doctrine in order to spread it downward to the people, but instead they are like "Trojan horses" to the state, infecting the learned with their seditious doctrine.

Summary

In his preface and introduction to the translation of Thucydides, Hobbes makes it clear that he identifies with Thucydides on several levels. He shares what he perceives as Thucydides' strong critique of democracy and endorsement of monarchy. Hobbes writes that Thucydides showed the damaging effects of a democracy's inconstancy and the fear it generates in its various leaders. Hobbes notes that ambition among both democratic and oligarchic leaders damaged policy, as demagogues used deceptive rhetoric to win the people and oligarchs competed for power. In this way, he asserts the private and selfish nature of all actors' motives and the effect that assumption has on different forms of government.

In *De Cive* Hobbes undertakes to educate his readers about why obedience to the sovereign is always in their self-interest, even if the sovereign's rule is autocratic. Hobbes shows that democratic and aristocratic decision making is unwieldy compared with monarchical rule. He points out that ambition, in democracies or aristocracies, leads to a prevalence of orators plying their self-interested rhetoric and competing with each other for popularity. But self-interest leads a monarch to avoid enriching other contenders for power, to seek wise advice in private, and to punish fewer people more purposefully. The quality of deliberation increases as the number of deliberators decreases because there will be less competition and therefore more advice in the common interest.

Although given less space, the argument that the power of the sovereign is only as great as the power of his citizens remains an important part of the thesis in *Leviathan*. It is clear that a king may be as corrupt as anyone in a public assembly, but it is the nature of having more than one man compete for power that leads to conflict and confusion in decision making. In addition, in *Leviathan* we are given more extensively the argument that the duty of the sovereign consists in keeping and maintaining power and teaching his subjects why it is good for him to do so.

Thus Hobbes writes about what naturally happens among men when they are left to make decisions in groups, small or large. Human nature being constant, all men put private advancement ahead of civic duties. The advantage of a monarchy, then, does not lie in the hope that the monarch is genuinely public-spirited; the advantage lies in the hope that a monarch's interests and those of his subjects mesh not only legalistically (because the citizens have made a contract to subject their wills to those of their sovereign) or because the citizens are given the narrow choice between order and anarchy but also because the monarch knows that only if his kingdom is prosperous and happy can he be prosperous and happy. If he burdens his kingdom with too many taxes or oppresses his subjects to the point where they are seditious and unproductive, he hurts not only them but also himself.

When attributed to many men in an assembly, the same goal that motivates the monarch, namely, getting and retaining power, does not automatically mesh with the interests of the state in general. Many men compete with each other for power, and in their competition great harm may come to the state. Their private interests *rightly conceived* will lead to factions, sedition, constant confusion, bad policy, and finally civil war. It is this natural effect, and not the evil nature of human beings, that makes democracies unstable. Hobbes believes that monarchy is the best form of government not because the monarch is so wise but because cold calculations of self-interest will lead him to produce policy that is in general consistently to the benefit of all. This theory, while hopeful in tone, destroys the notion of statesmanship while supposedly making statesmanlike behavior more likely. It assumes that the desired outcome is better insured by enlightened self-interest than by altruism, which is too rare.

THUCYDIDES

There is a tension throughout the *History* between the Athenian people and their leaders, and between demagoguery and good policy. It reveals itself in actors' deeds, their speeches, and in what they do not say as well as what they do say. We must look at several personalities and episodes in the *History* in order to understand Thucydides' opinion on regimes, or more accurately his opinion on what makes regimes either good or bad. It would seem that for Thucydides, contrary to Hobbes, political success has more to do with the individual leader's personality and skill than with the type of regime he rules. This emphasis on character is a great difference between the Thucydidean and the realist approaches.

Pericles and the People

Pericles was chief strategist or president of the board of generals for more than thirty years, and at the beginning of the Peloponnesian War he was the most popular man in Athens. He was also the chief advocate of the war. As Thucydides puts it, "[B]eing the most powerful man of his time and the leader of the state, he was opposed to the Lacedaemonians in all things, and would not let the Athenians make concessions, but kept urging them on to the war" (1.127.3).

According to Thucydides, Athens at this time was a democracy in name; in reality "government ruled by its foremost citizen" (2.65.10). This statement made Hobbes and others think that Thucydides saw Pericles' government as a temporary monarchy superimposed on the Athenian democracy. However, Pericles' power was far from absolute. To avoid the people's suspicion, Pericles promised to donate his land to the state in the event that the Spartan king Archidamus fail to seize it out of friendship when he invaded Attica (2.13). Indeed, Pericles had to go to great lengths to motivate the Athenians and to maintain their support for his war policy. The rhetoric of the Funeral Oration shows us how Pericles motivated the people by convincing them that the city could fulfill their innermost needs. This, as later leaders—namely, Cleon and Alcibiades—proved, required a very skilled and dedicated orator indeed, one who commanded overwhelming popularity and whose motivations were, in Thucydides' estimation, selfless and patriotic. The Funeral Oration points, more than any other speech, to Pericles' reliance on Athenian love of glory to motivate the people. His ideal is for all individuals to be swallowed up in the common pursuit of glory. The soldiers who have died get scant attention. He gives the ancestors and former Athenian exploits little time, preferring to speak of Athens as it is, at the pinnacle of achievement. Athens is a democracy in that all men are treated equally regarding the settlement of their private disputes, but it is a meritocracy when it comes to public honors. It is merit, not class, that distinguishes Athenians. In private matters Athenians strive not to give offense, and in their public life they fearfully obey all laws, especially those laws for helping the needy and those unwritten laws whose transgression means disgrace (2.37).

Pericles praises Athenian culture, indicating how unlike the Spartans Athenians are. They find time for relaxation and entertainment. Their homes reveal their good taste and elegance. They enjoy a cosmopolitan life-style (2.38). Athens is superior to Sparta in training for warfare: her excellence stems not so much from training as from their native courage (2.39). Athenians are lovers of beauty and wisdom but without extravagance or weakness. They find it a disgrace not to care about public matters, and, according to Pericles, "Athenians decide public questions for [themselves] or at least endeavour to arrive at a sound understanding of them, in the belief that it is not debate that is a hindrance to action, but rather not to be instructed by debate before the time comes for action" (2.40.2–3). They are kind, generous, liberal. Their city is "the school of Hellas." They shall be a wonder today but also in the future, needing no Homer to sing their praises: they will build by their actions their own monuments of good to their friends and of evil to their enemies. This is the city for which these soldiers paid the highest price (2.41–42). Such is the devotion Pericles wishes to foster in all Athenians that he wants them to think of themselves as "lovers" of Athens (2.43). He calls them as individuals to find a greatness, just as the eulogized soldiers did, that most of them would otherwise never know. This is the type of rhetoric that won for Pericles such a devoted following that Athens might be termed a government by its foremost citizen instead of a democracy. It was a rhetoric designed to enthrall and to bolster the Athenians while at the same time instilling in them high-minded feelings and goals. While he lived, Pericles continued to make great efforts to persuade the people in order to "rule" them. In his third speech, Pericles noted the fickle character of the Athenian people. The plague had fallen on Athens and the people in their suffering had turned on him. He attempted to defend himself against their charges and to chastise them for not standing firm, placing on them the responsibility for past decisions and forcing them to live up to their title of democracy: "For my part, I stand where I stood before, and do not recede from my position; but it is you who have changed. For it has happened, now that you are suffering, that you repent of the consent you gave me when you were still unscathed, and in your infirmity of purpose my advice now appears to you wrong" (2.61.2).

Pericles tells the people that the reason for their change of heart is their shortsightedness. They feel their present hardships but cannot see the advantages to come. But being citizens of a great city, reared with customs corresponding to its greatness, they should bear everything and protect their great name (2.61.3–4). In this way, Pericles attempts to revive the motivation of personal and public glory in prior speeches. He tells them why they should not be so depressed: Athens holds "absolute mastery" of the seas through the possession of its great navy. The Athenians' houses and fields, which they abandoned in order to crowd within the city walls, are nothing compared with this asset—they can be easily restored as long as Athens retains her true source of power (2.62.3). Pericles reminds them that they are fighting not only for their own freedom but also against the wrath of the empire that would descend on Athens if it were to lose its "tyranny." He once more appeals to their love of Athens's greatness. Those who aspire to greatness (rule over others) have always been hated in their own time, he reminds them, but they are remembered forever:

> The memory of this greatness, even should we now at last give way a little—for it is the nature of all things to decay as well as to grow—will be left to posterity forever, how that we of all Hellenes held sway over the greatest number of Hellenes, in the greatest wars held out against our foes whether united or single, and inhabited a city that was the richest in all things and the greatest. (2.64.3–4)

Taking Pericles' political advice, the Athenians sent no more envoys to Sparta. But their anger at Pericles did not die until they had fined him, proving again that Pericles' power was far from absolute. Not long afterward, however, "as is the way with the multitude," they reelected him general, entrusting him again with the war policy (2.65.4).

It is at this point that we find Thucydides' early "eulogy" of Pericles, his evaluation of the man and his importance. The Athenians' failure after the death of Pericles, he says, was due to their inability to follow the moderate Periclean strategy of defending the homeland and not embarking on any new foreign conquests. Instead, he continues, "they were led by private ambitions and private greed to adopt policies which proved injurious both as to themselves and their allies; for these policies, so long as they were successful, merely brought honour or profit to individual citizens, but when they failed proved detrimental to the state in the conduct of the war" (2.65.7–8).

Pericles could lead the people instead of being led by them. According to Thucydides, this was because the people recognized his standing and ability, and because he had proved himself incorruptible. Because of his stature and reputation, he did not have to resort to lying to them. When he thought they were too arrogant he would put fear in their hearts; when they were too afraid, as they were during the plague, he would remind them of their greatness. This is why Thucydides could say that Athens under Pericles was a democracy in name but gradually became a government ruled by its foremost citizen in reality (2.65.10). It was not that Pericles was virtually a monarch or tyrant but that his popularity eliminated all competitors. He was so popular that he overcame his setbacks and kept the volatile demos in line most of the time. He had to use skillfully the tactics of a democratic politician to obtain and retain the great power he had. But, by implication, no future Athenian leader was able to command such popularity and power. Those who followed Pericles gave in to the whims of the multitude:

> But the successors of Pericles, being more on an equality with one another and yet striving each to be first, were ready to surrender to the people even the conduct of public affairs to suit their whims. And from this, since it happened in a great and imperial state, there resulted many blunders, especially the Sicilian expedition, which was not so much an error of judgment, when we consider the enemy they went against, as of management; for those who were responsible for it, instead of taking additional measures for the proper support of the first troops which were sent out, gave themselves over to personal intrigues for the sake of gaining the popular leadership and consequently not only conducted the military operations with less rigour, but also brought about, for the first time, civil discord at home. (2.65.11–12)

Tragically, Thucydides observes, the Athenians were so well prepared to win the war that they didn't lose it until they became victims of their own "private quarrels." Thus, at the time he made it, Pericles had abundant grounds for his claim that the Athenians could easily win if they would simply fight the war at hand and not become involved in other adventures until victory (2.65.13).

Michael Palmer has given us the basis of Periclean motivation: that glory is the greatest good for the individual and that the means to the greatest glory for the individual is the greatest devotion to the common good. Noting that Pericles does not even mention the names of the soldiers he is eulogizing in his Funeral Oration, Palmer asks if one can really win immortal glory from dying in battle. Especially in a city like Athens, would not some men want more glory than others? To have an equal amount of glory is to have no glory at all. Should a Cleon or an Alcibiades be persuaded by Pericles' argument? Can the private and the public good truly coincide as Pericles says they can? Perhaps, but only with a leader such as Pericles to define the public good and persuade the people of its value.[6]

From this vantage point, Pericles begins to look a little less responsible and moderate than he did at first. Because he based Athenian motivation for the war primarily on glory, a strategy admittedly well fitted to Athenian nature, Athens needed a Pericles to keep demagoguery at bay and to restrain the natural urges of the people. How many leaders could get the Athenians to combine such an inspiring message with restraint? With him gone, what was to keep men less talented but more ambitious from exploiting the demos for their own ends? As we will see, after Pericles' death glory remained the goal for both Athenian leaders and the people as a whole, and this goal became more and more destructive.

Cleon and Diodotus

The next leader who had the greatest influence in Athens for a time was the demagogue and war-hawk Cleon, whose first important appearance is in the debate about what to do with the rebellious Mytilenaeans. As we have seen, it is on "the impulse of anger" that the Athenians initially decide to pass the death sentence on Mytilene. However, the next day brings "repentance" of the cruelty of the decree, and the people call for a second debate. In this debate both Cleon and Diodotus lie to their audience to persuade them. Ironically, the one who lies best, and truly does so for the Athenians' good, wins.

Cleon, speaking first, begins by criticizing the democracy, the very institution that has rewarded him for his considerable skill as an orator. Democracy, he says, is incompetent to govern other cities. The Athenians have forgotten that their empire is a despotism (something Pericles had also said); they want to treat their allies the way they treat one another. They forget that their allies' obedience is due to Athenian strength, not goodwill (3.37). He then attacks Diodotus by insinuating that anyone who would try to persuade the Athenians to quell their anger must have been bribed by the Mytilenaeans. But, he says, in the final analysis it is the Athenians themselves who are to be blamed for requiring these "contests" of orators. They are swayed by hearsay, style, novelty:

> It is your wont to be spectators of words and hearers of deeds, forming your judgment of future enterprises according as able speakers represent them to be feasible, but as regards accomplished facts, not counting what has been done more credible, because you have seen it, than

what you have heard, you are swayed in judgment by those who have made an eloquent invective. (3.38.4–6)

Cleon states that the people are "in thrall to the pleasures of the ear," wishing to be orators themselves and, if not that, to appear wise in their applause for one speaker or another. The irony of his rhetoric is that, at the time, it was Cleon more than anyone else who was concerned with his own political interests and power and who used his speech primarily for that purpose.

To rescue the Athenians from their own inconstancy, Cleon will show that "Mytilene has done [them] more injury than any single state" (3.39.2). As we know, he argues that Mytilene is guilty of aggression, not of the more understandable rebellion, since it is an independent ally of Athens. He takes advantage of the Athenians' immediate wrath by telling them that justice is best served when anger is hot, and he capitalizes on their inclination to be persuaded by calculating arguments, that is, on their need to be sophisticated.

It is Cleon's strategy first to point out the weakness of democracy (making them question their toughness), thus shaming his audience into giving him a serious hearing. Next he casts suspicion on his opponent to discredit him, making him appear unpatriotic at best and foolish at worst. Finally his argument primarily concerns cold, hard, Athenian interest. Cleon's speech seems tailor-made to convince the citizen who does not want to seem a member of the unsophisticated and inconstant democratic mass Cleon has just described.

Diodotus, speaking next, follows Cleon's pattern by first chastising his opponent. He criticizes him for trying to stifle debate. It is this type of attitude, he argues, that makes for haste and passion instead of calm deliberation, "of which the one is wont to keep company with folly, the other with an undisciplined and shallow mind. As for words, whoever contends that they are not to be guides of our actions is either dull of wit or has some private interest" (3.42.2). He disparages Cleon's intentions for accusing him of being bribed, but he essentially makes the same charges against Cleon. Such accusations, he says, deprive the city of advice because potential advisors fear the wrath of the people if their advice is thought unworthy. Diodotus outlines how orators should be treated in order to assure the Athenians' good counsel. It would be best if citizens like Cleon, who try to make gains by accusing others, were not eloquent, so that the people would not be misled by them. The good citizen "ought to show himself a better speaker" not by attacking his opponents but by giving a good argument. The city should be impartial to its advisors, neither rewarding those who give good advice nor punishing or showing any disrespect for those whose advice is not taken. Ideally, all should be allowed to speak without disgrace, whether or not their counsel is good or bad, successful or unsuccessful (3.42). But this is not done, with the result of great disadvantage to the state. This, we must assume, is why Diodotus himself has engaged in the practice of disparaging his opponent.

Diodotus seems to be assuming that the demos is capable of intelligent policy decisions if given a variety of policies from which to choose. But this seems only to be the case when there are no unscrupulous leaders such as Cleon around to cloud the debate with their trickery. On top of this, Diodotus complains, even if all speakers were allowed to speak freely and without fear, the demos would still assign full responsibility for policy, good or bad, to those speakers. This abdicating of responsibility on the part of the people leads to rash decisions (3.42.5).

Diodotus himself thinks that under the circumstances he must fool the demos into accepting his good policy. Diodotus tells the people that the best counselor has to lie, because the people automatically suspect that all advice is privately motivated. Athens, he says, is the only state in which a man cannot do a good deed for his country without deceiving it (3.43.3). He indicates that this has not always been so but that it has now become an insidious problem in Athenian politics: "And *it has come to such a pass* that good advice frankly given is regarded with just as much suspicion as the bad, and that, in consequence, a speaker who wants to carry the most dangerous measures must resort to deceit in order to win the people to his views, precisely as the man whose proposals are good must lie in order to be believed" (3.43.2–3).[7] As we have seen, Diodotus sways the audience with highly sophisticated arguments, employing the Athenian thesis in order to win a moderate judgment for the Mytilenaeans. And he does so even while it is clear he does not believe in the truth or practical utility of the Athenian thesis.

When all has been said, Cleon and Diodotus both accuse the Athenian demos of being inconstant, easily swayed, and changeable, unlike Pericles, who reminded the people of their greatness in order to edify and motivate them. Both have felt the need to emphasize (at least openly) expedience over considerations of justice, although Diodotus has emphasized it more than Cleon. Diodotus's strategy is particularly interesting. Lacking the stature of a Pericles and confronted with an anti-Pericles in Cleon, Diodotus has to manipulate and deceive the people in order to induce them to observe prudent moderation. Diodotus's argument combines reason with appeals to the irrational: "toughness" and sophistication. It is an admirable performance, a feat of statesmanship under conditions that Pericles did not have to face: competition with a wily, more hotheaded opponent.

Considering the decline in democratic politics Athens experienced, would government by king, by tyrant, or by the few be more capable of sound action than the democracy? I hope to show that Thucydides does not think so. Because he depicts Pericles and Diodotus as capable of leadership marked by rational moderation, he affirms that even in a democracy leaders will *not* always be controlled by their private passions to please the multitude. Some leaders can be guided by reason and moderation. The problem with democracy seems to be its dependence on men like Pericles and on the frequent intervention of speakers such as Diodotus to maintain a reasonable and moderate policy. But, as we will see, another type of government is not necessarily a better alternative.

Cleon and Nicias

Another interesting case of the democracy's interaction with its leaders revolved around the final taking of Sphacteria. As we have seen, after the Athenians rejected the Spartans' peace offer, they languished in their siege of Pylos. The Spartans on the island had managed to circumvent the Athenian blockade, and so the operation was bogging down. The Athenians knew that if the Spartans had still not surrendered by winter, the siege would have to be abandoned because there would be no way to get enough supplies to the soldiers. The Athenians were also troubled by the fact that the Spartans had not come to them with any new peace offers. They began to resent Cleon for his role in rejecting peace when it was available (4.27). Cleon, trying to save face, accused the messengers from Pylos of lying about the conditions there. The messengers then suggested that commissioners be sent to verify their reports, and Cleon was chosen by the Athenians to go check the situation for himself. Knowing that he would bring back the same news and thus lose credibility, Cleon urged the Athenians that if they believed the messengers' reports, they ought to send a fleet to bring the soldiers back home. He taunted his political enemy, Nicias, saying that he would already have taken the island by force if he were in charge (4.27.4–5). In this episode, Cleon shows his true character.

The people began to clamor for Cleon to attempt to take the island, if he thought it was so easy. Nicias, who had command, became tired of Cleon's boasts and was aware of the public sentiment, so he decided to resign in Cleon's favor. At first, Cleon thought Nicias was bluffing and so said he was eager to go. But when he realized Nicias was serious, he tried to back down. Understanding the politics of the situation quite well, the crowd caught on to Cleon's game and urged him more eagerly to go (4.28.3). Seeing no other way out, Cleon accepted, even claiming that he could do it without using any Athenian soldiers and in only twenty days. The Athenians laughed at this vain talk, and sensible men thought that either they would gain a victory at Pylos or they would lose Cleon altogether, which was what they preferred (4.28.5).

Strangely enough, Cleon succeeded in fulfilling his grandiose promises, although much of it was due to a freak fire on the island that solved the problem of visibility and allowed his partner, Demosthenes, to carry out and win a rare land battle (4.29–38). Thucydides clearly did not think that Cleon's military expertise was the most important factor in the victory. Much like the Athenians' initial victory on Pylos, he made it look like a product more of luck than of skill.

The entire decision-making process seems more a game than serious deliberation. Unlike the Mytilenaean Debate, there seems to have been no deliberation whatsoever about what option was best for Athens's strategic interests. Instead, a game of dare and double dare took place between two politicians who were enemies, with one effectively accusing the other of not being man enough to make a bold attack, and the other, exasperated, likewise daring his opponent to prove that he was as tough as he claimed to be. Cleon tried to persuade the demos that Nicias was a weakling in order to earn political points with the people. Nicias seemed likewise compelled to preserve his reputation by abdicating command and goading Cleon, along with the people, into fulfilling his promises. Nicias's decision to abdicate responsibility was irresponsible and self-serving. This contest was egged on by the Athenians, who, considering the leadership they had to work with, were not behaving unreasonably. When even "sensible men" decided to endorse Cleon's plan on the basis of a personal dislike of him, actually preferring that he lose, it is clear that the democratic process in this case had become a sham due to the grasping, self-interested efforts of these two politicians.

Nicias and Alcibiades

Alcibiades was the next demagogue to assert himself forcefully on Athenian war policy. His was a truly spectacular career of manipulation, both of his countrymen and of foreigners. But, as we will see, Thucydides was not completely critical of this most interesting character. Instead, he developed this multifaceted man at more length than any other person in the *History,* allowing us to see what was good and bad about Alcibiades' leadership.

Head of the war party after Cleon's death, Alcibiades first appears in a significant way after the first peace treaty with Sparta has been signed (the Peace of Nicias) and the Athenian-Spartan alliance has been concluded (5.16–22). Angry because the Spartans had not consulted him when negotiating for an alliance with Athens, Alcibiades spoke against that alliance and supported one with Argos instead (5.43). Later, the Spartans sent an embassy to Athens to discuss their alliance with Boeotia in an attempt to keep the irritated Athenians from concluding a treaty with Argos. They prepared to speak to the senate, saying that they had full powers to settle all the issues set forth between themselves and Athens. But Alcibiades, fearing that the commons would reject his plans to ally with Argos if they heard this plea from the Spartans, improvised a "trick" to make the Spartans look untrustworthy in the assembly. He told them he would give them back Pylos if they did not mention in the assembly what they had in the senate—the fact that they had full diplomatic powers to settle outstanding disputes. In response, the Spartans did not tell the assembly the extent of their diplomatic powers, and the assembly, upon discovering that the Spartans had not been candid with them, rejected their advice and clamored for an alliance with Argos, urged on by Alcibiades (5.44–45). Alcibiades must have used this trick because he assumed that otherwise, with all the information they needed, the democracy would make a reasonable decision. Indeed, the next day, Nicias advised the assembly that they should still seek friendship with the Spartans (5.46.2). Agreeing with this moderating advice, the assembly sent envoys, including Nicias himself, to urge the Spartans to drop the alliance they had made with Boeotia earlier. The envoys told the Spartans that if they would not drop their alliance with Boeotia, Athens would ally with Argos and its confederates. The Spartans refused to give up Boeotia:

> but the oaths they renewed on Nicias' request; for he was afraid that he would return with nothing accomplished and be exposed to calumny, as indeed happened, since he was generally regarded as having been responsible for the treaty with the Lacedaemonians. On his return, when the Athenians heard that nothing had been done at Lacedaemon, they flew into a rage, and thinking they had been wronged, when Alcibiades brought in the Argives and their allies, who chanced to be present, they made an alliance. (5.46.5)

Alcibiades had successfully used the Athenian demos for his own purposes. In this case, his manipulation was indirect. He had made the Spartans look like liars, allowing the hostility already present toward them to vent itself for his benefit. He (not Nicias) became known as the author of the new alliance with Argos. This outcome fulfilled or superseded his initial wish to be included in negotiating the peace treaty with Sparta, the treaty attributed to the skill of his rival, Nicias. He had brought Athens one step closer to breaking that treaty and thus one step closer to outright war with the Spartans, and he had fulfilled his personal need to be the center of attention. Alcibiades' main motive for all this was to avenge the insult perpetrated against him by Nicias and others, who had left him out of the original peace negotiations with Sparta, probably (among other reasons) because of his young age. Alcibiades was obviously selfish and egotistical in his political dealings.

Later, Alcibiades was chosen along with Nicias and Lamachus to lead the expedition to Sicily. Tempted by the love of glory and the offer of their kindred Egestians to provide the money for the war, the Athenians voted to send sixty ships to fight the Syracusans and their allies. Nicias, chosen for the voyage against his will, advised the Athenians against committing themselves to anything other than a token display of power. Like Diodotus, he said he would not speak contrary to his judgment simply to gain honor, even though he would "consider that he is quite as good a citizen who takes some forethought for his life and property; for such an one would, for his own sake, be most desirous that the affairs of the city should prosper" (6.9.2). Alcibiades told the Athenians that the treaty with Sparta had been concluded under pressure and could easily be broken if Spartan interests changed. Some of Sparta's allies did not even subscribe to the treaty and were either at open war with Athens or in a posture of war. To go to Sicily now would be too much of a risk and would have Athens "reach out after another empire" before they had secured their own empire (6.10.5).

Nicias implied that Alcibiades was advocating the expedition for his own glory and profit and that he was too young to command or even to give advice (6.12). Thucydides soon repeats Nicias's criticism, thereby confirming it: Alcibiades spoke against Nicias's advice because of their general political disagreement and because Nicias had just insulted him. He wanted to command the expedition to gain wealth and glory. The young commander's extravagance—indulging beyond his means and keeping horses—soon enough made the majority fear him. Still, Thucydides' evaluation of Alcibiades is ambivalent. He does not wholly disapprove of Alcibiades, as he does of Cleon. This seems to be because Alcibiades was genuinely talented as a general, whereas Cleon, according to Thucydides, was wholly inept. Thucydides states that the blame for Athens's failure in the war ultimately rested with the people, not with Alcibiades or Nicias. The people, after giving Alcibiades an important position, became afraid that he had tyrannical ambitions. They chose to reject the one person who could have produced success:

> And it was precisely this sort of thing that most of all later destroyed the Athenian state. For the masses, afraid of the greatness of his lawless and sensual self-indulgence in his manner of living, as also of his designs as revealed in every single intrigue in which he was involved, became hostile to him on the ground that he was aiming at a tyranny; and, though publicly he managed the affairs of the war most excellently, in his private life every man had been offended at his practices, and so entrusting the city to other hands after no long time they brought it to ruin. (6.15.4)

Thucydides thinks that Alcibiades might have been good for Athens even though he was motivated by self-interest. Yet it was this very selfishness, absent in Pericles, that made them reject Alcibiades in the end. And this rejection, despite Thucydides' ambivalence about Alcibiades' character, seems reasonable for all but the most bold and enlightened (not to say clairvoyant) democracy.

Alcibiades tried to defend his self-centeredness. He claimed that what Nicias would call his "reaching for glory" or "extravagance" were things that brought fame to himself, his ancestors, and the city. People who disliked him were simply jealous of his success (6.16.3). He pointed out that he had given the Hellenes an impression of Athens's greatness through his chariot racing at Olympia. Alcibiades claimed not that he did these things primarily in order to benefit the state but only that the state had indeed profited by his pursuit of glory. His greatness had made the city great. The city basked in his glory.

This is a glaring inversion of Pericles' invitation in the Funeral Oration for individual Athenians to obtain glory by basking in the city's fame and exploits. Alcibiades, satisfied with Pericles' appeal, seems to answer Pericles when he claims, "Nor is it unfair, either, that one who has a high opinion of himself should refuse to be on an equality with others, since he who fares ill finds no one to be an equal participator in his evil plight" (6.16.4).

Great men, he continued, are in their own lifetime an offense to their fellow citizens, most of all to their equals but also to others. But when they die, everyone wants to be associated with them (6.16.6). Such lasting fame is Alcibiades' ambition. Pericles, it will be remembered, said that great *cities* would always be resented at the moment but that the glory for their deeds would long outlast the odium. Once again, Alcibiades shows himself unable to accept the glory of the city over his own glory. Thucydides points out that the demos did not avail itself of the talents of this man, whose main concern was his own aggrandizement. But he does not go so far as to say the demos was unreasonable or stupid not to have taken advantage of Alcibiades. It seems Alcibiades' only fault was not selling himself well enough to the people; this failure had to do with Alcibiades' character, and in that way Alcibiades is also to blame.

Heeding Alcibiades, the Athenians became more eager for the expedition than before. Seeing that his old, honest argument would not work with the Athenians, Nicias decided to frighten them away from the expedition in a second speech. He told them of the great numbers of men and materiel they would have to send and the huge expense that awaited them if the expedition was to be a success (6.20–23). But instead of backing off from such an exertion, the Athenians took his advice, dazzled by the grandiosity of the scheme. Those who opposed it kept quiet, fearing to seem unpatriotic. Nicias's plan to frighten them backfired. Even his attempt to be dishonest and therefore to manipulate them into being sensible failed (6.24; 6.26). Nicias was not as eloquent as Diodotus and not as popular as Pericles. And, most importantly in this case, he did not understand what oratorical maneuvers would move the Athenian people.

But just when it seemed that everyone was behind the plan, the launching of the expedition was tainted by vandalism. All over the city, stone busts of Hermes were mutilated. The demos took this impiety very seriously both as a possible omen against the expedition and as part of a conspiracy to overthrow the democracy (6.27). Of course, Alcibiades had many enemies, and they took this opportunity to cast a shadow of blame on him. Those most jealous of him accused him of plotting against the democracy, the proof being the aristocratic character of his personal habits. Alcibiades pleaded to be tried immediately on these charges, instead of being sent on the expedition with suspicion hanging over him. But his enemies thought that his popularity with the army and people was so high that if he was charged immediately he would easily be acquitted. And so they told him to go, meanwhile plotting to bring worse charges against him in his absence (6.29).

Thus, this grandiose expedition began in an air of political turmoil and rivalry in which competing private interests had more influence than any concern for the common good. Nicias had implied that his (in hindsight good) advice was privately motivated, because public prosperity is also a private concern. This is a sentiment more in line with the Diodotean notion that, rightly conceived, a speaker's private interests do coincide with the common good. In contrast, Alcibiades attempted to identify his personal aggrandizement with the good of the city, saying the city should obtain its glory from his own glory. Alcibiades' rhetorical strategy was as ineffective as that of Nicias in the long run, since it made the Athenians overly suspicious of him.

Given the riskiness of the expedition, no doubt Nicias's original advice to leave Sicily alone was the best because of its caution and honesty. It made sense to finish up one war completely before embarking on another. The demos, however, was initially more impressed with Alcibiades' attempt to make his personal largess into a public treasure than with Nicias's admission that the public concerns were also his private concerns. But as quickly as it had accepted Alcibiades' policy, the demos turned on him, thereby endangering the expedition from the start. It was the people's fear of tyranny, Thucydides says, that led them to cripple their own cause. When he eulogized Pericles, Thucydides said that the leaders who came after him were unable to attain the stature of their great predecessor. It was because Cleon, Nicias, and Alcibiades were all lacking something that Pericles had—character, intelligence, eloquence—that Athenian politics began its slow descent toward disintegration.

Only after Alcibiades had begun operations did word come from Athens that he must go back to answer charges concerning the Hermae. The Athenians were becoming more and more afraid of a tyranny such as that of the old Athenian tyrant Peisistratus (6.53.3; 6.60–61). As if to refute that fear, Thucydides stops here to tell an odd story that ends up being a defense of the tyrants and consequently a critique of the Athenians' alarm at Alcibiades' growing power. He attempts to rehabilitate the reputation of Peisistratus, a tyrant who he says was generally not oppressive: "And indeed the Peisistratidae carried the practice of virtue and discretion to a very high degree, considering that they were tyrants. . . . In other respects the city itself enjoyed the laws before established, except in so far that the tyrants took precaution that one of their own family should always be in office" (6.54.5–6).

What follows this explicit praise of the tyrannies is a digression on the story of Harmodius and Aristogeiton, who, as popular belief had it, killed the tyrant Hippias, Peisistratus's son. This digression is important because it exposes the popular opinion of the two heroes as false, undermining one of the main "myths" supporting the view of the tyrants as oppressive. According to popular opinion, Harmodius and Aristogeiton attacked Hippias because they were lovers of their city and of freedom and he was a ruthless tyrant like his father. However, Thucydides points out that the real reason for their attack was a jealous lovers' squabble. Thucydides thus questions popular understanding of the supposed heroes and the tyrants.

Coupled with his personal comment on the Athenian tyrants, that they practiced virtue and discretion to a high degree, it is likely that Thucydides thought the tyrants were better equipped to think about the public good than were most democratic leaders during the current war. Thucydides' archaeology depicts the early tyrants as making caution the first aim of their policy because of their concern for their own safety and prosperity. The discussion of the tyrants in the archaeology and that in the story of Harmodius and Aristogeiton largely agree, but here the tyrants are depicted more favorably as public spirited, not oppressive. They practiced thrift and did not overburden the people with taxes. They preserved most of the laws of the previous democracy, except those that would have threatened their rule.

Placed as it is, as an interjection between the persecution of Alcibiades and his escape from Athenian justice, Thucydides' digression carries an important message. Given this background on the tyranny, perhaps having an Alcibiades in charge would have been worth risking the democracy. However, one is invited to compare Alcibiades' potential "tyranny" to that of the tyrants of old. Would he be as conservative? Would he understand, as they did, that limiting one's desires increases one's power and longevity? Given what Thucydides has shown us of Alcibiades' character, the answer would have to be negative. Perhaps the demos's fear of encouraging an Alcibiadean tyranny was not so ill-founded, since Thucydides emphatically shows us that the characters and virtues of the tyrants and Alcibiades are very different indeed. It is because of this story of Harmodius and Aristogeiton that Hobbes says that Thucydides "best approved of the regal government" (HT, "Life," par. 5). But it is more likely that Thucydides best approved of any leader who could be effective under the particular circumstances he faced; ultimately, that effectiveness had a lot to do with a certain prudence that Alcibiades lacked.

Meanwhile, with their hatred of him growing, the Athenians send for Alcibiades in order to confront him with the accumulated charges. Alcibiades goes willingly enough but disappears with his friends upon landing at Thurii. The Athenians pass a death sentence on him in his absence (6.61). Alcibiades next appears as a betrayer of Athens. He reveals to the Messinians an Athenian plan to take Messine (6.74). Then he arrives in Sparta and tries to persuade the Spartans to send help to Syracuse, to carry on the war more openly at home, and to fortify Deceleia in Attica. He excuses his treachery by claiming the Athenians had wronged him and that he was actually being a patriot by helping the Spartans to recover the true Athens, an endeavor that had gone astray (6.89–92). With this, the Spartans embraced the ideas of aiding the Sicilians and fortifying Decelea.

After Alcibiades' advice took effect, the war in Sicily quickly deteriorated for the Athenians. The Spartan commander Gylippus arrived with thirty ships to fight the Athenians. The Corinthians also arrived and urged the Syracusans on. The Athenians rejected Gylippus's offer to let them withdraw peacefully, and the stage was set for one of the most tragic military disasters in history. Low on water, firewood, and other supplies, and having his wall cut off by the Syracusans' counterwall, Nicias decided that he must ask Athens for reinforcements. He wrote a letter to the Athenians so that the messengers would not say whatever would please the crowd (7.8.2). In it Nicias told the Athenians that the besiegers had in fact become the besieged. The navy was crippled and the Athenian forces were vulnerable to attack by land and sea. They were low on supplies and many of their slaves, soldiers, and allies were deserting. He concluded:

> I could have written you things more pleasant than these, but certainly not more useful, if you are to have full knowledge of the situation here before deciding upon your course; and, besides, knowing as I do your tempers—that you do indeed prefer to hear what is most pleasant, but afterwards find fault if the results are in any respect disappointing—I have thought it safer to reveal the truth. (7.14.4)

Nicias tells them that they must either recall the fleet immediately or send another force equal to the first. Also, he asks to be replaced, because he is ailing from a kidney infection (7.15). But apparently respecting his candor, the Athenians did not let Nicias resign and sent Demosthenes and Eurymedon to help him.

But after Demosthenes arrived, Athens suffered still another reverse.[8] At this point, Demosthenes advocated returning to Athens. It would be better, he said, to fight the Peloponnesian fortifications in Attica than to squander more wealth in Sicily (7.47.3). But now Nicias did not want to go. He had information that soon the

Syracusans would run short of money and also that a pro-Athenian party in Syracuse was going to revolt. But actually, Thucydides writes, Nicias was afraid of what the Athenians would say if he left without them voting for it. They would be turned against him by the first clever speaker, and his soldiers returning would change their story and say he had taken bribes to leave (to take the blame off themselves). He knew the Athenian temperament, Thucydides says, and preferred a just death with the enemy rather than an unjust death at the hands of his countrymen (7.48). Just as Nicias had abdicated responsibility for taking Pylos to Cleon in order to save his reputation, he was prepared to risk the lives of an entire army in order to save his posterity. Thucydides writes, "For those who would vote on their case would not be men who would form their judgments from seeing the facts with their own eyes, as they themselves had seen them, and not from listening to the harsh criticisms of others; on the contrary, whatever calumnies any clever speaker might utter, by these the Athenians would be persuaded" (7.48.3–4).

Demosthenes strongly objected to not seeking safer territory to wait for the Athenians' decision. But a Spartan-like hesitation came over Nicias and the rest (7.49.4). When the Spartan commander Gylippus came back with troops from Sicily and the Peloponnesus, the Athenians finally decided to leave. But an eclipse of the moon stopped all, including Nicias, who was "somewhat too much given to divination and the like. . . . " He listened to his soldiers, who were superstitious, and would not even discuss moving until the prescribed twenty-seven days had passed (7.50.4). This strange and sad victory of superstition over reason was the death knell of the expedition. After a series of disastrous sea battles and a humiliating and bloody retreat, the Athenians suffered utter defeat. Eventually, Nicias, Demosthenes, and their respective troops were captured, after many had already been slaughtered. Both commanders were executed, and those soldiers who had survived the battle were either killed or sold into slavery, or they died of exposure during their long captivity.

Nicias risked his life, the lives of all his soldiers, and Athenian prestige because he preferred to go down in a fight rather than risk being charged with treason and sentenced to an ignominious death at home. Nicias's equivocation led not only to total defeat in Sicily but also indirectly to the eventual conquest of Athens by the Peloponnesians. It was self-love that caused Nicias to act.[9] In the end, Nicias could not summon the courage to act boldly in the face of the possible (even probable) persecution of the people.

Nicias's case is troubling because he is not a bad man. Thucydides eulogizes him, saying that he "of all the Hellenes of my time, least deserved to meet with such a calamity, because of his course of life that had been wholly regulated in accordance with virtue" (7.86.5). The virtue or *arete* of this passage is, as Leo Strauss translates, "virtue as understood by old established custom," or "law-bred" virtue.[10] This virtue or concern with piety was a Spartan characteristic, and as Strauss points out, it is not the unqualified *arete* that Thucydides uses to describe Brasidas (4.81.2), the tyrants (6.54.5), or Antiphon (8.68.1).[11] By showing us how dangerous was Nicias's Spartan-like concern for piety given the unusual circumstances that confronted him, Thucydides is indirectly criticizing his inflexibility, not piety itself. Why does Thucydides seem more critical of Nicias's final self-destructive act than those of the Plataeans or Melians? Probably because it is an act imbued mainly with self-love, not love of country, love of glory, or love of the gods, all of which Thucydides thought better qualities in leadership than narrow self-interest.

It should be clear by now that, contrary to the claims in his speech advising against the expedition to Sicily, Nicias's personal interests when put to the test did not coincide with the public good. Thucydides earlier in the *History* has said that Nicias desired peace in order to preserve his good reputation. Nicias felt that peace removed him as far from chance as possible, so that he could "preserve his good luck to the end" (5.16). At the beginning of the deliberation over the expedition, it seemed plausible that Nicias's private concerns might be compatible with his public duties. But by the time he decided to stay at Syracuse instead of leave for Athens, it can no longer be said that his private interests were identical to the true public good.

Nicias's overconcern for piety was matched by concern for his reputation, and these concerns of course intermingled. Alcibiades had left Athens in order to save his life. In Nicias's case it was not fear of death at the hands of the demos that caused him to do the state such a disservice but fear of disgrace. Still, ironically, the two men had much in common: their main concern was for themselves, not for the state, and in trying to preserve their own interests in the face of a real or imagined hostile democracy, they damaged the common good of Athens. But neither is wholly condemned by Thucydides because each had virtues of which he approves. Unfortunately for Athens, they lacked others.

Breakdown of Leadership

When the Athenians at home heard the terrible news, they were—as predicted—angry at the orators who had advocated the expedition, "as though they had not voted for it themselves" (8.1). They became afraid that the Sicilian forces would now join the Peloponnesians in attacking them at home. But they decided to fight to the last and began to prepare accordingly a belated dose of pragmatism that Thucydides describes: "In the panic of the moment they were ready, as is the way with a democracy, to observe discipline in everything" (8.1.4). Finally realizing where their leaders had led them, they decided, temporarily, to act independently.

The Spartans now escalated their attacks on Athens, while Alcibiades continued to help them by instigating revolts in pro-Athenian cities. But as soon as the Spartans began to suspect his loyalty, Alcibiades went to a Spartan ally, the Persian Tissaphernes, and advised him to pay the Peloponnesian army less money more irregularly. This was the beginning of Alcibiades' "intrigues," in which he tried to play one great power against another. By this time, he was trying to show the Athenians that he had Tissaphernes' confidence and could influence him on their behalf, because he wanted to be recalled to Athens. He tried to convince the notables among the Athenian armament at Samos to establish an oligarchy at Athens in exchange for his return (8.47.2). If they could bring this about, he would produce an alliance with Tissaphernes. Upon hearing this, the officers at Samos embraced the idea of subverting the democracy. Thucydides writes:

> [T]he influential citizens, who are apt to bear the heaviest burdens, had great hopes for themselves personally that they would get the government into their own hands and prevail over the enemy as well. So they went to Samos and set about combining in a conspiracy such men as were suitable, at the same time saying openly to the people that the King would be a friend to them and would furnish money if Alcibiades were restored and they were not ruled by a democracy. (8.48.1–2)

But the general stationed at Samos, Phrynichus, did not approve of Alcibiades' proposals. Thucydides says that Phrynichus rightly thought Alcibiades wanted to change his country's institutions simply in order to be recalled, no matter what turmoil it caused (8.48.4–5). However, the members of the conspiracy accepted Alcibiades' proposition and sent an embassy to Athens to ask for Alcibiades' restoration. Upon being told by the envoys that Alcibiades' plan was the only way to save the state, the demos pragmatically gave way, promising that soon it would change the government back to a democracy. But when the Athenians asked for the alliance Alcibiades had promised, they were disappointed. Alcibiades, really unsure of whether Tissaphernes wanted a closer relationship with Athens at that point, pretended to represent the king and purposefully asked for so many concessions from Athens that the Athenians eventually left without any agreement (8.56.3–5).

The island of Samos became the site of a contending government for the control of Athens. Alcibiades refused to join the oligarchical faction at Samos; the members of the faction decided to have nothing further to do with him because, ironically, they thought he was not the right leader for an oligarchy (8.58.4). By the time the faction's envoys arrived at Athens, they found that their friends in the city were already actively promoting insurrection and assassinating democratic leaders. They called for Pericles' democratic official and jury pay to be abolished and for a government of the Five Thousand (unpaid, and therefore composed of the rich only) to be established (8.67.3). Thucydides tells us that this government, when established, was meant to make the people think they were being represented by five thousand, but in reality it did not exist. Actually, the authors of the revolution would govern alone. This small group began a reign of terror in Athens. The people, thinking that there *were* possibly five thousand conspirators promoting this terror, kept their mouths shut. Thus divided, the commons could not oppose the oligarchs in charge, though there were only a few. They were, Thucydides writes, "unable to find out the facts."

Thucydides evaluates these oligarchical conspirators. Peisander, he says, appeared to most to be the chief agent of the overturning of democratic rule in Athens. But it was Antiphon, "a man inferior to none of the Athenians of his own day in force of character and one who had proved himself most able both to formulate a plan and to set forth his conclusions in speech," who was the mastermind of the plan. Antiphon was looked down upon by the multitude "on account of his reputation for cleverness." He stayed out of public contests because of this but was the best man available for giving others advice on how to behave in court or before the assembly. Eventually, when the oligarchs were overthrown, he made the best defense of himself of "all men up to my time" (8.68). Here, Thucydides praises these and other subverters of democracy, Phrynichus and Theramenes being the other two mentioned specifically. Phrynichus showed himself most zealous for the oligarchy, while Theramenes is praised for his "no small capacity in speech or in judgment" (8.68.4). Thucydides writes:

> Consequently, conducted as it was by many able men, the plot not unnaturally succeeded, even though it was an arduous task; for it was difficult, after the lapse of almost one hundred years since the tyrants had been overthrown, to deprive of their liberty the Athenian people, who had been, not only not subject to anyone else, but for more than half of that period had themselves been accustomed to rule over others. (8.68.4)

Thucydides' praise for these men must be weighed against his praise of the more moderate government to follow (8.97.2–3), his assessment of all Athenian politicians after Pericles (2.65.11–12), and his general distaste for extremism displayed in his account of the Corcyraean Civil War. He is praising some of their personal qualities, not their objectives, just as he has praised certain characteristics of Nicias. It is likely that Thucydides did not think highly of their tactics, which included assassination, repression, and terrorism. As Arnold W. Gomme points out, "[T]he whole passage in some degree looks forward to the summation . . . that it needed men of the highest quality to overthrow the well-established democracy of Athens."[12]

The oligarchs ruled the city by force. Alcibiades was not recalled, since the conspirators were unsure of his loyalty and probably feared his skill with the people. The oligarchs had been against the war from the start, and they now had the power to act upon their desires. They sent messengers to Agis to say they wanted peace and thought he might be more accommodating because the democracy was no longer in charge (8.70.2). But when they heard of the Athenian oligarchical revolution and its exaggerated cruelties, the Athenian detachment at Samos did an ideological about-face as quickly as the Samians, swearing oaths that Samos's constitution would be democratic from now on and that they would oppose the repressive Athenian government while continuing to fight the Peloponnesians (8.72–73).

The soldiers decided to operate a second government from Samos, using their fleet (which was most of what was left of the Athenian naval power) to get tribute from Athens's subject cities. Now they wanted to guarantee Alcibiades his security and recall him in exchange for getting Tissaphernes to help them (8.76). Alcibiades took their offer and immediately went about deceiving both sides, magnifying his influence with Tissaphernes and the king's concern for the Athenian cause. When he was elected general of the forces at Samos, he stopped the soldiers from sailing against Athens in their anger: if he were eventually to be recalled to Athens, he wanted an Athens to be recalled to. Thus, Thucydides comments ironically, Alcibiades' own interest and the public interest were for that moment the same. For once Alcibiades' leadership became moderate, at least in effect if not in intention: "And Alcibiades seems then in an eminent degree, and more than anyone else, to have benefited the state. . . . And in that critical moment no other man would have been able to restrain the crowd, but he stopped them from sailing, and reproaching those who were on their own private account angry at the envoys, he caused them to desist" (8.86.4–6).

Alcibiades sent word to the oligarchs that they should keep fighting the Peloponnesians and he would try to reconcile them with the Athenians at Samos. Sensing the trend toward democracy, the oligarchs urged that the government of the Five Thousand be truly instituted and claimed that a fairer constitution was needed. Thucydides remarks that there emerged a race among the various oligarchs as to which would first become leader of the commons. His assessment of their motivations agrees with that given much earlier in his eulogy of Pericles. They were less leaders than led, willing to compromise their principles to maintain power and to save their skins:

[I]n their personal ambitions most of them eagerly pursued the sort of methods by which an oligarchy formed out of a democracy is most sure to come to ruin; for all demand forthwith, not equality, but each that he shall be quite the first himself; whereas under a democracy an election is held and every man acquiesces more readily in the result because he feels that those whom he owes his defeat are not his equals. . . . Each one, therefore, strove to become the foremost leader of the people himself. (8.89.3)

The extreme oligarchs at Athens such as Peisander and Antiphon now felt endangered and asked Sparta for peace on almost any terms: they would rather be subject to Sparta than be victims of the coming democracy. Their desperate machinations got some of them killed and others arrested. For awhile, the Athenians came close to civil war in their confusion as to who was in charge (8.92.9). Thucydides twice refers to the Athenians as being in a "state of sedition" (95.2; 96.2). The hoplites were about to attack the oligarchs but were persuaded by them that the safety of the city was more important than immediate restoration of democracy (8.93).

Despite all this, even after the Athenians had lost Euboea and were afraid of a direct Peloponnesian attack on Peiraeus, they managed to cooperate to wage war. They manned twenty ships and called a meeting of the assembly. At this assembly, the Athenians established the government of the Five Thousand and decided on the oligarchical elements of no pay for jury duty or for any other political office and citizenship for men who could outfit themselves as hoplites only (8.97). This was the government of Theramenes to which Thucydides gave (with a qualification) his highest praise: "And during the first period the Athenians appear to have enjoyed the best government they ever had, at least in my time; for there was a moderate blending of the few and the many, and this it was that first caused the state to recover from the wretched plight into which it had fallen" (8.97.2–3).

That Thucydides calls this regime the best Athens ever had in his time suggests that he ranked this government above that of Pericles but not necessarily above the government of the tyrants of the Athenian past. If he did not have reservations about giving the mixed regime his highest praise, he would not have felt the need to say "at least in my time." His analysis of the Peisistratid tyrants combined with this comment means that Thucydides might have favored the tyrants' benevolent rule. The mixed regime was the best government possible, given the material it had to work with—the Athenian character at that time and the Athenians' now established tradition of democracy. It was a government that attempted to substitute institutional stability for reliance on the character of leaders when it was clear there was no stability to be had. It combined the Spartan values of the oligarchs with the Athenian values of the demos. This moderate regime, which lasted only two months,[13] was to lead Athens to the short resurgence in fighting spirit and strength with which Thucydides ends his *History*.

Summary

We must ask why Thucydides seems to deal out praise and criticism in equal measure to so many Athenian leaders. Why does he seem as impressed at times with the talents and virtue of men like Alcibiades and the Athenian oligarchs as he is with Pericles himself, even though they were not as civic minded? Does he really have a preference for one type of regime?

Pericles' power came from his unique ability to lead the demos, which in turn came from the people's conviction that Pericles was a man of rare unselfish character who truly had their interests at heart. After Pericles, when there was no one great enough to unify the state, competition among rivals often ruined policy. Then, the only type of regime that could overcome the narrow self-interest of all individuals was the mixed regime. The regime was stabilized through institutional mechanisms, in which a broadly based but not completely open ruling group exercised power in important offices. This regime, although Thucydides does not mention it, was more an "academic experiment" than an effective, working government.[14] Its greatest impetus was fear of defeat at the hands of Sparta.

The norm for Athens was the clash between the interests of the state and of the individual, and the *History* shows us how this affected Athens's foreign policy. Competing leaders' interests in their own advancement led them to fear the judgment of the demos. Even Pericles tried to avoid suspicion by promising to donate his property to the state should Archidamus not destroy it when invading Attica. Generally, however, Pericles was more impervious to this hazard than any other Athenian leader. Diodotus, unlike Pericles, had to lie and attack his opponent's character, so that his advice would not appear to be privately motivated. Alcibiades abandoned Athens at Thurii because he feared the worst if he were to be delivered to the assembly. After being sent on the Sicilian Expedition, Nicias seemed compelled by his fear of the demos's judgment. When their position became precarious, the Athenian oligarchs attempted to negotiate with Sparta because they did not want to be victims of the renewed democracy.

The Athenian assembly was portrayed as emotional, easily swayed, and quick to reverse previous decisions. This changeableness of the assembly was, however, largely produced and manipulated by demagogues using deceptive rhetoric for their own purposes. Thucydides emphasized the power of oratory as the chief tool the Athenian leaders used to sway the multitude, even though it had a mixed record of success. The credulity of the demos that Cleon criticized lended itself well to such manipulations, but it also lent itself to miscarriages of the speakers' intentions when the people took their advice all too seriously. Cleon's oratory, designed only to strengthen his stature and to diminish that of Nicias, caused the people to goad him into actually doing something at Sphacteria. Nicias's strategy of frightening the assembly with enormous figures of what it would take to succeed in the Sicilian Expedition brought about opposite results. But the Athenian assembly, despite these handicaps, was capable of making informed, moderating decisions, not only under Pericles but also when listening to an orator such as Diodotus, even though his rhetoric had to match the baseness of his opponent to be persuasive. The Athenians could, in a crisis, realize supreme necessity and cooperate in order to keep on fighting. They even could surrender their democracy in order to save the state, realizing the danger of chaos inherent in democracies during extreme crises. This was truly an act of patriotic sacrifice.

With the probable exception of Diodotus, all those who used deceptive or manipulative rhetoric had their own narrowly defined interests in mind. While Diodotus admitted that a speaker must lie about his private motivations in order to convince the people, it is not clear what private motivations Diodotus could have had, other than a recognition that what was best for the state in this case was what was best for him as an individual. Pericles did not have to deceive the people at all. But Cleon, Alcibiades, Nicias, and the oligarchs, while portrayed as good *or* bad men, clearly acted primarily on their private self-interests, not concern for the public welfare, and the people could sense it.

This emphasis on private motivation reflects Thucydides' generally pessimistic view of human nature. But given the right combination of character, intelligence, and ability, a leader or leaders could be master of any type of government. Thus Thucydides' praise of the democratic leader Pericles is perfectly consistent with his praise for the mixed regime and the tyrants of old. His admiration for the few also serves this point. He praised the oligarchical subverters of democracy, such as Peisander and Antiphon, when it came to their personal virtues. But he also pointed out the cruelty and infighting among these "better" men. Eventually, they were driven by private ambition to the point of destroying themselves, unable to truly identify their interests with the common good.

The main difference between men such as Peisander and Antiphon and men such as Pericles and the tyrants is character. Because of their relatively selfish characters, the dynamic of numbers came into play as oligarch competed with oligarch and as individuals did what it took to advance themselves relative to their competitors. This dynamic made an oligarchy not much better than a democracy when it came to consistency and ability to weather storms.

Clearly, Thucydides focuses quite a bit of attention on the moral and intellectual character of leaders. But despite the fact that Thucydides concentrated on the value of individuals, not regimes, have we come closer to a Thucydidean position on regimes? The mixed regime of Theramines represented the compromise between Athenian and Spartan values that Thucydides thought was desirable. Theoretically, it would have put an end to the ill effects of complete democracy: the dysfunctional interaction between the demos and its demagogues that led to bad policy. The moderating influence of the ruling class's desire for the status quo would have dampened the natural inclination of the people for innovation and adventure. But the size of the ruling body meant that it would not allow the state to ossify, since anyone who could afford to outfit himself as a hoplite could be a part of the government of the Five Thousand. These are the types of benefits Thucydides must have thought the mixed regime held in store, besides the obvious benefit of ending class-based strife. Thucydides thought more highly of this regime than he did of the Periclean regime. He praised Pericles because he was so extraordinarily talented as to make himself a virtual monarch, and even then he praised him not for his moderation but for his ability to handle a daring policy while not letting it get out of control. But Thucydides' evaluation of those who followed Pericles shows just how rare such talent is. A pure Athenian democracy had to count on the chance appearance of a Pericles, or even a Diodotus, if it was to hope for good leadership. With a mixed regime, Athens would not have to rely quite so much on luck. The tension between the few and the many, constitutionally fixed, might produce moderation.

Thucydides believed some men acted for reasons higher than base self-interest, but he presents them as exceptions to the rule. Still, he obviously believed that statesmanship—the ability of an individual to put the needs of the whole before his own—was the ideal for politicians. Great statesmen, such as Pericles and Diodotus, were especially gifted in character as well as in oratorical skills. Given the fact that the mixed regime of Theramines was mainly an "academic experiment" and that most of Athens's experience revolved around democracy and tyranny, the role of individual statesmen cannot be overemphasized. Great statesmanship remained the only real vehicle for moderation and prudence in Athenian foreign policy throughout virtually the entire recorded war.

A COMPARISON OF HOBBES AND THUCYDIDES ON LEADERSHIP AND REGIMES

There are two broad points on which the history of Thucydides and the philosophy of Hobbes seem to agree concerning leadership and regimes. First, both seem to agree that human nature is basically self-centered. However, Thucydides allows for nonselfish or virtuous action (as well as foolish and rash actions), even though it is the exception rather than the rule. He must do this to explain some of the greatest decisions of the Peloponnesian War and to evaluate the failure of others. This indicates that Thucydides has more of a normative focus; he evaluates individuals based on their characters as well as on their effectiveness, and the two are often shown to be related. Hobbes does not allow for exceptions to his view of human nature. Since the human material is constant, Hobbes's focus is on structure and is solely concerned with result. The variety of political actions is accounted for by what self-interest dictates in any particular situation. The only reason monarchs are more apt to rule reasonably is that, having no competitors, their interests and the interests of the people coincide.

Second, both Thucydides and Hobbes seem to agree on the general nature of democracies: they are inconstant and often ignorant. For Thucydides, however, this also is not an ironclad law. The Athenian democracy was capable of recognizing and submitting to a truly great leader: Pericles. The Mytilenaean episode proves that the people could recognize a well-fashioned argument, contrary to Hobbesian expectations. The fact that the democracy could decide well changes Thucydides' evaluation of the Athenians' errors. Thucydides' tone is one of chastisement when the democracy makes mistakes because he believes it is possible for the Athenians to do better. He places blame in both leaders and led because he can point to examples of good behavior for both. For Hobbes, democratic assemblies are always going to behave badly—they are compelled to do so by their natures and their situation. Thucydides' criticism of democracy is true criticism, while Hobbes's is utter rejection. Thucydides' work teaches us that what is needed is better leaders and a less excitable public. Thucydides will not absolve leaders and their followers from responsibility for their actions, because their actions are not determined simply by their situation.

Strauss has hypothesized that the "antithesis of fundamentally unjust vanity and fundamentally just fear of violent death is the basis of Hobbes's political philosophy."[15] That is, Hobbes believed vanity or pride to be the cause of conflict among men, and he believed that fear of death was the only passion that could override their vanity and make them cooperate. This antithesis led to Hobbes's preference for monarchies over democracies and aristocracies. Strauss thinks that Hobbes formed the connection between the vanity/fear and democracy/monarchy antitheses as early as his writing of the introduction to his translation of Thucydides, a conclusion with which I agree. Hobbes's conclusions about monarchy in his introduction to the translation are based on his criticism of the ambition or pride of individual leaders in Athenian democracy and oligarchy. It is not that monarchs are not ambitious; it is rather that their ambition does not have to compete with others' interests.[16]

As early as his translation of Thucydides' *History*, then, Hobbes held that "vanity is the most dangerous passion." Vanity blinds men to the realities of their situations. Competition can lead to sedition, not to mention politics driven by glory instead of the common good. Pride prevents men from giving good counsel, because they must not show their weakness (fear) to one another. Hence egoism, or self-interest, which is normally a rationalizing influence, is corrupted by pride in any arena in which competition with other men is necessary. But a man whose pride is not threatened can make policy in accordance with rational principles. Hobbes saw in Thucydides a host of examples supporting this thesis. Hobbes, as we have seen, thought Thucydides best approved of monarchy. The fact that he saw in Thucydides such a clear argument for monarchy is evidence that his ideas were already formed in the 1620s concerning his solution to social disorder, not that he derived these ideas *from* Thucydides. Indeed, it appears from the preceding analysis that Hobbes misread Thucydides or robbed him of his subtleties in many places.

Hobbes thought Thucydides proved that human nature is entirely uniform and determined. Hobbes interpreted the *History* as illustrating that people were motivated by self-centered, narrow passions: fear, honor, and profit. These passions led human reason. The passions that led individuals to ruin were pride or ambition and shortsighted interest. The passions that led them to unite to save themselves were fear and long-term self-interest. The ambition of the Athenian demagogues caused them to compete among each other, leading to the downfall of the state and the loss of the war. The only times in which ambition coincided with the welfare of Athens were when the city was ruled by one: either the tyrants or Pericles. The ambitions of the various factions in Corcyra and elsewhere made for the worst kind of bloodshed. There were two ways to counteract the negative effect of human pride: either by forcing men to unite due to a common threat or by turning the usually negative influence of ambition and interest into a positive influence by placing all power into the hands of one. The best possible regime was rule by one, in which the people had no chance of being manipulated by competing leaders and there would be no factions to increase the chances of civil war. Athens's troubles were due more to her regime than to human nature.

How did Hobbes deal with Thucydides' praise of the mixed government of the Five Thousand? This problem was no doubt partially assuaged by Thucydides' statement that this government was the best Athens had *in his time*. As has been noted, this would mean that the government of the Five Thousand was preferable even to Pericles' government but not necessarily better than that of the tyrants. But how could Hobbes agree as he does that "government mixed of the few and the many" was better than Pericles' regime? Schlatter gives us a possible and telling answer when he says that Hobbes interpreted the government of the Five Thousand as the creation by the people of a sovereign, unmixed regime. Hobbes translates the crucial passage: "The Athenians . . . called an Assembly . . . in which, having deposed the Four Hundred, they decreed the Sovereignty to the Five Thousand." Schlatter points out that Hobbes's use of the word *sovereignty* is unique among translators:

> But if the Five Thousand had the sovereignty . . . then according to Hobbes' later thinking the government was not mixed, but a simple aristocracy. In fact, the creation of the aristocracy of the Five Thousand by the Athenian people is a perfect illustration from the history of Hobbes' later description of how a true, unmixed, aristocratic government is instituted: the people come together and agree to give the sovereignty by majority vote to a particular group of men.[17]

This alone is enough to show that Hobbes's interpretation differed from Thucydides' meaning. If Hobbes did see the government of the Five Thousand as an unmixed aristocracy, then he could rank it second to the tyrannies as the best form of government Athens ever had, and he would of course still rank democracy last.

Hobbes distorts Thucydides' message in other ways. Hobbes thought that the *History* supported his utter disdain for rhetoric and its role in deliberation. And yet, although oratory was misused and the demos was manipulated by unscrupulous orators, it cannot be concluded from a careful evaluation of the *History* that oratory always had a negative influence or that it always led to defective decision making. Pericles' relatively successful use of speeches allowed him to lift his democratic rule to one that more resembled monarchy. Pericles' "monarchy" was built on his popularity—his ability to project his personal integrity through his speech. Hobbes could not have acknowledged this and maintained his opinion that democratic oratory is always divisive, narrowly self-interested, and therefore bad. To say that Thucydides showed his preference for monarchy partly by his praise for Pericles and also to say that Thucydides proves the universally detrimental character of democratic oratory is to contradict oneself. Hobbes did not recognize that Pericles held his so-called monarchy not by force but by persuasion. If Hobbes had recognized this he would not have been able to maintain his strict antithesis between democracy and monarchy. To further say what Thucydides said—that it was the special character of Pericles, his integrity and patriotism, that made him an uncontested democratic leader—would have struck a blow to Hobbes's thesis that all men are alike in their motivation and that the only way to obtain order is to impose upon them the correct kind of institutions. In short, Thucydides thought Pericles was successful because he was special. Hobbes says that Pericles was successful because he was uncontested, but he does not, and cannot, ask why.

Even though some have interpreted Pericles' speeches as indicating that he, too, was primarily motivated by self-interest—retaining power by flattering and cajoling the demos—Thucydides himself did not see Pericles that way. Thucydides believed Pericles was a unique leader capable of controlling the volatility of the demos and moderating its sometimes excessive enthusiasm. It is this aspect of Pericles (and Diodotus)—the possibility of a leader whose interests are raised to the common good by sheer integrity—that cannot be tolerated by the Hobbesian notion of universal selfishness in human nature. The idea of the great man is still alive, if threatened, in Thucydides; it is essentially dead in Hobbes. Hence, ironically, we find an optimism in the usually pessimistic Thucydides, while we find complete pessimism on this issue in Hobbes, who unlike Thucydides believed in the possibility of linear progress. Hobbes's progress hinges on imposing on men his form of education and the correct institutions to harness and use their basic self-centeredness. Thucydides did not have a conception of linear progress and hinged his hope on the impossibly poetic notion that occasionally a unique leader of genius and vision could for a time lift a nation to greatness, possibly helped along by Thucydides' own wisdom. There was no necessity for this and no way to make it happen—greatness was based on individuals, not institutions.

But for Hobbes, uniform mediocrity prevails. Any hope for greatness is sacrificed for order and longevity. Indeed, any man who considers himself great exhibits the dangerous delusion of pride and desire for preeminence. This is why there is no place for the statesman for Hobbes, whereas, regardless of what kind of government he preferred, Thucydides recognized the pivotal role of individuals in history. Personal character, eloquence, virtuosity—and their absence—could mean a great deal. When one believes, as Thucydides did, that wars and stasis will recur and governments will change and that the fortunes of the human race will decline as well as rise in cycles that no human intervention is capable of stemming, one is naturally concerned with individual excellence—or evil. Both depend largely on chance, the one thing above all else that Hobbes would banish from the political universe.

Here we come to the ultimate difference between Thucydides and Hobbes. Thucydides recognizes and respects statesmanship because, for him, there are standards that exist independent of power relationships, and these are more than the dictates of right reason in any given situation. He thought that power and justice could compromise (not coincide) in the practice of moderation and restraint. Practicing restraint or decency within the confines of what was possible, given the nature of foreign politics, was an ideal that existed independent of either Spartan or Athenian practice. For the Athenians to show reasoned restraint required a Pericles or a Diodotus. The Spartans did not have a corresponding statesman to move them away from their often damaging caution and reticence (although they had the military counterpart in Brasidas) or their cruelty. Statesmanship requires some form of restraint on a nation's impulses. It requires following a standard based not simply on what can be done but also on what should be done, given a realistic assessment of the circumstances.

If no standards exist independent of power relationships, then no statesmanship—no wisdom, prudence, or judgment—is really needed. The actor's power weighed against the power of his competitors dictates what will be done, according to reason. Hobbes relies on the ability of the sovereign to use reason correctly, in his enlightened self-interest. If he does this, the outcome may be a certain moderation, but not necessarily, since human character and intelligence do vary. In international relations, a leader's enlightened self-interest might demand preemptive elimination of all present and possible future enemies. In the domestic arena, it might call for the destruction of a particular class. As we have noted already, reason can easily become rationalization when put into practice. Hobbes hopes for enlightenment, for the possibility that his philosophy will be read and understood correctly. Thucydides' hope lies in the appearance of statesmanship, while Hobbes's hope rests in his ability to educate sovereigns and subjects. Whose expectations are more realistic?

Conclusion

Realism and the Thucydidean Alternative

As indicated in the Introduction, one major purpose of this book is to focus on the political philosophies of Thucydides and Hobbes in the hope that international relations theorists will be able to draw further insights and to shape directions in either agreeing or disagreeing with my argument. While much of this must be left for another occasion, perhaps I can indicate a few areas where the ideas expressed here have an impact on theoretical debates in the study of international relations.

I am sure it has become clear that I find Thucydides' approach to politics preferable to Hobbes's. I have tried to prove that Hobbes, despite his pessimistic assumptions about human nature, is not realistic. Is it realistic to assume that all people act predictably, that they are always guided strictly by self-interest, that all other motivations are a sham—or, if genuine, so rare that to take them into account is useless? This is the false sophistication Diodotus serves the Athenians to make them recoil from a massacre, and its use in political science today is being questioned in the area of rational choice theory, among others.[1] According to Thucydides, human beings are multifaceted, so that it becomes necessary, for example, to examine individual leaders and to listen seriously to their reasons for acting a certain way. Thucydides shows that there is a natural sociability in people that goes beyond vying for power and glory and, indeed, coexists with these urges, so that, as Jane Mansbridge would maintain, it is unrealistic not to take into account a certain amount of genuine altruism.

Does Hobbes's account of leadership deal with the impact of great individuals on history? Thucydides' *History* contains individuals with varying motivations, some altruistic, some self-interested, some acting on rage and revenge. In other words, it reflects reality. Because Thucydides' human nature is so much richer than Hobbes's, it follows that no particular type of regime will *of necessity* yield better results than another. Instead, good results depend largely on the quality of leadership. Our concern that a king will not become a good sovereign simply by listening to the Hobbesian argument results from our doubt that human nature conforms to Hobbes's specifications. If by realistic, then, we mean reflecting reality and being useful, the Thucydidean account of political behavior is more realistic.

Is Hobbes realistic in assuming that justice has no meaning outside of power relationships? Does this account for the way most people actually think and behave? If so, then to believe only in positive law makes perfect sense. But isn't it more realistic to recognize that some ethical norms exist (or are, at least, generally assumed to exist) independent of any particular actor or action and to accept them as valid even though they are often violated? Don't we assume something like this every time we make the argument that a particular law is wrong or is applied wrongly to a particular case, or when we react with revulsion at some international atrocity committed by superior force? Even if one is a true Machiavellian, it would be better to operate on the assumption that human beings generally recognize a certain common sense of morality, even if they do not always follow it. Only then would a Machiavellian be able to effectively manipulate his victims.

Of course, neither man can be said to fall neatly into one category or another of modern international relations theory, but Hobbes is clearly a forerunner of today's structuralists or systemic thinkers, political scientists who have often opposed or even ridiculed the classical realism of, for example, Martin Wight[2] as intuitive, unsystematic, and even poetic.[3] Thucydides, in contrast, might have had something of a "scientific" method in that he was concerned with the gathering of facts, not the perpetuating of the poetic or mythical style of past historians. But his findings demonstrate elegantly why

politics is essentially impervious to the permanent solutions proposed by Hobbes and his latter-day disciples in the social sciences.

Despite this, Thucydides, as often as Hobbes, has been dubbed
the father of international realism. As Michael Doyle recently put it,
"To most scholars in international politics, to think like a Realist is to
think as the philosophical historian Thucydides first thought."[4]
However, both realism and neorealism are more correctly thought of
as the offspring of Hobbes, whereas Thucydides presents us with an
alternative approach. In this conclusion, I will begin by arguing that
realism and neorealism, despite their differences, share the same
philosophical roots. This is not to deprecate the differences between
them but to show in what ways both types of realism can be contrasted with the Thucydidean approach. I will then turn to some recent attempts by international relations scholars to locate Thucydides
within their field. Finally, I will suggest that Thucydides has been
misunderstood and that he actually provides an interesting alternative approach to realism in the study of international politics.

THE PHILOSOPHIC ROOTS OF
REALISM AND NEOREALISM

The greatest division among realists today seems to be between
"classical realists" and "structural realists," or between realism and
neorealism. Classical realists supposedly identify with the tradition
of E. H. Carr, Hans Morgenthau, Raymond Aron, and Martin
Wight.[5] They explain states' actions through a theory about human
nature. As Morgenthau puts it, man is characterized by egoism and
animus dominandi, lust for power.[6] Human beings are driven by their
passions and assumed to be interested primarily in self-preservation
and enhancement of their power. Neorealists, in contrast, insist that
they differ from classical realists inasmuch as they have a theory that
excludes all factors except the structure of the international system
itself—how power is distributed within the system. They concentrate on questions of how different power distributions might affect
or determine the actions of states.[7]

But is the distinction between realism and neorealism entirely
valid?[8] Though there are differences, classical realists such as Morgenthau can be seen as having one foot in the traditionalist camp and
the other in the structuralist camp, peeking over the shoulders of
statesmen and rummaging through history while at the same time

coldly calculating power configurations. Classical realists attribute to the system much, if not all, of the motivation for those statesmen. A critique of neorealism that leads to further questions about distinguishing it from realism has come from those who find separating the system from its parts logically impossible. This critique questions the neorealist theory's logical validity and does not simply ask that more be added to the neorealist insight in order to make it more inclusive or useful. Ernst Haas argues that regardless of what structuralists might think, it is quite impossible to divorce the system from the heads of its constituent parts. "Do systems have needs," he writes, "and do the operation of systems serve functions *other than* the goals and purposes in the minds of the people who inhabit them?"[9] Even Morton Kaplan, a systems theorist once much derided by the classical school, admits this truth and even goes beyond it to hint at the possibility of human freedom to willfully change the system.[10] Others have argued both that structuralism has some logical flaws and that old-fashioned realism has, contrary to neorealist professions, a structural element.[11]

Neorealists might argue that even though they tend to talk about states as though they are "billiard balls," they too realize that it is statesmen who do the acting. They posit an anarchical world in which each state must fend for itself, faced with the "security dilemma."[12] Statesmen make decisions based on this world and this dilemma, and that is why statesmen, as individuals, do not have to be considered at all in neorealist analysis.

But in saying this neorealists are readmitting the realist's ideas on human nature. In order to forego consideration of individual wills, the neorealist theorist has to assume (in theory) a uniformity of human nature such that all statesmen will respond to particular situations in the same way (in accordance with the national interest, for example, to balance power with power). Given the anarchical world and given this assumption about human nature, neorealist theorists think they can predict what states will do, even if they know nothing of the character of the leaders in question. This is the most fundamental reason classical realism and neorealism are in some very important regards inseparable: the assumptions that classical realists make about statesmen are the very assumptions neorealists have to make about the "motivations" of states. These are Hobbesian assumptions.

The "Structuralism" of Thomas Hobbes

Hobbes's image of human nature conditioned his entire theory. His mechanism made it possible for him to depict men as uniformly egocentric individuals naturally at odds with one another.[13] This depiction, along with the assumption of rough equality among people (L, 13, para. 3), made a war of all against all the necessary result of the absence of government, necessitated a social contract as the basis of government, and made fear the prime motivator for individuals to enter into any such contract (L, 11, para. 2).[14] Hence, once he had thus defined the nature of men, it was easy for Hobbes to predict their behavior within different "structures," one being anarchy and the other being rule under a potent sovereign. The structure then could be thought of, for all practical purposes, as the only important factor to consider when determining what human behavior would be.[15] The transformation from the state of nature to civil society occurred because human beings in the state of nature led such a fearful, miserable life that they could not enjoy any of their rights in repose but were constantly threatened with extinction. Fear then prodded reason into accepting the social contract.

Hobbes points out that the state of international relations is a different matter. To be sure, it is a matter of a state of nature or a state of war.[16] But the level of insecurity within this condition differs from that of the individual. The passions that incline individuals to peace are fear of death, desire for things necessary to commodious living, and hope that by their industry they will attain them (L, 13, para. 14). But the creation of the state takes away the extreme fear that individuals have for other individuals in the state of nature. States also provide the protection necessary for commodious living and the industry to obtain it. The international state of nature therefore does not directly threaten most individuals. For these reasons, peace will not be such an urgent priority. International relations will continue to be driven by this security dilemma, each state striving for more power, which often means going to war.[17]

Hobbesian assumptions about human nature, when one considers them at the level of international relations, produce continued anarchy. Relative levels of power among states are the only factors to consider when analyzing relations among states. Given human nature, kings will always react to threats in the same manner. Notice that if Hobbes's vision of human nature is wrong, because the actions of humans are less predictable (many being more sociable, less selfish, or motivated more by an ideology or creed than by pure self-interest as he defines it), the structure would no longer have a determining character. Hobbes's prediction of continual war in international relations relies on the accuracy of his depiction of human nature. Notice also that under the right circumstances—for instance, complete environmental breakdown that would threaten individuals' security—states could conceivably agree to a social contract.

In the latter vein, as proof of realism's kinship with Hobbes, we find the realist John Herz able to make the argument *within the realist tradition* that since the dangers to states have changed dramatically with the onslaught of nuclear terror and environmental breakdown, states must reconsider giving up a portion of their sovereignty to some international body in order to protect the common good of survival.[18] Richard Ashley, in commenting on Herz's fearful predictions and exhortations, depicts Herz as proffering "Kantian themes of emergent holistic imperatives in a world becoming 'one.' " Whether or not Ashley is correct in invoking Kant in this context, he is wrong in suggesting that Herz is rejecting Hobbesian imagery with its "pervasive insecurity, recurring violence, generalized expectations of war, and self-animating strategic logic against strategic logic."[19] As Herz himself claims in response, he is working precisely *within* that imagery.[20]

Due to his similar assumptions about human nature, Morgenthau recognizes the powerful influence of anarchy and power relationships among states. Morgenthau tells us that there can be no international peace without a world state. Since the probability of such a world state materializing is slight, the (anarchical) world will continue to be plagued by conflict, which we must try to deal with in less dramatic ways.[21] He tells us that in anarchy "all nations do what they cannot help but do: protect their physical, political and cultural identity against encroachments from other nations."[22] Morgenthau's structural aspect and its source shine through when he writes, "[T]he concept of the national interest, then, contains two elements, one that is logically required and in that sense necessary, and one that is variable and determined by circumstances. . . . The former is, then, of necessity relatively permanent."[23] Although Morgenthau accuses Hobbes of "scientism" for believing that the problems of human nature can easily be overcome with the use of scientific reason,[24] Morgenthau on the whole accepts Hobbes's depiction of human nature. He simply rejects Hobbes's monumental faith in reason as the cure.

Waltz's mistaken reading of Morgenthau's theory, and his disconnection with the origins of his own, is shown clearly in the following statement: "Both Hobbes and Morgenthau see that conflict is in part situationally explained, but both believe that even were it not so, pride, lust, and the quest for glory would cause the war of all against all to continue indefinitely. Ultimately, conflict and war are rooted in human nature."[25] Waltz does not seem to realize that it is a particular human nature, which Hobbes and Morgenthau supply, that necessarily brings about predictable actions at the level of structure or system. Hobbesian men, like states, will react differently in anarchy than upon submitting to an overarching power. Their reactions, at all times, will uniformly be motivated by self-interest or self-preservation. It is because of this uniformity of interests that structure becomes the unit of analysis, that structure is able to determine what individuals, or states, will do. Depending on the given structure, individuals or states will interact differently. Morgenthau simply is aware of the interconnectedness of the realist theory of human nature and the realist theory of structure.

Perhaps it would be useful to attack this issue from another angle, from the realist and neorealist definition of theory. Contrary to the opinion of Waltz, who seems to think that neorealism embodies the only true theory of international relations, Morgenthau *does* put forth his own theory.[26] If theory, according to Waltz's definition, involves an artificial abstraction from the variety of human experience for the sake of isolating an important causal factor, then Morgenthau's theory is as much a theory as Waltz's. Indeed, Morgenthau sounds very much like Waltz when he claims, "It is no argument against the theory here presented that actual foreign policy does not or cannot live up to it."[27] He, too, believes theory is, and must be, a set of abstractions from reality. Morgenthau is simply focusing on a different actor: human beings instead of the structure of the international system. But it is not as simple as that, because Waltz must, as I have said, implicitly accept Morgenthau's abstract theoretic ideas of human nature in order for the theory to work.

Therefore, although there are differences of emphasis, methodology, and "elegance" or simplicity between realism and neorealism, it is wrong to juxtapose them as does Richard Ashley.[28] The essential philosophic underpinnings are the same for both, so that Herz is correct in rejecting Ashley's attempt to make two theories out of them.

Realism and Neorealism: Major Points of Agreement

It is worthwhile to briefly summarize the common properties of realism and neorealism more systematically than has already been done. Both assume, first of all, a uniformity of human nature. As in Hobbesian theory, although realists and neorealists do not think it always pertains, this human nature is ubiquitous enough to be used for prediction. In this way, human beings can be seen as predictable units, and one can focus on the conditions surrounding them: anarchy, or the state of nature. It is this theory of human nature that is projected on the state by realists. Human beings, as Morgenthau so aptly puts it, are driven by their passions—especially the passion of self-interest.[29] States in anarchy, likewise, must be expected to pursue their interests, which can be summed up in security and in the pursuit of power.[30] Human reason is driven by these passions; reason is instrumental and does not rule.

The emphasis that realists place upon the environment or circumstances in which actors are placed is a direct result of the uniformity that they posit in human nature. Upon this uniformity both theories stand or fall. Robert Gilpin must assume that an increase in physical power will of necessity induce the newly powerful to challenge other states or that other states will perceive it naturally as a threat in order to be able to put forth his theory of hegemonic war. Realists' assumptions about human nature and therefore the nature of states produce the conditions for structuralism.

As in Hobbesian theory, realist assumptions produce a kind of determinism, a problem that is not often addressed directly by realists or their critics, although it is often indirectly criticized by questioning any or all of the above tenets of realism.[31] Stanley Hoffmann long ago touched on the heart of the matter when he wrote, "[A]s a general theory, the realist analysis fails because it sees the world as a static field in which power relations reproduce themselves in timeless monotony."[32] The realists' scheme is one in which human beings have little or no free will, since they are driven by their passions to conform to the behavior that the given international system dictates. But if they lack free will and are expected to behave mechanistically in reaction to one another, there is little point in commenting on them or recommending one policy over another.[33]

This is the reason realism can purport to be a field of study that puts aside the issue of values, or is positivistic: actors in such a deterministic world cannot help but do "evil" and so do not really do evil. Guiltlessness on the part of individual leaders for their decisions is implied in the theory. And yet, contradicting their own determinism, as did Hobbes, realists seem to put forth their wisdom about how the world really works with the hope that someone will be educated by their studies. They warn that not conforming to their theory will be the demise of the negligent state.[34] As Haas notes, within systems theory "the 'right' relationship [of the units] must (ought to) conduce to some condition which is 'needed,' 'requisite,' 'optimal,' or 'natural.' "[35] Yet if the world is such as they describe, why is this information needed? What happens will happen. This was a problem that at least Hobbes never overcame: as long as men remained driven by their passions, indeed by their very physical composition, how could they ever attain the freedom of will to learn from Hobbes?

THE USE AND ABUSE OF THUCYDIDES

There is a proclivity among scholars to describe Thucydides and Hobbes as similar in their thinking, or as both being realists.[36] Gabriella Slomp has argued that Hobbes got much of the inspiration for his theory of the three greatest human passions, fear, glory, and interest, from Thucydides and that the two thinkers are therefore very similar.[37] According to Randall Collins, Thucydides revealed a world of "conflict and brute force."[38] And yet, all the attempts to identify Thucydides with one variant of realism or another, and even recent, thoughtful attempts to set the record straight within the scholarly discourse of international relations, have failed to do justice to the reality of Thucydides.[39]

Gilpin, a neorealist, has put forth a view of Thucydides' *History* as representing "the general law of the dynamics of international relations."[40] He believes the basic insight Thucydides offers us is that distributions of power and changes of that power determine the actions of states within the international system. A state's power increases when "economic, technological, and other changes" occur that make it superior (or potentially superior) to the current hegemon. Such a state is naturally a challenger and is viewed as a challenger of the hegemon for dominance. This situation will likely result in a hegemonic war. Gilpin terms this a "structural theory of war."[41]

Gilpin, however, acknowledges that this theory, which is represented by Thucydides' work, is useful but incomplete. It cannot predict specific actions of states or which way a war will go once it is started. It does not take into account the effect of perceptions or personality on the actions of states. Gilpin also raises some of the problems with his own view of Thucydides by observing in him elements of analysis that do not enter into the "theory of hegemonic war." For instance, he notes that Thucydides sometimes attributes the actions of states to human nature instead of to the determinative power dynamic of systems; he points out the importance that Thucydides places on the differing national characters of Athens and Sparta as causes of the two states' behavior; he tells us that what impelled Sparta to wage war was the belief or perception of Athens's growth of power, regardless of the reality of that growth.[42] Yet he still identifies Thucydides' understanding of the war he chronicled as basically that of a structural realist. As he declares, "Underlying this analysis and the originality of Thucydides' thought was his novel conception of classical Greece as constituting a system, the basic components of which were the great powers—Sparta and Athens."[43] Gilpin and others find their evidence for the above claim in a statement by Thucydides: "The truest explanation [for the war], although it has been the least often advanced, I believe to have been the growth of the Athenians to greatness, which brought fear to the Lacedaemonians (Spartans) and forced them to war" (1.23.6).[44]

It would be wrong to deny that Thucydides acknowledges underlying power changes as a factor in producing the war. But whether or not these changes are seen by him as determinative is the question. Daniel Garst begins a very useful rethinking of this neorealist reading of Thucydides when he presents an alternative: the actions of states have to be understood as grounded in the decisions of individuals taking part in a political process within certain social contexts that provide rules and norms.[45] Thucydides presents speeches as the precursors of action, and Garst argues that neorealists' narrow readings of Thucydides are exposed by ignoring these speeches or as seeing them as epiphenomenal. Indeed, Gilpin fairly ignores Thucydides' speeches. Considering that Gilpin seems to know the *History* well, the only explanation is that he believes that for Thucydides the speeches are simply reflections of necessity, that they are justifications or explanations of already determined action, or that they are epiphenomenal. But Garst rightly sees Thucydides' use of these speeches as quite important and in themselves at least partly determinative: "Though various sorts of 'laws' are invoked in the speeches put forward by individual actors, Thucydides makes no attempt to explain them in the course of his narration; indeed, he rarely puts forward explicit laws of his own."[46]

Hence, Garst must consider Thucydides' statement in 1.23.6 to be only part of the picture and must not read it to mean that changing power configurations between Athens and Sparta in and of themselves made war inevitable. But Garst does not follow through on the ramifications of the above statement that Thucydides presents theories about the laws of human nature or war mainly (although not wholly) through speeches. For, indeed, Thucydides does present in speeches and not in narrative the strongest statements about laws of human nature and the behavior of states that correspond generally to the realist approach. Specifically, it is the Athenians who consistently purport to hold such a theory.

The Athenian thesis is first stated at the Spartan War Conference in an attempt to dissuade the Spartans from declaring war. Athenians there on other business decide to speak for their city. Their tactic seems to be to frighten the Spartans by giving them a piece of the Athenian mind-set. They assert that human nature is under the influence of certain passions, which are universal, lawlike, and compelling: "It was under the compulsion of circumstances that we were driven at first to advance our empire to its present state, influenced chiefly by fear, then by honour also, and lastly by self-interest as well" (1.75.3–4). Afterward, they say, it would have been dangerous to give up the empire, especially since all defectors would fall into Spartan hands (1.75.5). Thus the Athenians excuse their actions and at the same time impress the Spartans with the resolve and vigor of their city.

Later, as the war raged throughout Greece, the Athenians repeated their thesis in order to persuade the small island city of Melos, which wanted to be neutral in the war, to become a tribute-paying ally of Athens. With a tremendous advantage in power over Melos, the Athenians argued that the Melians' deaths would be inevitable if they did not submit and that the Melians' decision to resist would be entirely foolish. They state:

> of the gods we hold the belief, and of men we know, that by a necessity of their nature wherever they have power they always rule. And so in our case since we neither enacted this law nor when it was enacted were the first to use it, but found it in existence and expect to leave it in existence for all time, so we make use of it, well aware that both you and others, if clothed with the same power as we are, would do the same thing. (5.105)

Hence, in order to identify Thucydides' position, as opposed to the Athenian position, which in its essence is the realist position, one must ask whether and how Thucydides' view differs from this Athenian thesis and how and for what purpose Thucydides uses this thesis within the overall *History*.

AN ALTERNATIVE VIEW OF THUCYDIDES

In this book I have tried to argue that Thucydides' *History*, if read carefully, presents a picture of human nature that is neither wholly free of nor wholly slave to exterior forces. Unlike realists, Thucydides chooses for his analysis the moral and political clashes between participants depicted in speeches as well as in deeds. Because of this alternative focus, much of Thucydides' *History* bears on questions of national or personal character. Next I will reiterate some of my main points in this context, with the hope of removing Thucydides from the list of "fathers of realism," and will suggest that Thucydides might offer an alternative approach to analyzing international relations.[47]

As I have argued above, the most important component of the realist theory, upon which it stands or falls, is the assumption of a uniformity of human motivation defined as narrow self-interest driven by compelling passions. The foremost evidence that Thucydides does not subscribe to such a view of human nature is that he makes much of the difference, not the sameness, in national character between the two great "superpowers" of the war, Sparta and Athens.

National Character

Thucydides describes Sparta before the war as sitting by, sometimes worrying over Athens's progress, sometimes disbelieving its allies' reports, always tolerating Themistocles' protestations and artful dodges until Athenian power was secure (1.90). She was aware of Athens's growing military might and chose to do nothing until her allies became abusively insistent that she consider war. The speeches that make up the Spartan War Conference show how ingrained was Spartan reticence, for the Corinthians tried to shame them into declaring war by proclaiming that their old-fashioned, timid style would never be a match for Athenian boldness and innovation (1.71). According to the Corinthians, the Athenians were risk takers, and they were very much unlike the Spartans. They were innovative, imaginative, and decisive (1.70). They were active simply because they enjoyed activity, while the Spartans acted only if fear compelled them (1.71). The Spartan king Archidamus, proud of his nation's character, in response to the Corinthians told his fellow Spartans to "be not ashamed of the slowness and dilatoriness for which they censure us most" (1.84). He praised characteristic Spartan hesitation as prudence and depicted the allies, like the Corinthians, as trying to maneuver Sparta into war for their own particular interests (1.84.2–3; 82.6).

In the end, the Spartans were prodded by their allies,[48] but though they went to war with Athens the *History* is rife with examples of how their character affected their waging of the war.[49] While Thucydides mentions that fear of a slave uprising made the Spartans less willing to extend themselves at times, it is far from clear that Thucydides would attribute to this one factor the difference in the two nations' characters.[50]

Individual Character

Thucydides' working assumption is that individuals such as Themistocles, Pericles, and their successors made decisions that led to the buildup and imperial policy of Athens and that differences in their character were operative in policy outcomes.[51] Themistocles and Pericles are both depicted as innovators with powerful, persuasive personalities who convince the Athenians first of the need to build up Athenian strength and independence after the Persian War and later of the need to defend the empire by war. The successors of Pericles are described as being ambitious and self-interested, while Pericles is described as patriotic and more interested in the common good than himself (2.65.7–8). It was the difference in character between Pericles and these future leaders that Thucydides said caused Athens's decline and eventual defeat (2.65.11–13). Thucydides says that the reason Pericles was able to lead the people in a more measured war policy than his successors was that the Athenian people could recognize his selflessness and submitted to his rule (2.65.10).

How can one reconcile this Thucydidean reason for why Athens lost the war with the realists' assumption that all people are motivated alike? It is precisely because they were not all motivated alike that Athens's chances for victory were greatly lowered in Thucydides' judgment after Pericles died. Athens's resources, he wrote, were so great that even with all the conflict caused by ambitious politicians, Athens held out for an amazingly long time (2.65.13). But in the end, it was not Athens's capabilities or lack thereof that was to blame for her failure. It was a failure of leadership. That much is crystal clear in the *History*. Yet leadership would not be so vitally important in Thucydides' explanation if he conceived of human motivation as being as predictable as the Athenians wanted to make it at the Spartan War Conference and at Melos.

The fact that Thucydides makes much of individual character as well as differences in national character between Athens and Sparta disproves the Athenians' thesis, which was promoted by them throughout the war, that such violence is natural, ungoverned by free will, and therefore blameless. Let us now look again at the statement by Thucydides that Gilpin points to in support of the idea of Thucydides as realist: "The truest explanation [for the war], although it has been the least often advanced, I believe to have been the growth of the Athenians to greatness, which brought fear to the Lacedaemonians [Spartans] and forced them to war" (1.23.6).[52]

This statement does not obviate the observations I have made above, since the growth of Athens to greatness could be and was caused by human decision in a noncompulsory fashion and with the knowing acquiescence of Sparta until the point when Sparta's allies convinced her that Athens's actions were actually sufficiently threatening to declare war. If, however, my reading of the meaning of this passage is correct, then it is not particularly useful for proving Thucydides to be a structuralist, an adherent of the theory of hegemonic war, or even a theorist who believed that the power relationship between Athens and Sparta represented a system. That is because such a structuralist theory, as I have shown above, is dependent upon an assumption of consistent human motivation and behavior that is absent in the information behind Thucydides' statement. If that nature is not consistent enough, then one will not be able to predict how structure will affect the actions of individual states.

What if, Thucydides seems to ask us, leaders do not *have* the interests of their state as the first priority? What if, as were later Athenian leaders, they are willing to forfeit the safety of the state for their personal ambitious pursuits? What if, like the Spartans, they are extremely reluctant to confront a challenger? What if they believe, as did the leaders of the Plataeans and Melians, that pursuit of the national interest is pursuit of something beyond self-preservation? What happens with states in which there are leaders, and followers, prepared to die for love of political principles or religion?

The Role of Speech

Thucydides' statement that the truest cause of the war was Sparta's fear of Athens's growing power seems to diminish the speeches to mere appendages of action. The speeches leading to war revolved around the apparent causes, according to Thucydides. This can be taken to mean that the speeches must deal only with the surface or superfluous details. This appears to be the opinion of neorealists such as Gilpin, who would not find the speeches to be causal. Yet if Thucydides relied so much on underlying power and psychological factors to explain human behavior, why did he need speeches? He could have simply reported what he thought was the motivation of the speakers. Or he could have done away with speeches and speakers altogether. Yet as Mark Cogan has pointed out, all underlying causes need a spark to set them off and human beings must be persuaded to follow a policy before it can be implemented.[53] Speech is the instigator of cooperative actions within nations as well as among them. Even if underlying hostility exists, it will remain nebulous until a decision is made to go to war. This decision must involve identifying both the threat and why a particular policy is best able to deal with that threat.

There are many instances in the *History* in which rhetoric is clearly more than a formality. Were it not for Pericles' oratorical combination of reason and passion, content and form, would the Athenians have waged such a conservative war for the first two and a half years, letting the Peloponnesians ravage their countryside and contenting themselves with raids on the Peloponnesian coastline? Would they have consented to abandoning their possessions to Spartan pillage and crowding within the city walls? Would they have continued the war at all, once the plague had left them weak and disheartened, unless Pericles had been uniquely capable of commanding their respect and continued support? Judging by his evaluation of future leaders, Thucydides does not think so. With Pericles, the Athenians "stayed the course" with only momentary lapses. After he died, Thucydides says, men of less stature emerged. They could not lead the people as well as Pericles. Indeed, they became followers of the demos, in that they were concerned only with their own particular political survival and advancement. With this type of evidence, can we dismiss the speeches of Pericles as trivial or epiphenomenal?

Thucydides characterizes Pericles mainly through his speeches, whereas he could have devoted more time to describing his democratic reforms or his military record. The essence of Pericles' importance for Thucydides was his leadership of the Athenians, and that leadership was in large part due to his rhetoric, which skillfully manipulated and accurately attuned itself to the nature of its audience without pandering to it. Thucydides' treatment of Pericles and the other Athenian leaders who came after him reveals his interest in and emphasis on statesmanship; this is evidenced in his detailed portraits of Pericles, Cleon, Nicias, and Alcibiades, in which he delves into their intellectual capabilities and characters and does not simply report their actions.

Pouncey observes that the quality and importance of rhetoric as a conduit for deliberation eroded as the war progressed; by the seventh and eighth books of the *History* Thucydides has eliminated the long speeches, debates, and dialogues with which he populated the earlier books, leaving only dispatches, military harangues, reports of decisions made, and the texts of treaties.[54] I agree with Pouncey that this is not the product of an unrevised eighth chapter but is deliberate. The importance of speech declined as the war became more vehement and extended. Speech lost its meaning in domestic politics as stasis spread. Corcyra differed not much from Athens late in the war in this respect, as both societies disintegrated in the conflict between democrats and oligarchs. Because decisions were made more and more haphazardly as reactions to immediate threats or as manifestations of personal interest, Thucydides naturally stops giving us full speeches. Important speeches that could change the course of events no longer occurred. It is no coincidence that Athens lost its unity at the same time Thucydides stops giving full speeches. In the *History,* effective leadership and meaningful deliberation are inextricably intertwined.

Thucydides' Treatment of Realism as Political Rhetoric

Thucydides uses the speech of Diodotus at Mytilene to comment upon the ultimate outcome of the strict assumptions of the Athenian thesis: a determinism that numbs all morality and threatens to remove all judgment. Diodotus is arguing against Cleon's demogogic call for a death sentence against the entire town of Mytilene. Mytilene's oligarchs had effected a revolt from Athens's suzerainty, and Cleon's reasoning was that even if it was unjust to kill all the Mytilenaeans, it was nevertheless supremely expedient (3.40.4–5). If the Athenians did not punish the Mytilenaeans severely, other cities would more easily revolt. In this case, Cleon claims, the action would be both expedient and just since the Mytilenaeans had indeed revolted and the common people had acquiesced, injuring Athens severely (3.40.1–2).

Diodotus also professes to look only at questions of expediency (3.44.4). But employing the assumptions of the Athenian thesis, he claims that the Mytilenaeans could not but revolt since it is human nature to try to claim as much power and control as possible. Since people will always be able to convince themselves of the certainty of their success, a death sentence for the Mytilenaeans will not deter anyone (3.45.5–7). Therefore he recommends a moderate sentence for the Mytilenaeans, whereby only the ringleaders will be put to death and Mytilene will be returned to Athenian control (3.47.4–5). This, he claims, will encourage those who could not help but revolt to give up willingly and more quickly when they see that they are faced with a siege. If they know they will receive death, they will hold out forever and make Athens spend much money and time in an effort to punish them.

Diodotus uses the Athenian thesis that men are compelled to grasp for power to argue that the only way Athens can control her allies is to exercise an ever-present vigilance and terror over them so that they will never consider revolting in the first place (3.46.6). This, however, is not his recommendation to the Athenians. Instead the argument serves to illustrate the ultimate outcome of the Athenian thesis in practice. In the end, the Athenians effected his more moderate recommendations (and more just, considering the circumstances, since the oligarchs were mostly to blame for the revolt and the people actually helped turn the town back over to Athens). Hence Diodotus has used the Athenian thesis, emphasizing its determinism, both to plead for relief for the Mytilenaeans and to show the extreme outcome of wholeheartedly believing the thesis. According to the thesis, only constant forceful repression—and not good, respectable leadership—would keep states from rising up against stronger states. And yet it was good, respectable leadership, as Garst points out, that originally earned Athens the loyalty and respect of its allies; and it was the deterioration of this leadership into imperialistic repression that caused the allies to resent Athens and revolt in increasingly greater numbers as the war went on.[55]

Too much realism, it seems, was unhealthy for Athens and her empire. At the Spartan War Conference, the Athenians insisted that all are compelled to follow their passions—namely, fear, interest, and honor—to grasp for power and dominion wherever and whenever they can. At first, the Athenians themselves did not seem to take this thesis entirely seriously, insisting that the allies had become impudent precisely because Athens had provided them with more justice than she had to. At the Mytilenaean Debate, the element of compulsion or determinism in the thesis was used to obtain a moderate, even just, sentence for the Mytilenaeans. Only when we arrive at the Melian Dialogue do we see the Athenians acting in accordance with the theory they put forth. Thucydides' History implies that as the Athenians came to believe and to act on their thesis more and more, their legitimacy declined among their allies and empire and their domestic political order became corrupt and disintegrated amid politicians who each followed their own selfish interests.

Thucydides finds the thesis useful for describing a particularly popular way of thinking (sophistic), as one strain in a moral discourse that, when acted upon, is successful. That is, it is successful in the short run. For him it is proof that, for better or worse, human beings can create their own world instead of being created by it. In that sense, Thucydides looks on the thesis in a very different light than the modern realist.

Detached Observer?

If Thucydides believed in the Athenian thesis, he would have no reason to dwell on moral arguments and would not attempt to display the obvious immorality of certain incidents in the war both in speeches and deeds. This is because if he believed in the Athenian thesis, there would be no real choice and therefore no real decision, and no blame or praise to be placed. Justice would be something that could take place only among equals, as the Athenians claim at Melos (which would be more like forced accommodation), or within states as enforced laws. But obviously justice is something more than that for Thucydides. Not only does he eloquently provide us with three great moral dramas that bring out quite starkly the conflict between brute force and justice (and the notion of the common interest as justice) but he also, in his own words, provides us with standards of justice. His description of the Thracian massacre at Mycalessus is plainly one of outrage for barbarous atrocities:

> For the Thracian race, like the worst barbarians, is most bloodthirsty whenever it has nothing to fear. And so on this occasion: in addition to the general confusion, which was great, every form of destruction ensued, and in particular, they fell upon a boys' school, the largest in the town, which the children had just entered, and cut down all of them. And this was a calamity inferior to none that had ever fallen upon a whole city, and beyond any other unexpected and terrible. (7.29.5)

Thucydides' idea of justice can be seen even more clearly in his commentary on the Corcyraean revolution. Echoing the Melians' notion of justice, Thucydides writes that during this time men abrogated "in advance the common principles observed in such cases—those principles upon which depends every man's own hope of salvation should he himself be overtaken by misfortune—thus failing to leave them in force against the time when perchance a man in peril shall have need of some one of them" (3.84.3). Thucydides does write that "human nature, now triumphant over the laws," delighted in giving the passions full sway. But he treats this as an inversion of the normal, with the result of producing inverted values. Noble simplicity was laughed at, while shrewd sophistication was considered admirable. Intelligent men were bested by those who could use crude force, and they feared those who were more clever. Words changed their meanings so that prudence was considered cowardice and impulsiveness was seen as manliness (3.82.4–8). What Robert W. Connor refers to as "revolutionary newspeak" took over.[56] Thucydides places the blame for this inversion of normalcy on "the desire to rule which greed and ambition inspire, and also, springing from them, that ardour which belongs to men who once have become engaged in factious rivalry" (3.82.8).

Would Thucydides so strongly censure these things if in his mind they were the normal condition of human beings or beyond the will of man to control? While Thucydides may depict the influence of this baser side of human nature as quite strong, particularly in times of war, he could not have thought of it as insurmountable.

By lamenting the inversion of customary values, Thucydides reasserts their objective meaning and indicates that what occurred during the civil wars was an inversion or perversion of human nature that occurs from time to time. The distortions of self-interest, Connor observes, are the "drive for dominance, self-aggrandizement, and ambition."[57] Not to make the observation that war, the "rough schoolmaster," brings most people down to the level of their condition would be to ignore the obvious (3.82.2–3). But this does not mean that it must happen this way. To say that such behavior will recur "while human nature is the same" is not to say that this behavior is an adequate representation of the whole of human nature at all times. If it did mean the latter, again there would be no way to criticize such behavior, as Thucydides does.

THE THUCYDIDEAN SCHOLAR

Perhaps both classical and modern realism are too much of the same stripe, too rigid in their expectations, and too lacking in their practical, predictive roles to be realistic. And yet, retort the realists, their theories have given us the closest thing to a unifying theory of international relations; and for doing so it continues to play a central role in international relations scholarship—until someone comes up with a better unifying theory.

Ought we to give unifying theory such pride of place if it serves only as a sterile heuristic device? Yale Ferguson and Richard Mansbach's *The Elusive Quest* questions the utility of both quantitative research and theory building in international relations. After making their careers largely on such work, Ferguson and Mansbach have admitted that what they and others have produced has little utility in the world of the practitioner. A large part of their explanation for this failure is that because the social context of the research changes, research goals and values change; and because they do change, cumulative knowledge is impossible.[58] But they also note that theorizing has been largely unproductive from the standpoint of practical usage, because the laws it discovers do not seem to apply to any particular case:

> The sad truth, of which there appears to be growing recognition and acknowledgement, is that international relations practitioners in governments, some of whom (perhaps mistakenly) in the 1950's and 1960's looked to the academic world for guidance in matters like deterrence, find very little of either interest or relevance in contemporary theory and therefore make little attempt to read it.[59]

Closer to the debate on realism, Ashley launched a controversial attack in 1984 on the accuracy and practical use of neorealist theory according to Kenneth Waltz, Robert Keohane, Stephen Krasner, Robert Gilpin, Robert Tucker, George Modelski, and Charles Kindleberger.[60] Neorealism, he said, is

> a positivist structuralism that treats the given order as the natural order, limits rather than expands political discourse, negates or trivializes the significance of variety across time and place, subordinates all practice to an interest in control, bows to the ideal of a social power beyond responsibility, and thereby deprives political interaction of those practical capacities which make social learning possible. What emerges is an ideology that anticipates, legitimizes, and orients a totalitarian project of global proportions: the rationalization of global politics.[61]

Ashley repeats all the arguments against neorealism that have been made in the past and many against its classical forerunner that have also been made. Neorealism's structuralism emphasizes the international system and its inherent dynamic without realizing that a crucial part of the calculation of power has to do with leadership and will to exercise power or with recognition of a state's legitimacy. It is guilty of concentrating on the state to the exclusion of other actors, such as statesmen as individuals and outside international organizations. It commits utilitarianism, by which Ashley means a sort of means-ends rationality that fails to account for norms prior to or independent of states' driving interests and capabilities. Neorealism is positivistic, in that it treats the knowledge it accumulates as in itself value neutral. This knowledge is designed to give others information about the most efficient means to ends determined in another manner.[62]

I agree with much of Ashley's critique of neorealism and extend it to much of classical realism, although I would not go so far as to characterize it as a totalitarian project, since such thinking has been a part of political currency since the Melian Dialogue and the Mytilenaean Debate and probably long before that. International relations scholars were already familiar with Ashley's criticisms before he renewed the debate, and many agree with him on at least some of his points. But they still struggle with the notion that their primary task must be theory building, and theory building of an altogether too demanding sort for the complex human subject with which it must deal. Is there a point to this obsession? Do we fear being called unscientific, or worse yet mere historians?

In the latter vein, one alternative, which Ferguson and Mansbach offer, is for more analysts to turn to "policy questions or purely descriptive analyses of current events and issues, without attempting to explore the theoretical implications of their work." But they describe these efforts as "merely journalistic"—current history—work that easily becomes outdated.[63] Much of the problem, as they see it, is that students of international relations, unlike students of the hard sciences, not only are faced with "a staggering number of potentially relevant variables with which to wrestle outside of a closed laboratory setting but also, unlike the physical scientists, must proceed with precious little agreement as to how variables should be labeled and defined."[64] Ultimately these students, they say, must arrive at gross simplifications. Theorists are then left open to the timeworn criticism that their definitions are too narrow and that they have excluded much relevant evidence. Theory, by its very nature, must simplify.

But is it possible that politics, especially international politics, are so exceedingly complex and—as Friedrich Kratochwil and John Gerard Ruggie put it[65]—"intersubjective" that theoretical simplification will not yield enough leftover truth to make generalizations worthwhile? Is it possible that high-quality historically and *philosophically* informed journalism is desirable? In practice, journals such as *Foreign Affairs* and *Foreign Policy* are read by foreign policy makers. These are largely filled with well-informed, quasi-theoretical essays. And they and other texts dealing with current or past events in this manner yield a good amount of political knowledge, and perhaps political wisdom, as increasingly more are digested. This approach to scholarship goes along well with Ferguson and Mansbach's final recommendation for salvaging the discipline of international relations. They call for a "fundamental transformation" in scholarship, "abandoning the explicit and implicit analogies to the natural sciences and, instead, trying to make sense of the way in which humanists approach their materials."[66] Agreeing with this ironic conclusion, this book has intended in part to show that the Thucydidean approach to international politics is one well worth considering as an alternative to Hobbesian social science.

Such an approach, as we have seen here, embraces the concept of character and holds that individuals can and do have enormous impact on world events. This individuals-as-actors orientation has often been given short shrift in international relations texts or has been unnaturally narrowed into psychological, biological, or content analysis.[67] But individuals are the essence of Thucydidean realism, every bit as much or more important than the great forces (the drive for power and power relationships among states) that supposedly dictate what leaders will do in the name of national interest. A realist and a neorealist, Morgenthau and Kenneth Waltz, concentrate on great forces, sometimes almost to the exclusion of individual involvement. Thus, while they (especially Morgenthau on the morality of statesmanship) may agree with many of Thucydides' themes, they too try to systematize and detach their subjects from human involvement in a way Thucydides does not and so devise theories (especially Waltz) that are too abstract to yield any predictions. If systemic or structuralist theories such as Waltz's are too abstract to bear any significance at any given time, are they at all meaningful?

John G. Stoessinger, who leans more toward the Thucydidean approach than any of the above theorists, assesses Woodrow Wilson in a way Thucydides would understand: "Wilson's personality collided with the conditions of the time. . . . In his dream was his greatness, in his rigid personality his tragedy."[68] Stoessinger assumes that individuals are responsible for great events in international relations and that they are therefore to be praised or blamed for their decisions. His studies of the beginnings of World War I and America's conduct in the Korean war, as well as his open admiration for Henry Kissinger, are examples of his Thucydidean worldview. Kaiser Wilhelm made a crucial mistake in guaranteeing Serbia's security and *letting* himself be overtaken by war paranoia; Douglas MacArthur was a great general who tragically became a victim of his own hubris; Henry Kissinger made the world safer because of his ability to apply his intellect to politics without being obsessively uncompromising.[69]

Stephen Krasner is similar to Stoessinger in his insistence that individuals must be held responsible for their political acts. In Krasner's case, the alternative that scholars have employed of blaming seemingly autonomous bureaucracies is not only factually wrong but also morally dangerous.[70] He writes: "Both psychologically and politically, leaders may find it advantageous to have others think of them as ineffectual rather than evil. But the facts are otherwise—particularly in foreign policy. There the choices—and the responsibility—rest squarely with the president."[71]

Scholarship in the Hobbesian mode that has resulted in removing responsibility from particular leaders includes all efforts to identify political actions as resulting from forces beyond individual control. These forces may be economic or material determinism, the compulsory human drive for power or glory, the determining effects of the international *system* apart from its particular units, and the underlying psychological forces at the individual and social levels that are determined by environment and history. As is evident, realism and neorealism are part of a larger way of thinking that includes Marxism, psychologism, and all other brands of determinism. All deny, as did Hobbes's theory, any genuine moral responsibility.

It would shock many political scientists to find that their thought bears any resemblance to totalitarianism. Nevertheless, it is the opinion of many political scientists today that it is unnecessary to look seriously at political deliberation in order to understand and to evaluate politics. Following Hobbesian assumptions, political behavior is attributed to irrational compulsions such as greed or the need for power. Often these compulsions are said to be the motivations of elites who control government to obtain more resources for themselves and who use political rhetoric (consciously or not) only for the purpose of, in Hobbes's words, "cozening" the public. Thus Murray Edelman characterizes hortatory speech as concealing "emotional appeal under the guise of defining issues. . . . While these phrases may seem to be objective definitions of issues and are discussed as if they were, they are nothing more than emotional appeals for public support."[72] This dismissal of political rhetoric tends to make molehills out of mountains. David M. Ricci has captured this effect: "If human actions and motivations flow from irrational and unreliable impulses linked to various sorts of personal and collective compulsions, the affairs of even well-known men and women can hardly inspire us as they might have in the past."[73]

Ricci attributes this trend in modern scholarship to a reaction against the excesses of the twentieth century and to the fact that words "have been used to justify political falsehood, massive distortions of history, and the bestialities of the totalitarian state."[74] A similar reaction was the impetus for Hobbes's science; his horror at civil violence led him to lose faith in ordinary human reason. It is because he (and we) lost all faith in the ability to reason without the security blanket of method that scientific reasoning emerged as a powerful alternative in politics. But if people are so irrational and compulsive that we can no longer take seriously what they say, how can we expect them to be reasonable enough to accept peacefully the solutions proposed by social scientists? Is not the inevitable consequence of such beliefs about human nature a need for control?

Surely democracy actually operates on the assumption that, and is effective because, people are independent moral agents, not the drones of history, the market, or their psychological urges. We now have proof beyond argument in Eastern Europe and the former Soviet Union that the same human nature that sometimes causes chaos also revolts against too much social planning and will not be kept down unless the government is continually ready to use deadly force. This is the ultimate implication of the Hobbesian approach. At least Hobbes foresaw the possibly negative consequences of his assumptions. But as we have seen, he could produce no effective way to avoid them. This unfortunate hangover of the scientific solution makes the Hobbesian approach to political problems more dangerous than the Thucydidean approach, which emphasizes the importance of political deliberation and ordinary judgment and tolerates a good amount of chaos. The price to be paid for accepting Thucydides' approach is abandoning the notion that we can produce a formula that will bring about perpetual progress and therefore acknowledging a greater role for chance or fate than we are usually willing to tolerate. Yet the benefit is the elevation of the human spirit, free of the godlike and mistaken attitude that science will solve all our problems.

In the realm of scholarship one pressing danger (at least in this country) is that social scientists' findings will become self-fulfilling prophecies, that students who are taught that all political speech is empty will allow politicians to say and do anything, and that students who are told that their vote doesn't matter and that democracy is a sham will stop voting and will turn to either apathy or violence. Indeed, given what we have seen in the 1980s and so far in the 1990s, these statements may no longer be warnings; they may be explanations.

Hobbesian thinking and the corresponding scientific social planning that Friedrich Hayek warned of in *The Road to Serfdom* are attempts to deal with the fact that one cannot hope for the rare combination of intelligence and integrity to solve all our problems. The assumptions by which such thinking is guided are inaccurate, and the solutions it proposes do not work. But influenced as we are by the pervasive modern notion of progress, how can we live with the Thucydidean alternative in which neither nature nor man can force history to be progressive for long? This is, of course, the assumption behind Paul Kennedy's assessment of previous and present empires—history has its peaks and its valleys, both of which people are responsible for.[75] It would seem, as Bishop Bramhall might observe, that both approaches tend to make human efforts for progress seem futile.

But a Thucydidean rejection of rationalism does not have to imply despair simply because it rejects the possibility of linear progress. Thucydides' judgments on individuals use standards that are constant. These individuals are usually not pacific, nor do they always have the common good foremost in their minds, but they are judged by standards that Thucydides considers to be true even when they are repeatedly violated. It is true, as Mansbach and Ferguson claim, that social contexts change enough to render much theory that is attached to its historical experiences and goals of little use. Thucydides' work proves false the notion that societies change so much that we cannot identify the high points and have reasonable assurances that most peoples at all times and places had similar sensibilities about greatness and magnanimity on the one hand and the penchant for wanton slaughter and destruction on the other. Despite our different social backgrounds, we probably would not have to argue too much about *why* Periclean Athens was great (and also why it was destined to fall). As we have seen, Thucydides' values and insights are still recognizable today, just as they were in Hobbes's day. Because some type of barbarism is always a possibility, civilization has the potential for true greatness, not just the Hobbesian delusion of pride.

Rather than make individual effort futile, then, Thucydidean thinking makes it supremely important: even though human drives and external forces may exert much force, we are aware of right and wrong and we can blame only ourselves for our failures. The example of Thucydides' *History* presents an alternative to present-day scholarship, but it also presents us with a challenge—the same challenge put forward by many of the classics. It dares us to take ourselves and our leaders seriously, to trust ourselves to evaluate them and their actions based on their personal qualities, and not to rely solely on the system to produce good results regardless of who is elected or appointed. It challenges us to listen carefully to political arguments, to assume at least at the outset that these arguments are made with the intent to persuade, not to "cozen," and to force ourselves to come up with counterarguments if we disagree. That may be more difficult over the long haul than producing a unifying theory of international relations.

The word *character* has been used in this book in the sense of national as well as personal character. Yet this dimension of human concerns that is clearly emphasized in Thucydides is largely forgotten in realist interpretations of Thucydides due to a modern prejudice against such supposedly ambiguous notions as "character." Perhaps the greatest use of Thucydides' work is in helping us identify more accurately what that term means and what difference it can make in politics. At any rate, scholars following in Thucydides' footsteps would have to show how great, as well as mediocre, leaders affect their nations' destinies. They would have to concentrate on what we call the "individuals-as-actors" approach, with a twist: well-founded moral judgments would be allowed. Thucydidean scholars, by consequence, would have to study the political rhetoric of leaders and assume that their rhetoric has some connection with their actions, even if that connection is sometimes only deception. The rhetoric would have to be analyzed and judged against a leader's actions; the content would be subject to a reality test.

These scholars would view varying political theories and ethical claims as part of the political rhetoric among nations and would try to determine the effect of various theories and claims on practice. Theory would be seen not as a benign and objective instrument of analysis for the scholar so much as an object for analysis. Whether and to what extent the theory is practiced, whether it is successfully practiced, and whether it is met with acceptance or resistance are the types of questions Thucydidean scholars might ask in the process of studying political rhetoric.

One theoretical principle these scholars would hold is the existence of free will. That is, they would deny any determinism, either from human passions or from the international system. It is this principle that would turn them to an earnest study of individual leaders, their rhetoric, and their decisions. They would be able, therefore, to praise good statesmanship and blame its opposite. They would be able to condemn truly abysmal failures of leadership, or morals, guided by a commonsense understanding of justice.

But might not such a scholar be seen as naive, not to mention unscholarly, for not being objective? Perhaps this is the greatest secret of Thucydides—he manages to encompass much more of political reality and still come across as a hardheaded realpolitiker. He manages to do so because he believes that the rise and decline of states and the emergence of violence and peace are due to the decisions of leaders and the particular character of those leaders and their nations. Because of this belief, Thucydides sees no end to the up-and-down cycle of human fortunes. According to him, the depths to which Greece sank will recur countless times, and by the same token civilizations will reach their peaks before collapsing again under their own weight. History, in his eyes, is cyclical.[76] It is this dependence on the emergence of greatness, this "fatalism," that ultimately makes him appear to be the realist.

If scholars' distaste for this mind-set can be overcome, the Thucydidean approach offers an ennobling, and perhaps more practically useful, analysis of international politics than does realism. This is because leaders are not seen as the instruments of exterior forces. They are held responsible for their actions, and they are shown that they and their societies have much to lose if they abandon thinking about and acting on the common good.

NOTES

INTRODUCTION

1. Richard K. Ashley, "Political Realism and Human Interests," *International Studies Quarterly* 25, 2 (June 1981): 205; Ashley, "The Poverty of Neorealism," *International Organization* 38, 2 (Spring 1984): 259; Hedley Bull, *Anarchical Society* (New York: Columbia University Press, 1977); Bull, "Hobbes and the International Anarchy," *Social Research* 48, 4 (Winter 1981): 717–38; Robert G. Gilpin, "The Richness of the Tradition of Political Realism," *International Organization* 38, 2 (Spring 1984): 90–294; Joseph S. Nye, Jr., *Nuclear Ethics* (New York: The Free Press, 1986), 6–7; Kenneth Waltz, *Man, the State and War* (New York: Columbia University Press, 1959), 210–12, 216.

2. Waltz, *Man, the State and War*, 159.

3. Robert O. Keohane and Joseph Nye, *Power and Interdependence* (Boston: Little, Brown and Company, 1977), 42.

4. Bull, *Anarchical Society*.

5. The most common sentence to be misconstrued is: "The truest explanation [for the war], although it has been the least often advanced, I believe to have been the growth of the Athenians to greatness, which brought fear to the Lacedaemonians [Spartans] and forced them to war" (1.23.6; cf. 1.88).

HUMAN NATURE

1. Cf. Clifford W. Brown Jr., "Thucydides, Hobbes, and the Derivation of Anarchy," *History of Political Thought* 8, 1 (Spring 1987): 33–62; George Klosko and Daryl Rice, "Thucydides and Hobbes's State of Nature," *History of Political Thought* 7, 3 (Winter 1985): 405–9; Michael Palmer, "Machiavellian *Virtu* and Thucydidean *Arete*: Traditional Virtue

and Political Wisdom in Thucydides," *Review of Politics* 51, 3 (Summer 1989): 366; Peter R. Pouncey, *The Necessities of War: A Study of Thucydides' Pessimism* (New York: Columbia University Press, 1980), 151–57.

2. Cf. Michael Doyle, "Thucydidean Realism," *Review of International Studies* 16, 3 (July 1990): 223–37; Robert Gilpin, "The Theory of Hegemonic War," *Journal of Interdisciplinary History* 18, 4 (Spring 1988): 591–613.

3. Cf. H, 32; L, 6, 57.

4. C. B. MacPherson, *The Political Theory of Possessive Individualism: Hobbes to Locke* (Oxford: Clarendon Press, 1964), 20.

5. MacPherson, *The Political Theory of Possessive Individualism*, 22.

6. Cf. C, 3.2.

7. John W. Danford, "The Problem of Language in Hobbes's Political Science," *The Journal of Politics* 42, 1 (February 1980): 129.

8. Cf. Raymond Poulin, *Politique et Philosophie Chez Thomas Hobbes* (Paris: Presses Universitaires de France, 1953), 6n.2.

9. Miriam M. Reik, *The Golden Lands of Thomas Hobbes* (Detroit: Wayne State University Press, 1977), 72; cf. L, 4, par. 6.

10. Danford, "The Problem of Language in Hobbes's Political Science," 125.

11. Reik, *The Golden Lands of Thomas Hobbes*, 58.

12. David Johnston, *The Rhetoric of Leviathan: Thomas Hobbes and the Politics of Cultural Transformation* (Princeton: Princeton University Press, 1986), 61.

13. See Johnston, *The Rhetoric of Leviathan*, 61; John W. Ray, "The Place of Oratory in the Political Philosophy of Thomas Hobbes," *Western Speech* 37, 1 (Summer 1973): 173; cf. James P. Zappan, "Aristotelian and Ramist Rhetoric in Thomas Hobbes's *Leviathan*: Pathos Versus Ethos and Logos," *Rhetorica* 1, 1 (Spring 1983): 82.

14. Johnston, *The Rhetoric of Leviathan*, 56.

15. Cf. L, 25.

16. Poulin, *Politique et Philosophie Chez Thomas Hobbes*, 7.

17. Cf. 1.88.

18. Cf. 1.103.4.

19. Clifford Orwin, "Stasis and Plague: Thucydides on the Dissolution of Society," *Journal of Politics* 50, 4 (November 1988): 831–47.

20. Arnold W. Gomme, *A Historical Commentary on Thucydides*, vol. 2 (Oxford: Clarendon Press, 1959), 359.

21. Orwin, "Stasis and Plague," 836.

22. Orwin, "Stasis and Plague," 836.

23. Robert W. Connor, *Thucydides* (Princeton: Princeton University Press, 1884), 102.

24. Orwin, "Stasis and Plague," 384n.5.

25. Conner, *Thucydides,* 101.

26. Cf. John Wilson, "The Customary Meanings of Words Were Changed—Or Were They? A Note on Thucydides 3.82.4," *Classical Quarterly* 32, 1 (Winter 1982): 19.

27. Connor, *Thucydides,* 96.

28. Leo Strauss, *The City and Man* (Chicago: University of Chicago Press, 1964), 147.

29. Connor, *Thucydides,* 102.

30. Lowell Edmunds, "Thucydides' Ethics as Reflected in the Description of Stasis (3.82–83)," *Harvard Studies in Classical Philology* 79, 4 (Winter 1975): 88.

31. Francis MacDonald Cornford, *Thucydides Mythistoricus* (London: Routledge & Kegan Paul Ltd., 1965); Steven Forde, "Thucydides on the Causes of Athenian Imperialism," *American Political Science Review* 80, 2 (June 1986): 210; Christopher Bruell, "Thucydides' View of Athenian Imperialism," *American Political Science Review* 68, 1 (March 1974): 68.

32. As Steven Forde writes, "It invites compassion more than condemnation for those overcome by the hubristic impulses of human nature, but also yields a counsel of prudence to future statesmen." *The Ambition to Rule: Alcibiades and the Politics of Imperialism in Thucydides* (Ithaca, N.Y.: Cornell University Press, 1989), 205.

33. Cf. 7.23.3–4; 7.40.2–5; 7.43.7; 8.25.3–4; 8.105.3; 8.106.2–3.

34. See J. L. Creed's discussion, in "Moral Values in the Age of Thucydides," *Classical Quarterly* 23, 2 (November 1973), of the various uses of the term *arete,* and especially its use in this case (p. 220).

35. Hunter R. Rawlings III, *Structure of Thucydides' History* (Princeton: Princeton University Press, 1981), 232.

36. Cornford, *Thucydides Mythistoricus,* 90.

37. See Leo Strauss's "Preliminary Observations on the Gods in Thucydides' Work," *Interpretation* 4, 1 (Winter 1974): 1–16, for a complete analysis of the limited use of godly influence in the *History.*

38. Cornford, *Thucydides Mythistoricus,* 95.

39. Strauss, *The City and Man,* 228–29.

40. Cleon's victory is depicted as due to a freak fire on the island, which solved the problem of visibility and allowed his chosen partner, Demosthenes, to carry out a rare land battle between Athens's surrogates and the besieged Spartans (4.26–38). The action itself is depicted as Cleon's unwitting response to a dare—the Athenians (and Nicias) called his bluff, thus forcing him to make the attempt.

41. Cf. Forde, *The Ambition to Rule,* 199–210.

42. Cf. Pouncey, *The Necessities of War.*

43. See Michael Palmer, "Love of Glory and the Common Good," *American Political Science Review* 76, 4 (December 1982): 825–36.

44. L, 15, par. 21.

45. It might be useful for those especially interested in this aspect of my analysis to turn to the Conclusion now for specific applications.

JUSTICE

1. This is the case because of the relative security of people *within* states. However, I will argue in the Conclusion that given the correct circumstances Hobbesian logic may allow for international agreements that would lessen or curtail the sovereignty of individual states. Hobbes himself, of course, could not have foreseen such dire circumstances as the threat of global nuclear war or environmental catastrophe.

2. Here we will see the Athenian thesis being used in two ways: rhetorically by Diodotus in order to procure moderate Athenian policy; and in action by the Athenians at Melos, producing immoderation and injustice.

3. Cf. B, 388–89, 404, 418.

4. This question has a bearing on realists who make prescriptions for a moderate foreign policy based solely on what is rational behavior given international anarchy and the particular circumstances of the time and who scorn injunctions based on some higher morality or law.

5. Cf. Raymond Poulin, *Politique et Philosophie Chez Thomas Hobbes* (Paris: Presses Universitaires de France, 1953), 167.

6. Cf. L, 46, par. 28.

7. Cf. L, 46, par. 31.

8. Cf. LNC, 216–21.

9. Cf. 13.7; L, 13, par. 2.

10. The following is my attempt to determine how Hobbes's laws of nature would apply to international relations, taking as many clues as possible from Hobbes. The readers should understand that Hobbes did not *systematically* apply the laws of nature to the international case.

11. David Johnston, *The Rhetoric of Leviathan: Thomas Hobbes and the Politics of Cultural Transformation* (Princeton: Princeton University Press, 1986), 37.

12. Cf. L, 15, par. 4.

13. Cf. DC, 13.7.

14. Cf. PR, 45n.

15. Cf. B, 200–201, 203, 384.

16. These terms are borrowed from John G. Stoessinger's *Crusaders and Pragmatists: Movers of Modern American Foreign Policy* (New York: Norton, 1985).

17. Hans J. Morgenthau struggled with this moral dilemma in many of his works. See *Scientific Man vs. Power Politics* (Chicago: University of Chicago Press, 1946), 176, 201–3; *Dilemmas of Politics* (Chicago: University of Chicago Press, 1958), 55; *Politics Among Nations,* 5th ed. rev. (New York: Alfred A. Knopf, Inc., 1978), chaps. 31 and 32, especially p. 263.

18. Morgenthau, *Scientific Man vs. Power Politics,* 176.

19. Morgenthau, *Scientific Man vs. Power Politics,* 202.

20. Lowell Edmunds, "Thucydides' Ethics as Reflected in the Description of Stasis (3.82–83)," *Harvard Studies in Classical Philology* 79, 4 (Winter 1975): 74.

21. Edmunds, "Thucydides' Ethics," 82.

22. Much of this section appears in my "Rethinking the Diodotean Argument," *Interpretation* 18, 1 (Fall 1990): 53–62.

23. Clifford Orwin, "The Just and the Advantageous in Thucydides: The Case of the Mytilenaean Debate," *American Political Science Review* 78, 2 (June 1984): 491.

24. Orwin, "The Just and the Advantageous in Thucydides," 487.

25. Leo Strauss, *The City and Man* (Chicago: University of Chicago Press, 1964), 191.

26. The one partial exception is David Cohen, "Justice, Interest, and Political Deliberation," *Quaderni Urbinati di Cultura Classica* 16, 1 (Spring 1984): 35–60. Cohen very usefully devotes seven pages to the debate in the context of all the events in book 3. I agree with the major points of his Plataean commentary, but it is necessarily limited by the fact that he is devoting himself to an analysis of several events.

27. A complete list of books that do not make use of the Plataean Debate would be too lengthy to give here. Francis MacDonald Cornford does not treat it at all, even though it suggests a purpose of Thucydides, because it does not reflect the Thucydidean "methodology" that Cornford's thesis explicates (*Thucydides Mythistoricus* [London: Routledge & Kegan Paul Ltd., 1965]). Virginia Hunter mentions Plataea only twice in passing, even though a study of it could have helped her thesis that Thucydides was not a scientific and objective reporter but a historian who selected facts in order to demonstrate certain patterns in history (*Thucydides, the Artful Reporter* [Toronto, Canada: The Hunter Rose Co., 1973]). Peter J. Fliess mentions the debate only briefly, even though it could serve as an excellent example of a state caught up in the bipolar struggle between Athens and Sparta (*Thucydides and the Politics of Bipolarity* [Baton Rouge: Louisiana State University Press, 1966]). Dennis Proctor devotes four pages (*The Experience of Thucydides* [London: Aris & Phillips Ltd., 1980], 91–95), and Hunter R. Rawlings contributes eight pages, although he proceeds from the vantage point of Sparta, not the parties of the debate

themselves (*The Structure of Thucydides' History* [Princeton: Princeton University Press, 1981]). Strauss does not treat it in depth, but he mentions it on many pages and integrates its meaning into his overall analysis (*The City and Man*).

28. For Orwin's contributions, see "The Just and the Advantageous in Thucydides," 485–94; "Stasis and Plague: Thucydides on the Dissolution of Society," *Journal of Politics* 51, 3 (Summer 1988): 345–64. See also "The Drama of the Melian Dialogue Revisited," a paper presented at the annual meeting of the Northeast Political Science Association, Philadelphia, Penn., 17–19 November 1983.

29. To my knowledge, no other author has made this argument, even in passing, about the Plataean Debate.

30. The best treatment of the Corcyraean revolution from the point of view of elucidating Thucydides' ethics is Edmunds's "Thucydides' Ethics," 73–92. See also John T. Hogan, "The [axiosis] of Words at Thucydides 3.82.4," *Greek, Roman and Byzantine Studies* 21, 2 (Summer 1980): 139–50; Orwin, "Stasis and Plague" 831–47; and John Wilson, "The Customary Meanings of Words Were Changed—Or Were They? A Note on Thucydides 3.82.4," *Classical Quarterly* 32 (Winter 1982): 50–56.

31. Proctor, *The Experience of Thucydides*, 92.

32. Arnold W. Gomme mentions that the "*fall* of Plataia was of little military importance and had not much effect on the issue of the war; but all its circumstances illustrated the *mores* of men at war in a most vivid way; and for that reason Thucydides treats it at such length and in so impressive a manner" (*A Historical Commentary on Thucydides* [Oxford: Clarendon Press, 1959], 2: 354).

33. John H. Finley calls this, quite aptly, a coup d'etat attempt by the oligarchs (*Thucydides* [Cambridge: Harvard University Press, 1942], 178).

34. According to the Thebans, Thucydides says, the Plataeans promised to restore the prisoners if the Thebans withdrew from their territory, even taking an oath to that effect. The Plataeans told a different story, saying they did not promise to restore the men at once but only if an agreement was made after preliminary negotiations.

35. Peter R. Pouncey sees Archidamus' statement as a sincere example of the Spartans' "respect for the history and conventions of the past," which were soon lost (*The Necessities of War: A Study of Thucydides' Pessimism* [New York: Columbia University Press, 1980], 17). In contrast, Finley sees it as a cynical example of "customary Spartan piety," indicating that there was no change in Spartan character over time but that Archidamus demonstrated typical Spartan cynicism (*Thucydides*, 179). I do not believe, from the evidence that Thucydides gives us, that it is possible to unequivocally embrace Pouncey's distinction.

36. Pouncey has noted that this effect occurs without any explicit moralization on the part of Thucydides. He writes, "Apart from the single comment at the end about the 'profitable' alliance with Thebes, Thucydides will not make the connections for us by any explicit moralization. His own device is to envelop the reader almost claustrophobically in *details* about the siege and its progress" (*The Necessities of War*, 18; emphasis mine).

37. Again, as Pouncey points out, "they have the innocence of all victims, and we admire their tireless intelligence for self-preservation and their solidarity . . . foredoomed as they are" (*The Necessities of War*, 18).

38. Finley notes that Thucydides' "account of Plataea is defective, in that he does not tell why the Athenians ever encouraged the unfortunate city to resist if they were not going to support it more strongly" (*Thucydides*, 179).

39. After briefly describing the Plataeans' speech, Rawlings describes the Theban's speech in one sentence, as "sophistical and vengeful" (*The Structure of Thucydides' History*, 200). While this may be true, it is a mistake to so quickly dismiss the content of the speech as unimportant.

40. Proctor disagrees in *The Experience of Thucydides*, 92. It is true that the Thebans appeal to loyalty to Boeotian tradition and institutions (as a guise for the quest for hegemony), but their greater appeal is to the ideology of the current conflict, what they feel the Spartans are most concerned about. Thucydides decries this type of ideological attachment in his description of the Corcyraean Civil War.

41. Strauss sees more justice in this Theban claim or perhaps thinks that Thucydides is trying to show the partial reasonableness of both sides' claims by allowing the Thebans this argument. He writes, "The rights and wrongs of the case are not entirely clear, for whereas the Thebans (Sparta's ally) had invaded Plataeae (Athens' ally) while the treaty was still in force, yet there was already 'confusion' of the treaty, they had been called in by a respectable part of the Plataean citizenry" ("On Thucydides' War of the Peloponnesians and the Athenians," in *The City and Man*, 176).

42. Cohen writes, "The final comment is precisely the theory of Cleon that deliberation should be reduced to a criminal trial, and the manifest hypocrisy of the sham procedure employed at Plataea is sufficient commentary on the consequences of adopting this mode of deliberation" ("Justice, Interest, and Political Deliberation," 55).

43. This is what Cohen must mean when he writes, "Thucydides does not analyze this perversion of justice and its consequences, nor does he need to, for the analysis is implicit in the presentation" ("Justice, Interest, and Political Deliberation," 55).

44. Cohen makes a similar observation that the themes of the Corcyraean episode, as well as those of the Mytilenaean Debate, resonate in the

Plataean Debate ("Justice, Interest, and Political Deliberation," 56–60).

45. Edmunds's study, "Thucydides' Ethics," 73–92, points out that Thucydides censures the following qualities: false piety, abandonment of debate in favor of bold deeds so as not to be "worsted in words," the desire for revenge, overweening ambition, and zealous attachment to party above family and community. This rather direct censure is the most reliable source for Thucydides' ethical views. A close second would be his eulogy of Pericles, in which Thucydides praises Pericles for his integrity, honesty, patriotism, love of the common good, and lack of selfish ambition (2.65.10–12). Pericles' successors, through their intrigues and grasping for power, brought about the collapse of the Sicilian expedition. His admiration for the Plataeans and his foiling of the Thebans' argument are in basic agreement with these two more overt ethical statements.

46. Gomme, *A Historical Commentary on Thucydides,* 5: 157.

47. Orwin, "The Drama of the Melian Dialogue Revisited," 487.

48. Cf. Strauss, *The City and Man,* 191.

49. George Kennan, *American diplomacy 1900–1950* (Chicago: University of Chicago Press, 1951), 86–87.

LEADERSHIP AND REGIMES

1. I explicitly introduce the idea of a "Thucydidean model" as an alternative to the realist model here for the first time, although I have implicitly been describing it throughout. An attempt to flesh out certain aspects of this model by applying it to contemporary scholarship can be found in the Conclusion.

2. David Johnston, *The Rhetoric of Leviathan: Thomas Hobbes and the Politics of Cultural Transformation* (Princeton: Princeton University Press, 1986), 76.

3. Johnston, *The Rhetoric of Leviathan,* 76.

4. Johnston, *The Rhetoric of Leviathan,* 59.

5. Cf. L, 11, par. 20.

6. See Michael Palmer, "Love of Glory and the Common Good," *American Political Science Review* 76, 4 (December 1982): 825–36.

7. Emphasis mine. This phrase is important because it denotes the acknowledgment of a change in the style and substance of Athenian leadership over time.

8. At Epipolae—7.43–45.

9. Cf. Arnold W. Gomme, *A Historical Commentary on Thucydides* (Oxford: Clarendon Press, 1959), 4: 460–461.

10. Leo Strauss, *The City and Man* (Chicago: University of Chicago Press, 1964), 208.

11. Strauss, *The City and Man,* 209n.79.

12. Gomme, *A Historical Commentary on Thucydides,* 5: 172.

13. Thucydides himself does not make mention of the regime's short life.

14. David Grene, *Greek Political Theory* (Chicago: University of Chicago Press, 1965), 78.

15. Leo Strauss, *The Political Philosophy of Hobbes: Its Basis and Its Genesis,* translated by Elsas M. Sinclair (Chicago: University of Chicago Press, 1952), 27–28.

16. Strauss, *The Political Philosophy of Hobbes,* 110–11.

17. Richard Schlatter, "Thomas Hobbes and Thucydides," *Journal of the History of Ideas* 6, 3 (June 1945): 360.

CONCLUSION

1. Jane Mansbridge, ed., *Beyond Self Interest* (Chicago: University of Chicago Press, 1990).

2. Cf. Hedley Bull, "Martin Wight and the Theory of International Relations," *British Journal of International Studies* 2, 2 (July 1976): 101–16; Herbert Butterfield and Martin Wight, eds., *Diplomatic Investigations: Essays in the Theory of International Politics* (London: Allen and Unwin, 1966); Martin Wight, *Power Politics* (London: Leicester University Press, 1978).

3. Cf. Roy E. Jones, "The English School of International Relations: A Case for Closure," *Review of International Studies* 7, 1 (January 1981): 1–13.

4. Michael Doyle, "Thucydidean Realism," *Review of International Studies* 16, 3 (July 1990): 223–37.

5. Hedley Bull lists these among others as "classical realists" in his classic article "International Theory: The Case for the Classical Approach," *World Politics* 18, 3 (April 1966): 361.

6. Hans Morgenthau, *Scientific Man vs. Power Politics* (Chicago: University of Chicago Press Midway Reprint, 1974), 191–96.

7. See Kenneth N. Waltz, *Theory of International Politics* (Reading, Mass.: Addison-Wesley Publishing Co., 1979); and Waltz, *Man, the State and War* (New York: Columbia University Press, 1959), for the best expositions of neorealist thought.

8. Alan James quickly dismisses any difference between realism and neorealism and goes on to analyze them as alike in their "basic approach" in "The Realism of Realism: The State and the Study of International Relations," *Review of International Studies* 15, 3 (July 1989): 216. There seems to be more than enough disagreement on this point to explore in what ways they can be taken together. Professor James has wisely taken the safer route.

9. Ernst Haas, "On Systems and International Regimes," *World Politics* 27, 2 (January 1975): 149.

10. Morton Kaplan, in "The Great New Debate: Traditionalism vs. Science in International Relations," *World Politics* 19, 1 (October 1966): 2, writes, "The politician who desires to change the world must also change the state of the system—in this case, the political system. He may do this by use of force, by the allocation of resources, or by means of verbal persuasion."

11. Friedrich Kratochwil, "Errors Have Their Advantage," *International Organization* 38, 2 (Spring 1984): 309; Robert Gilpin, "The Richness of the Tradition of Political Realism," *International Organization* 38, 2 (Spring 1984): 301–2.

12. See John Herz, "Idealist Internationalism and the Security Dilemma," *World Politics* 5, 2 (January 1950): 157–80.

13. See L, 1, par. 1, 4; L 6–7; HN, 4–5, 7–8, 25–26, 31–32.

14. See L, 13 and 14.

15. See L, 13.

16. See DC, 10, par. 17; 13, par. 7; L 13, par. 2.

17. Cf. L, 11, par. 3; 13, par. 12; 17, par. 2; 30, par. 30.

18. John H. Herz, "Political Realism Revisited," *International Studies Quarterly* 25, 2 (June 1981): 182–97.

19. Richard K. Ashley, "Political Realism and Human Interests," *International Studies Quarterly* 25, 2 (June 1981): 205.

20. John Herz, "Comment," *International Studies Quarterly* 25, 2 (June 1981): 237.

21. See Hans Morgenthau, *Politics Among Nations,* 5th ed. rev. (New York: Alfred A. Knopf, Inc., 1978), 503.

22. Hans Morgenthau, *Dilemmas of Politics* (Chicago: University of Chicago Press, 1958), 272–73.

23. Morgenthau, *Dilemmas of Politics,* 65–66.

24. Morgenthau, *Scientific Man vs. Power Politics,* 169.

25. Kenneth Waltz, "Realist Thought and Neorealist Theory," *Journal of International Affairs* 44, 1 (Spring-Summer 1990): 35.

26. See Waltz, "Realist Thought and Neorealist Theory," 32.

27. Morgenthau, *Politics Among Nations,* 8.

28. Ashley, "Political Realism and Human Interests," 204–36.

29. See Morgenthau, *Scientific Man vs. Power Politics,* 117–18; 196–201.

30. See Morgenthau, *Dilemmas of Politics,* 55.

31. This is the case whenever realists are accused of ignoring the problem of the fungibility of power, are taken to task for ignoring other actors besides states, or are accused of discounting the influence of individual statesmen and their personalities on the process.

32. Stanley Hoffmann, "International Relations: The Long Road

to Theory," *World Politics* 11 (April 1959): 350.

33. This is similar to the question Bishop Bramhall asked Hobbes in *On Liberty, Necessity, and Chance.*

34. Morgenthau, *Dilemmas of Politics,* 75–76; *Politics Among Nations,* 36; Waltz, *Man, the State and War,* 160.

35. Haas, "On Systems and International Regimes," 150.

36. See E. H. Carr, *The Twenty Year's Crisis: 1919–1939* (New York: Harper and Row, 1939); Morgenthau, *Politics Among Nations;* Waltz, *Theory of International Politics.*

37. Gabriella Slomp, "Hobbes, Thucydides and the Three Greatest Things," *History of Political Thought* 2, 4 (Winter 1990): 565–86.

38. Randall Collins, "Reassessments of Sociological History: The Empirical Validity of the Conflict Tradition," *Theory and Society* 1 (1974): 153–54.

39. The thoughtful essay to which I refer, and which I will discuss, is Daniel Garst's "Thucydides and Neorealism," *International Studies Quarterly* 33, 1 (March 1989): 3–27. Garst wrote his article largely in response to Robert Gilpin's views that Thucydides provides a model of the neorealist theory of hegemonic war, an argument that can be found in Gilpin's "The Theory of Hegemonic War," *Journal of Interdisciplinary History* 18: 4 (Spring 1988), 591–613. See also Doyle, "Thucydidean Realism," 223–37.

40. Gilpin, "The Theory of Hegemonic War," 591.

41. Gilpin, "The Theory of Hegemonic War," 592.

42. Gilpin, "The Theory of Hegemonic War," 593, 599, 605.

43. Gilpin, "The Theory of Hegemonic War," 595.

44. Cf. 1.88.

45. Garst, "Thucydides and Neorealism," esp. 3–7.

46. Garst, "Thucydides and Neorealism," 4.

47. I hope to have shown that Thucydides is not a realist even in Doyle's minimalist sense of viewing "interstate politics as a 'state of war.' " See Doyle, "Thucydidean Realism," 224. Even though Doyle's description of minimalist realism can be glimpsed in Thucydides' work, it does not adequately reflect Thucydides' method, purpose, or emphasis.

48. Thucydides tells us at the beginning of the Spartan War Conference that the Aeginetans and the Corinthians "took a leading part in fomenting the war" (1.67.2–4).

49. See 3.29; 3.31; 3.89; 4.55.1–3; 5.54.1–2; 5.55.3; 5.82.3–4; 5.113; 5.115.2–4; 5.116.1; 6.93.1–3; 6.95; 8.24.5; 8.96.5. The last passage reiterates near the end of the book, in Thucydides' own words, the judgment of the Corinthians near the beginning at 1.69.70.

50. For those passages mentioning the helots in this context, see 1.101.2–3; 4.55.1–3; 4.80.2–5; 5.14.4.

51. The reader will recall that on the Spartan side of the equation, it was a personality "problem" that led to Sparta's decision to retire their leadership of the postwar alliance in favor of Athens. Their decision was due to the abrasive character of the Spartan commander in chief, Pausanias, who engendered too much opposition among the allies, making Sparta generally unpopular and raising the esteem of Athens (1.94).

52. Cf. 1.88.

53. Marc Cogan, *The Human Thing: The Speeches and Principles of Thucydides' History* (Chicago: University of Chicago Press, 1981).

54. Peter Pouncey, *The Necessities of War: A Study of Thucydides' Pessimism* (New York: Columbia University Press, 1980).

55. Garst, "Thucydides and Neorealism," esp. 10, 13. Garst, however, seems to say that Athens got its empire, as opposed to simply its leadership of the alliance, by persuasion and voluntary consent. Actually, the *empire* commenced when the Athenians began to change their tactics to the international equivalent of a "protection racket." One could, however, surmise that Athens's decline began as soon as she changed her tactics.

56. Robert W. Connor, *Thucydides* (Princeton: Princeton University Press, 1984), 101.

57. Connor, *Thucydides,* 102.

58. Yale H. Ferguson and Richard W. Mansbach, *The Elusive Quest: Theory and International Politics* (Columbia: University of South Carolina Press, 1989), 13–31.

59. Ferguson and Mansbach, *The Elusive Quest,* 212.

60. Ashley, "The Poverty of Neorealism," 227.

61. Ashley, "The Poverty of Neorealism," 228.

62. Ashley, "The Poverty of Neorealism," 237–61.

63. Ferguson and Mansbach, *The Elusive Quest,* 212.

64. Ferguson and Mansbach, *The Elusive Quest,* 214.

65. Friedrich Kratochwil and John Gerard Ruggie, "International Organization: A State of the Art on an Art of the State," *International Organization* 40, 4 (Autumn 1986): 774.

66. Ferguson and Mansbach, *The Elusive Quest,* 222.

67. John T. Rourke, *International Politics on the World Stage* (Guilford, Conn.: Dushkin Publishing Group, Inc., 1989), 87–96.

68. John G. Stoessinger, *Crusaders and Pragmatists: Movers of Modern American Foreign Policy* (New York: Norton, 1985), 21.

69. Stoessinger, *Crusaders and Pragmatists; Nations in Darkness: China, Russia and America,* 4th ed. (New York: Random House, 1985); *Why Nations Go to War,* 4th ed. (New York: St. Martin's Press, 1986).

70. Stephen D. Krasner, "Are Bureaucracies Important? (Or Allison Wonderland)," *Foreign Policy* 7 (Summer 1972): 159–79; "A Statist Interpre-

tation of American Oil Policy Toward the Middle East," *Political Science Quarterly* 94, 1 (Spring 1979): 77–96.

71. Krasner, "Are Bureaucracies Important?" 179.

72. Murray Edelman, *The Symbolic Uses of Politics* (Chicago: University of Illinois Press, 1964), 137.

73. David M. Ricci, *The Tragedy of Political Science: Politics, Scholarship, and Democracy* (New Haven, Conn.: Yale University Press, 1984), 303.

74. Ricci, *The Tragedy of Political Science,* 304.

75. Paul Kennedy, *The Rise and Fall of the Great Powers: Economic Change and Military Conflict from 1500 to 2000* (New York: Random House, 1987).

76. George Will described the American reaction to this way of thinking well when he wrote: "Cyclical theories of history result from, and foster, fatalism: mankind is caught in a rut, going around in circles. But fatalism is, strictly speaking, un-American. As a quintessential American (Emerson) said, intellect annuls fate." *Newsweek,* 4 November 1991, 80. Fatalism, however, is not the cause but one emotional and mistaken result of viewing human nature in a Thucydidean way.

WORKS CITED

Ashley, Richard K. "Political Realism and Human Interests." *International Studies Quarterly* 25, 2 (June 1981): 204–36.

Ashley, Richard K. "The Poverty of Neorealism." *International Organization* 38, 2 (Spring 1984): 225–86.

Botwinik, David. *Hobbes's State of Nature Doctrine*. Ph.D. diss., Boston College, 1981.

Brown, Clifford W., Jr. "Thucydides, Hobbes, and the Derivation of Anarchy." *History of Political Thought* 8, 1 (Spring 1987): 33–62.

Bruell, Christopher. "Thucydides' View of Athenian Imperialism." *American Political Science Review* 68, 1 (March 1974): 68.

Bull, Hedley. "International Theory; the Case for the Classical Approach." *World Politics* 18, 3 (April 1966): 361–77.

——— . "Martin Wight and the Theory of International Relations." *British Journal of International Studies* 2, 2 (July 1976): 101–16.

——— . *Anarchical Society*. New York: Columbia University Press, 1977.

——— . "Hobbes and the International Anarchy." *Social Research* 48, 4 (Winter 1981): 717–38.

Butterfield, Herbert, and Martin Wight, eds. *Diplomatic Investigations: Essays in the Theory of International Politics*. London: Allen and Unwin, 1966.

Carr, E. H. *The Twenty Year's Crisis: 1919–1939*. New York: Harper and Row, 1939.

Churchill, Winston S. *The History of the English-Speaking Peoples*. London: Cassell, 1956. Vol. 2.

Cohen, David, "Justice, Interest, and Political Deliberation." *Quaderni Urbinati di Cultura Classica* 16, 1 (Spring 1984): 35–60.

Cogan, Marc. *The Human Thing: Speeches and Principles of Thucydides' History*. Chicago: University of Chicago Press, 1981.

Collins, Randall. "Reassessments of Sociological History: The Empirical Validity of the Conflict Tradition." *Theory and Society* 1 (1974): 147–78.

Connor, Robert W. *Thucydides*. Princeton: Princeton University Press, 1984.

Cornford, Francis MacDonald. *Thucydides Mythistoricus*. London: Routledge & Kegan Paul Ltd., 1965.

Creed, J. L. "Moral Values in the Age of Thucydides." *Classical Quarterly* 23, 2 (November 1973): 213–31.

Danford, John W. "The Problem of Language in Hobbes's Political Science." *The Journal of Politics* 42, 1 (February 1980): 102–34.

Doyle, Michael. "Thucydidean Realism." *Review of International Studies* 16, 3 (July 1990): 223–37.

Edelman, Murray. *The Symbolic Uses of Politics*. Chicago: University of Illinois Press, 1964.

Edmunds, Lowell. *Chance and Intelligence in Thucydides*. Cambridge: Harvard University Press, 1975.

Edmunds, Lowell. "Thucydides' Ethics as Reflected in the Description of Stasis (3.82–83)." *Harvard Studies in Classical Philology* 79, 4 (Winter 1975): 73–92.

Ferguson, Yale H., and Richard W. Mansbach. *The Elusive Quest: Theory and International Politics*. Columbia: University of South Carolina Press, 1989.

Finley, John H. *Thucydides*. Cambridge: Harvard University Press, 1942.

Fliess, Peter J. *Thucydides and the Politics of Bipolarity*. Baton Rouge: Louisiana State University Press, 1966.

Forde, Steven. *The Ambition to Rule: Alcibiades and the Politics of Imperialism in Thucydides*. Ithaca, N.Y.: Cornell University Press, 1989.

Forde, Steven. "Thucydides on the Causes of Athenian Imperialism." *American Political Science Review* 80, 2 (June 1986): 433–48.

Garst, Daniel. "Thucydides and Neorealism." *International Studies Quarterly* 33, 1 (March 1989): 3–27.

Gilpin, Robert G. "The Richness of the Tradition of Political Realism." *International Organization* 38, 2 (Spring 1984): 287–304.

Gilpin, Robert. "The Theory of Hegemonic War." *Journal of Interdisciplinary History* 18, 4 (Spring 1988): 591–613.

Gomme, Arnold W. *A Historical Commentary on Thucydides*. 5 vols. Oxford: Clarendon Press, 1959.

Grene, David. *Greek Political Theory*. Chicago: University of Chicago Press, 1965.

Haas, Ernst. "On Systems and International Regimes." *World Politics* 27, 2 (January 1975): 147–74.

Haugeland, John. *Artificial Intelligence*. Cambridge, Mass.: Cambridge University Press, 1985.

Hayek, Friedrich A. *A Road to Serfdom*. Chicago: University of Chicago Press, 1956.

Herz, John. "Comment." *International Studies Quarterly* 25, 2 (June 1981): 237–41.

——— . "Idealist Internationalism and the Security Dilemma." *World Politics* 5, 2 (January 1950): 157–80.

Herz, John H. "Political Realism Revisited." *International Studies Quarterly* 25, 2 (June 1981): 182–97.

Hobbes, Thomas. *De Cive*. Edited by Howard Warrender. Oxford: Clarendon Press, 1983.

——— . *The English Works of Thomas Hobbes of Malmesbury*. Edited by Sir William Molesworth. London: Scientia Aalen, 1962.

——— . *Hobbes's Thucydides*. Edited by Richard Schlatter. New Brunswick, N.J.: Rutgers University Press, 1975.

——— . *Leviathan*. Edited by C. B. Macpherson. Baltimore, Md.: Penguin Books Inc., 1971.

Hoffmann, Stanley. "International Relations: The Long Road to Theory." *World Politics* 11 (April 1959): 346–77.

Hogan, John T. "The [axiosis] of Words at Thucydides 3.82.4." *Greek, Roman and Byzantine Studies* 21, 2 (Summer 1980): 139–50.

Hunter, Virginia. *Thucydides, the Artful Reporter*. Toronto, Canada: The Hunter Rose Co., 1973.

James, Alan. "The Realism of Realism: The State and the Study of International Relations." *Review of International Studies* 15, 3 (July 1989): 215–29.

Johnson, Laurie M. "Rethinking the Diodotean Argument." *Interpretation* 18, 1 (Fall 1990): 53–62.

Johnston, David. *The Rhetoric of Leviathan: Thomas Hobbes and the Politics of Cultural Transformation*. Princeton: Princeton University Press, 1986.

Jones, Roy E. "The English School of International Relations: A Case for Closure." *Review of International Studies* 7, 1 (January 1981): 1–13.

Kaplan, Morton. "The Great New Debate: Traditionalism vs. Science in International Relations." *World Politics* 19, 1 (October 1966): 1–20.

Kennan, George. *American Diplomacy 1900–1950*. Chicago: University of Chicago Press, 1951.

Kennedy, Paul. *The Rise and Fall of the Great Powers: Economic Change and Military Conflict from 1500 to 2000*. New York: Random House, 1987.

Keohane, Robert O., and Joseph Nye. *Power and Interdependence.* Boston: Little, Brown and Company, 1977.

Klosko, George, and Daryl Rice. "Thucydides and Hobbes's State of Nature." *History of Political Thought* 7, 3 (Winter 1985): 405–9.

Krasner, Stephen D. "Are Bureaucracies Important? (Or Allison Wonderland)." *Foreign Policy* 7 (Summer 1972): 159–79.

———. "A Statist Interpretation of American Oil Policy Toward the Middle East." *Political Science Quarterly* 94, 1 (Spring 1979): 77–96.

Kratochwil, Friedrich, and John Gerard Ruggie. "International Organization: A State of the Art on an Art of the State." *International Organization* 40, 4 (Autumn 1986): 753–75.

Kratochwil, Friedrich. "Errors Have Their Advantage." *International Organization* 38, 2 (Spring 1984): 305–20.

Macpherson, C. B. *The Political Theory of Possessive Individualism: Hobbes to Locke.* Oxford: Clarendon Press, 1964.

Mansbridge, Jane, ed. *Beyond Self Interest.* Chicago: University of Chicago Press, 1990.

Morgenthau, Hans J. *Scientific Man vs. Power Politics.* Chicago: University of Chicago Press, 1946.

———. *Dilemmas of Politics.* Chicago: University of Chicago Press, 1958.

———. *Politics Among Nations.* 5th ed. rev. New York: Alfred A. Knopf, Inc., 1978.

Nye, Joseph S., Jr. *Nuclear Ethics.* New York: The Free Press, 1986.

Orwin, Clifford. "The Drama of the Melian Dialogue Revisited." Paper presented at the annual meeting of the Northeast Political Science Association, Philadelphia, Penn., 17–19 November 1983.

———. "The Just and the Advantageous in Thucydides: The Case of the Mytilenaean Debate." *American Political Science Review* 78, 2 (June 1984): 485–94.

———. "Stasis and Plague: Thucydides on the Dissolution of Society." *Journal of Politics* 50, 4 (November 1988): 831–47.

———. "Thucydides' Contest: Thucydidean 'Methodology' in Context." *Review of Politics* 51, 3 (Summer 1989): 345–64.

Palmer, Michael. "Love of Glory and the Common Good." *American Political Science Review* 76, 4 (December 1982): 825–36.

———. "Machiavellian *Virtu* and Thucydidean *Arete:* Traditional Virtue and Political Wisdom in Thucydides." *Review of Politics* 51, 3 (Summer 1989): 365–85.

Poulin, Raymond. *Politique et Philosophie Chez Thomas Hobbes.* Paris: Presses Universitaires de France, 1953.

Pouncey, Peter R. *The Necessities of War: A Study of Thucydides' Pessimism.* New York: Columbia University Press, 1980.

Proctor, Dennis. *The Experience of Thucydides*. London: Aris & Phillips Ltd., 1980.

Ray, John W. "The Place of Oratory in the Political Philosophy of Thomas Hobbes." *Western Speech* 37, 3 (Summer 1973): 166–74.

Rawlings, Hunter R. III. *The Structure of Thucydides' History*. Princeton: Princeton University Press, 1981.

Reik, Miriam M. *The Golden Lands of Thomas Hobbes*. Detroit: Wayne State University Press, 1977.

Ricci, David M. *The Tragedy of Political Science: Politics, Scholarship, and Democracy*. New Haven, Conn.: Yale University Press, 1984.

Rourke, John T. *International Politics on the World Stage*. Guilford, Conn.: Dushkin Publishing Group, Inc., 1989.

Schlatter, Richard. "Thomas Hobbes and Thucydides." *Journal of the History of Ideas* 6, 3 (June 1945): 350–62.

Slomp, Gabriella. "Hobbes, Thucydides and the Three Greatest Things." *History of Political Thought* 11, 4 (Winter 1990): 565–86.

Stoessinger, John G. *Crusaders and Pragmatists: Movers of Modern American Foreign Policy*. New York: Norton, 1985.

———. *Nations in Darkness: China, Russia and America*. 4th ed. New York: Random House, 1985.

———. *Why Nations Go to War*. 4th ed. New York: St. Martin's Press, 1986.

Strauss, Leo. *The Political Philosophy of Hobbes: Its Basis and Its Genesis*. Translated by Elsas M. Sinclair. Chicago: University of Chicago Press, 1952.

———. *The City and Man*. Chicago: University of Chicago Press, 1964.

———. "Preliminary Observation on the Gods in Thucydides' Work." *Interpretation* 4, 1 (Winter 1974): 1–16.

Thucydides. *Hobbes's Thucydides*. Translated by Thomas Hobbes. New Brunswick, N.J.: Rutgers University Press, 1975.

Thucydides. *History of the Peloponnesian War*. Translated by Charles Forster Smith. Cambridge, Mass.: Harvard University Press, 1980.

Waltz, Kenneth. *Man, the State and War*. New York: Columbia University Press, 1959.

Waltz, Kenneth N. "Realist Thought and Neorealist Theory." *Journal of International Affairs* 44, 1 (1990): 21–37.

———. *Theory of International Politics*. Reading, Mass.: Addison-Wesley Publishing Co., 1979.

Westlake, H. D. *Individuals in Thucydides*. Cambridge: Cambridge University Press, 1968.

Wight, Martin. "Why Is There No International Theory?" In *Diplomatic Investigations*. Edited by Herbert Butterfield and Martin Wight. London: George Allen & Unwin, Ltd., 1966, 17–34.

————. *Power Politics*. London: Leicester University Press, 1978.

Will, George. "Ahoy! Is That a Middle Class?" *Newsweek,* 4 November 1990, 80.

Wilson, John. "The Customary Meanings of Words Were Changed—Or Were They? A Note on Thucydides 3.82.4." *Classical Quarterly* 32, 1 (Winter 1982): 50–56.

Zappan, James P. "Aristotelian and Ramist Rhetoric in Thomas Hobbes's *Leviathan:* Pathos Versus Ethos and Logos." *Rhetorica* 1, 1 (Spring 1983): 65–91.

INDEX